KU-008-864

CONTENTS

NEW CURRICULUM – NATIONAL CURRICULUM

edited by
Bob Moon
at The Open University

Hodder & Stoughton

LONDON SYDNEY AUCKLAND TORONTO
in association with The Open University

This reader forms part of The Open University course E271 *Curriculum and Learning*. For further information on the course, write to School of Education (E271), The Open University, Walton Hall, Milton Keynes MK7 6AA.

This reader is one part of an Open University integrated teaching system and the selection is therefore related to other material available to students. It is designed to evoke the critical understanding of students. Opinions expressed in it are not necessarily those of the course team or of the University.

The E271 course team is against the use of sexist language and gender stereotyping. We have tried to avoid the use of sexist language in this reader but some examples may remain from the original articles, and for this we apologise.

British Library Cataloguing in Publication Data
New Curriculum – National Curriculum
—(Curriculum and learning)
 1. Great Britain. Schools. Curriculum
 I. Moon, Bob. II. Open University. III. Series
 375.00941

 ISBN 0-340-54006-0

First published 1990

Typeset by Wearside Tradespools, Fulwell, Sunderland.
Printed for the educational publishing division of Hodder and Stoughton Ltd, Mill Road, Dunton Green, Sevenoaks, Kent by Clays Ltd, St Ives plc

ACKNOWLEDGMENTS

The publishers would like to thank the following for permission to reproduce material in this volume:

Basil Blackwell Inc for 'Two National Curricula – Baker's and Stalin's. Towards a Liberal Alternative' by John White from the *British Journal of Education Studies*, Vol 36, No 3, 1986; *British Journal of Sociology*, 41:3 for 'Changes in the control of education and concerns for quality in Britain and other Western European Societies', by Bob Moon first published as 'Patterns of Control: School Reform in Western Europe'; Ivor Goodson for his article 'Curriculum Reform and Curriculum Theory, a case of historical amnesia' from the *Cambridge Journal of Education*, Vol 19, No 2; The Open University for 'French Curriculum Reform' by Anne Corbett and 'A Scottish Tradition of Curriculum Reform' by Jim Rand; Taylor and Francis Ltd for 'Central Control of the Curriculum' by Clyde Chitty from *History of Education*, Vol 17, No 4, 'The New Right and The National Curriculum: State control or market forces?' by Geoff Whitty from the *Journal of Education Policy*, Vol 4, No 4, 'Competition and Conflict in the Teaching of English: a Socio-Historical Analysis' by Stephen J Ball from the *Journal of Curriculum Studies*, Vol 14, No 1, 'Training the Mind: Continuity and Change in the Rhetoric of School Science' by Robin Millar from the *Journal of Curriculum Studies*, Vol 17, No 4 and 'Curriculum reform in mathematics: beyond the impossible revolution?' by Agnieszka Wojciechowska from the *Journal of Curriculum Studies*, Vol 21, No 2; Tony Taylor for his article 'An Early Arrival of the Fascist Mentality: Robert Morant's Rise to Power' from the *Journal of Educational Administration and History*, Vol 17, No 2; Trentham Books Ltd for 'The National Curriculum: A Black Perspective' by Conrad MacNeil from *Multicultural Teaching*, Vol 16, No 2 and 'Beyond Vocationalism: A new perspective on the relationship between work and education' by Ken Spours and Michael Young from *British Journal of Education and Work*, Vol 2, No 2; University of Tokyo Press for 'Conflicting Approaches to the Reform of Japanese Schooling: Economic Liberalisation versus Educational Liberation' by Teruhisa Horio from *Educational Thought and Ideology in Modern Japan*.

Every effort has been made to trace and acknowledge ownership of copyright. The publishers will be glad to make suitable arrangements with any copyright holders whom it has not been possible to contact.

Introduction

New Curriculum – National Curriculum is one of a series of Readers* prepared as a resource for an Open University course with the title 'Curriculum and Learning'. The aim of the book, like the course, is to explore a range of issues that are to the forefront of educational debate in the 1990s. There is therefore a concern with the important legislative changes that occurred in the 1980s. The introduction of a National Curriculum in England and Wales and its equivalent in Northern Ireland represented a highly significant reform affecting practice in the vast majority of schools. In the same period there was equally important rethinking of the post-16 provision in schools and colleges. Reforms in Scotland anticipated, paralleled or rejected the approach adopted in England, Wales and Northern Ireland. Examining at 16-plus and the introduction of a national system for schools, colleges and adult post certification were both introduced well ahead of reforms south of the border. On the other hand, there was a marked reluctance to embrace some of the ideas about testing and assessment pursued so vigorously by Mrs Thatcher's Conservative administration at the end of the 1980s. The changes in all parts of the British Isles have been highly significant and have attracted interest across the world.

A discussion of legislation reforms, however, should not divert attention away from underlying principles of theory and practice that inform our understanding of curriculum and learning. This book, therefore, looks at various aspects of national curricular reforms of the 1980s and certain broader key issues and themes that help place these in a historical and contemporary context.

New Curriculum – National Curriculum is divided into five sections. The first explores, from different contemporary and historical perspectives, the power of central government in attempting to determine curriculum policy and practice in schools. Clyde Chitty, in his analysis, looks at the evolution of government policies over a forty year period, up to and including the highly centralist attempt to control curriculum in Britain in the late 1980s. It is this most recent exercise of power that

---

* Other titles in the series are:
  Children's Learning in School edited by Victor Lee
  Assessment Debates edited by Tim Horton
  Judging Standards and Effectiveness in Education edited by Bob Moon with John Isaac and
    Janet Powney.

Geoff Whitty addresses. He examines the apparent tension within the Education Reform Act between the imposition of a National Curriculum and its stress elsewhere on parental choice and market forces in determining the shape of the school system. In concluding the section, Tony Taylor takes a step back in time to look at the late nineteent-h, early twentieth-century reform of schooling and curriculum. The parallel with contemporary experience hardly needs making explicit. Any comparison, however, between his portrayal of Morant's often fascist mentality with the politicians, civil servants, and other bureaucrats who administered the Education Reform Act in the 1980s and 1990s is left entirely to the reader's discretion!

The second section of the Reader looks at the relationship between curriculum structure and the concept of a National Curriculum. John White, disputably attributed with bringing such a concept to the fore in Britain over the last two decades, takes a critical look at the curriculum formulation as set out by Kenneth Baker and his advisers. Ivor Goodson, one of the pioneers of curriculum history, shows how important it is to look beyond the written curriculum and to find in its origins the social constructions that have influenced contemporary practice. Michael Young, whose work on the sociology of knowledge in the late 1960s and early 1970s did so much to establish curriculum as a focus for academic debate, contributes an article with Ken Spours on the highly contemporary issue of the relationship between work and education, and between the academic and vocational curriculum. A primary specialist, Robin Alexander, looks at the early compulsory years of schooling and points to the disjunction between the core subjects of the National Curriculum and the style and language of primary schooling. Finally Conrad MacNeil, writing between the publication of the Education Reform Bill and the passing in July 1988 of the Act, suggests that a radical rethink of the curriculum clauses is necessary if the format, content and implementation of the National Curriculum is to meet Black people's educational aims and aspirations for their children. In the 1990s, his perspective still merits a response.

In the third section, the origins of three subjects that have become core subjects within the National Curriculum are each considered in turn. The way this has come out (some have only existed as subjects in their own right for a relatively short period of time), and the attempts to establish status and influence by different interest groups within and around each subject area allows a fascinating insight into ongoing micro-political struggles. Stephen Ball, for example, sees subject disciplines as 'internally differentiated epistemological communities prone to disputation over the definition of subject knowledge and methodology'. Anyone observing the attempts to establish a National Curriculum in England and Wales would have had to concur. Robin Millar considers the emergence of the science 'lobby', a group (or groups) that has had a major impact on policy towards science and the structure of the whole curriculum in the contemporary period.

An international perspective is adopted in the paper by Agnieszka Wojciechowska in looking at two major changes in mathematics in the early 1900s and the 1960s. Many people will have experienced as a pupil or teacher the ferment surrounding 'new' or 'modern' maths and the way it became embroiled in the political debates of the 1960s and 1970s. This article provides a direct link into the introduction to the fourth section of the Reader. Here, I review the evolution of curriculum controls in a range of European countries since the early 1960s. The early research upon which this was based was centred on mathematics. In looking at the advent of new mathematics, as well as some of the more recent reforms, it is striking how frequently the way in which a curriculum system is expected to operate is confounded by empirical evidence about the system in action. Traditional central controls in France, for example, were almost totally ignored and bypassed by the new maths reformers. The structurally decentralised system of the Netherlands has failed to stem a highly centralist pursuit of National Curriculum style policies in the 1980s. The case studies by Anne Corbett and Jim Rand explore this dimension as well as illustrating just how European an experience the 1980s questioning of education, and curriculum, has been. Finally, in this section, we look across the world to Japan where, in parallel with European systems, there has been a national debate, along with Prime Ministerial proposals, to reform education and curriculum in particular. Teruhisa Horio, Professor of Education at the University of Tokyo, provides a critical analysis focusing on the role of the central ministry (Monbusho) in the reform deliberations.

In a postscript to the volume Michael Fullan's address to a 1988 conference on the proposed National Curriculum is reproduced. Whatever the merits or otherwise of the plethora of new policies that schools are required to implement, the process of change is ever present. Michael Fullan has established an international reputation for analysis, comment and practical advice and this short paper offers an introduction to some of his ideas.

part one
ORIGINS AND CONTROL

CENTRAL CONTROL OF THE SCHOOL
1.1 CURRICULUM, 1944–1987

CLYDE CHITTY

The issue of central control of the school curriculum which has aroused such controversy in recent years can be understood only in the context of the changing relationship between central government and local education authorities in the forty or more years that have elapsed since the passing of the Butler Education Act in 1944. This paper is an attempt to analyse the nature of that relationship and the reasons for its fracture as we approach the final decade of the twentieth century.

It is, on the face of it, a remarkable achievement that the 1944 Act should have acquired its formidable reputation as a monumental and seemingly indestructible piece of legislation. None of the previous major education acts – and those of 1870, 1902 and 1918 spring immediately to mind – could lay claim to such longevity. Timothy Raison described it in 1976 as 'a Rolls Royce among statutes';[1] more recently, Keith Evans has argued that it was 'probably the greatest single advance in English educational history, its provisions showing real breadth of outlook and considerable educational vision'.[2]

It can certainly be argued that the 1944 Act sought to extend educational opportunity by providing free secondary education for all. Yet its positive features have been generally overstated both within this country and by observers from abroad. Although it came to be regarded by many as a cornerstone of the Welfare State, it had a number of serious weaknesses and shortcomings which effectively undermined its good intentions. Above all, it provided no clear definitions of either the content of primary and secondary education or the structure of the education system itself. It was not felt necessary to tackle the issue of the curriculum. Until the legislation of 1988, there was no statutory requirement for the inclusion of any subject in the school timetable, except that of religious education. At the same time, little thought was given to the precise relationship between central and local authority. As Aldrich and Leighton have pointed out: 'the 1944 Act failed to provide either a clear definition of the duties and powers of the several bodies engaged in the educational process or a coherent framework to govern the relationships between them'.[3]

Source: C. Chitty (1988) 'Central Control of the Curriculum, 1944–87', *History of Education*, 17(4), pp. 321–34.

Butler sought to [...] defend the absence of any curriculum guidelines in the 1944 Act by stressing the need for partnership in matters relating to the school curriculum:[4]

> I propose to give, so far as I can, a definition, which we have in mind at present, subject to future negotiation, of the various bounds of responsibility of the local education authority, the governing body and the head teacher ... Taking the three bodies ... I will begin by saying that the local education authority, as I see it, will have responsibility for the broad type of education given in the secondary schools including the aided grammar schools and other aided secondary schools ... The governing body would, in our view, have the general direction of the curriculum, as actually given from day to day, within the school. The head teacher would have, again in our view, responsibility for the internal organization of the school, including the discipline that is necessary to keep the pupils applied to their study, and to carry out the curriculum in the sense desired by the governing body ... We ... suggest that, in future, major changes in the curriculum should be brought formally before the local education authority and the governors; and not done in some chance way.[5]

John White has argued that Butler deliberately left out any requirement for the school curriculum for the same political reason that, in his view, caused Lord Eustace Percy, the then President of the Board of Education, to abolish the Elementary Regulations in 1926: namely, the fear that a future Labour administration could use the power, existing in the Regulations, to control the school curriculum in an explicitly socialist way.[6] According to White's theory, it was Butler's idea to decontrol secondary curricula in order to prevent the Labour Party from ending the old dualism between elite and non-elite by parliamentary regulation – realising, of course, that the grammar and elementary traditions could be preserved by a continuation of 'indirect rule'. The publication of the pamphlet *The Nation's Schools* by the new and essentially conservative Ministry of Education in May 1945, which enjoined local authorities to organise secondary education on tripartite lines, could be seen as 'one impressive example of the way in which "indirect" control over curricula could be used to hamstring the progress of secondary education for all'.[7]

Opposition to this viewpoint has been expressed by Timothy Raison – at least as far as the abandonment of the Secondary Regulations is concerned. Raison argues that the neglect to make provision for the Regulations to continue was probably due to administrative oversight. He suggests that Butler did, in fact, envisage that the Minister should take on a positive role as far as content was concerned, but simply failed to make provision for the specific powers that would have been needed 'if leadership implied command'.[8] Whatever the motivation for Butler's omission, the implications were to prove far-reaching.

Since the Elementary Regulations had been abolished in 1926, and the Secondary Regulations were now allowed to lapse, primary and secondary teachers were about to enjoy a period of comparative autonomy in curriculum matters – even if they failed to take full advantage of it. Indeed, Denis Lawton has argued that the period from 1944 to the beginning of the 1960s may be seen as 'the Golden Age of teacher control (or non-control) of the curriculum'.[9] [. . .]

In 1960, however, there were some indications that this cosy era of partnership and teacher autonomy was coming to an end. Debating the 1959 Crowther Report in the House of Commons, Sir David Eccles (Conservative Minister of Education 1959–62) made it clear that there was a desire at the centre to gain more control over the school curriculum:

> I regret that so many of our education debates have had to be devoted almost entirely to bricks and mortar and to the organization of the system. We hardly ever discuss what is taught to the seven million boys and girls in the maintained schools. We treat the curriculum as though it were a subject, like 'the other place', about which it is 'not done' for us to make remarks. I should like the House to say that this reticence has been overdone. Of course, Parliament would never attempt to dictate the curriculum, but, from time to time, we could, with advantage, express views on what is taught in schools and in training colleges. As for the Ministry of Education itself, my Department has the unique advantage of the countrywide experience of Her Majesty's Inspectors. Nowhere in the Kingdom is there such a rich source of information or such a constant exchange of ideas on all that goes on in the schools. I shall, therefore, try in the future to make the Ministry's own voice heard rather more often, more positively, and, no doubt, sometimes more controversially. For this purpose, we shall need to undertake inside the Department more educational research and to strengthen our statistical services. Crowther . . . prodded us to do this and action is now in hand. In the meantime, the section in the Report on the Sixth Form is an irresistible invitation for a sally into the secret garden of the curriculum.[10]

Here in March 1960 was the first suggestion of a venture by the central authority into what had clearly become forbidden territory.

Two years later, in 1962, the Curriculum Study Group was established without prior consultation with organised educational interests. The Group was to involve HMIs, administrators and experts co-opted from the outside. It would provide a nucleus of full-time staff to organise and co-ordinate research studies. Its work would be linked with that of the universities, practising teachers, local authorities, research organisations, professional institutes and others concerned with the content of education and examinations. According to Ronald A. Manzer, 'Eccles envisaged the Group as a relatively small, "commando-like unit", making raids into the curriculum'.[11] Yet the hostility of professional educators was such that in 1963 the new Minister of Education, Sir Edward Boyle, decided that the Group should be replaced by a more acceptable organisation. The Lockwood Committee was set up and recommended that there should be a Schools Council for Curriculum and Examinations.

As well as being the years of 'teacher control (or non-control) of the curriculum', the period from 1944 to the beginning of the 1960s was also, according to Maurice Kogan, one of optimisim and consensus in education.[12]

Both Lawton and Kogan argue that by the 1960s, the end of the period of educational harmony and consensus was in sight with a swing back to central control. Yet, despite the declared wishes of Sir David Eccles, there is much evidence for thinking that teacher autonomy and educational harmony were not really under serious threat in the 1960s. According to Colin Hunter, it was in the mid-1960s that 'Crosland and Boyle presided over the benign consensus which was the basis of the organizational implementation of the comprehensive system'.[13] The Schools Council established in October 1964 certainly posed no threat to the concept of teacher autonomy: as Lawton himself has pointed out, 'its influence in curriculum development was considerable, yet it could never have been said to have possessed control, or even much power, in curriculum matters'.[14] Then again, the power and influence of HMI actually declined in the 1960s which represented, according to a recent study by Lawton and Gordon, 'probably ... the lowest period of HMI influence and morale'.[15] For one thing, there was the continuing problem of overlap between HMI and local authority inspectors; and HMI themselves felt that their professional expertise was not making itself felt. After 1968, their influence appeared to diminish still further when the emphasis was on advice and support with a much reduced role for the formal inspection of schools; and the confidential Yellow Book of 1976, prepared for the Labour Prime Minister James Callaghan by the civil servants of the DES, made reference to the reduced activity of the Inspectorate, attributing it largely to 'over-reaction to the emergence of the Schools Council'.[16] The Assessment of Performance Unit (APU) may be seen as an example of the DES trying to exert some central influence on the curriculum, but it was not established until August 1974. As late as 1975, Timothy Raison was arguing, in his pamphlet published in 1976, that 'to a considerable extent, the Secretary of State acts as the guardian of the educational system, rather than as its administrative head' enjoying the benefits of 'a substantial degree of consensus about what should be taught and how'.[17] In the Yellow Book, the period immediately prior to 1976 is described as 'the era of assertive "teacher power"'.[18] This may well be considered something of an overstatement; but it is still arguable that it is not until the mid-1970s that we find clear evidence of a concerted effort by both the civil servants and the politicians to influence directly the content of the whole secondary school curriculum and the future direction of secondary education. Indeed, we may single out 1976 as a year of special significance, since it saw the compilation of the confidential Yellow Book, the delivery of the Ruskin College Speech and the inauguration of the so-called Great Debate. These were all key manifestations of what Jackson Hall has described as 'the centralist tendency'.[19]

At least part of the explanation for the desire of the central authority to seek tighter control of the school curriculum, and particularly the secondary curriculum, must be sought in the changed economic circumstances of the mid-1970s. This was, after all, a period of profound crisis in the post-war development of British capitalism.

The policy-makers of the 1960s had seen a direct and indisputable correlation between educational reform and economic prosperity: a skilled and educated workforce would facilitate economic growth which would, in turn, constitute a firm basis for continuing educational expansion. But the period of the 1970s saw the steady demise of the old, confident, liberal dogmas. Expansion and optimism gave way to contraction and doubt. By the middle years of the decade, the post-war consensus was breaking down on a number of fronts. As the former Labour Minister Tony Benn has observed:

> The post-war consensus, built upon full employment and the welfare state, has failed to command the support of people because they have seen first that it did not contain within it any element whatsoever of transformation, and, secondly, that even by its own criteria it failed. That policy could not bring about growth, it could not extend freedom, it could not even maintain let alone develop welfare and it could not sustain full employment.[20]

As far as the economy was concerned, both in Britain and indeed throughout the Western world, the crucial years were 1973–5. The major world recession that erupted in 1974 marked the decisive end of what Andrew Gamble has described as 'the longest and most rapid period of continuous expansion world capitalism has ever enjoyed'.[21] The period 1971–3 had seen a sharp boom in each of the major advanced capitalist countries and a generally rising rate of inflation. Some downturn, it could be argued, was likely to occur in 1974 or 1975, simply as part of the usual rhythm of the business cycle. It is, after all, in the nature of capitalist development not to proceed smoothly but always unevenly, with great uncontrollable spurts followed by equally uncontrollable periods of slump and stagnation. However, in the event, the generality and depth of the recession were unprecedented in the post-war period and can now be seen as marking the end of the long expansionary phase of post-war accumulation.[22] While it would, of course, be wrong to see the recession as having a single cause, its onset was clearly marked by a very big rise in the price of oil in 1973. And the economic difficulties of Western societies in the years that followed served to challenge the liberal and expansionist beliefs of the 1960s. As Professor Bernbaum has pointed out: 'If economies are no longer characterized by high rates of growth, then the assumptions that growth is closely related to the benefits obtained through large-scale educational enterprises are more readily challenged.'[23]

In these circumstances, it was comparatively easy to select the education system as a convenient scapegoat for the nation's ills. Of the many factors which caused the Callaghan Government to launch the Great Debate in 1976, particularly important were the claims made by Conservative politicians, and in sections of the media, that standards in education were declining, together with the complaints from leading industrialists and employers that secondary schools were not doing enough to prepare their pupils for 'the world of work'. For obvious reasons, these were important considerations for Labour politicians and their advisors.

The confidential Yellow Book, *School Education in England: Problems and Initiatives*, prepared by the DES at the request of the Prime Minister,[24] suggested that 'the time has probably come to try to establish generally accepted principles for the composition of the secondary curriculum for all pupils, that is to say a "core curriculum"'.[25] It also recognised the need 'to explore and promote further experiment with courses of a higher level of vocational relevance likely to appeal to a significant number of 14 and 15 year olds';[26] though, drawing on his experience as Specialist Advisor to the 1976/77 Education, Arts and Home Office Select Committee enquiry into the attainments of the school leaver, Professor Ted Wragg has concluded that the DES was 'singularly unenthusiastic' about most aspects of the school-to-work debate.[27] It would seem to be true that, at this stage, leading members of the Department did not fully share the politicians' concern to vocationalise the curriculum for what was perceived to be the 'non-academic' section of the school population. In other words, the desire to exert direct influence over the curriculum was more important than the *precise nature* of its form and content. Yet the Yellow Book was at least quite frank about the need for more positive initiatives from the Centre:

> It will also be good to get on record from Ministers and, in particular, the Prime Minister, an authoritative pronouncement on the division of responsibility for what goes on in school, suggesting that the Department should give a firmer lead. Such a pronouncement would have to respect legitimate claims made by the teachers as to the exercise of their professional judgement, but should firmly refute any argument – and this is what they have sought to establish – that no one except teachers has any right to any say in what goes on in schools. The climate for a declaration on these lines may, in fact, now be relatively favourable. Nor need there be any inhibition for fear that the Department could not make use of enhanced opportunity to exercise influence over curriculum and teaching methods: the Inspectorate would have a leading role to play in bringing forward ideas in these areas and is ready to fulfil that responsibility.[28]

This document represented the bureaucratic view of affairs in 1976. A group of HMI was certainly developing its own ideas on the composition of the secondary school curriculum at this time, but the Inspectorate did not play a major role in the compilation of the Yellow Book.[29]

It was also, significantly, the year when Sir James Hamilton took over from Sir William Pile as Permanent Secretary at the DES. According to the recently published memoirs of Bernard (now Lord) Donoughue, who was at that time Head of the Downing Street Policy Unit, this important change at the top of the DES was secured by the intervention of the Prime Minister's political advisors, with the full support of the Cabinet Secretary: 'The existing Permanent Secretary was transferred to a more appropriate department and was replaced by James Hamilton, who had a background in science and engineering, and whom I had previously found encouragingly positive on Cabinet Office Committees.'[30] The new Secretary shared the politicians' concern for a stronger voice in curriculum matters and has been described by Stuart Maclure, editor of the *Times Educational Supplement*, as an 'unrepentant centralist'.[31] He made his position clear on the role of the DES soon after taking up his new post. Talking about Section 1 of the 1944 Education Act in the summer of 1976, he said: 'It means more than seeing that buildings, teachers and other resources are available. It must mean a much closer interest by the Department in the curriculum in its widest sense.' He added: 'The key to the secret garden of the curriculum has to be found and turned.'[32]

The Ruskin College Speech, which, contrary to popular belief, was prepared not within the DES but by Bernard Donoughue and others of the Downing Street Policy Unit,[33] was delivered by the Prime Minister on 18 October 1976 and was a clear indication that education was now at the forefront of the political debate. The Prime Minister was anxious to repudiate the suggestion that education policy in general and curriculum policy in particular could be said to be the exclusive concern of any one group:

> If everything is reduced to such phrases as: 'educational freedom versus State control', we shall get nowhere ... Parents, teachers, learned and professional bodies, representatives of higher education and both sides of industry, together with the Government, all have an important part to play in formulating and expressing the purpose of education and the standards that we need.[34]

The Ruskin Speech covered many of the issues and shared many of the assumptions to be found in the DES Yellow Book, but it also reflected the particular concerns of the Prime Minister. Interviewed by Professor Ted Wragg in the BBC Radio Four programme *Education Matters*, broadcast on 6 December 1987, James (now Lord) Callaghan made it clear that he had been influenced by the opinions of the CBI (Confederation of British Industry). He would also have been aware of the comments of Sir Arnold Weinstock (Managing Director, GEC) and Sir Arthur Bryant (Head of Wedgwood Pottery), which complemented those of Sir John Methven (Director General of the CBI). Given prominence in the media in 1976, these painted a picture of unaccountable teachers, teaching an irrelevant curriculum to young workers who were poorly motivated, illiterate and innumerate.[35]

With its veiled attack on teacher autonomy, the Ruskin Speech marked a clear shift on the part of the Labour leadership towards policies which would facilitate greater government control of the education system. As a *Times* leader writer pointed out,[36] the speech gave the DES the initiative to develop a policy of change from the Centre. This was obviously necessary if government ideas on the school curriculum were to be implemented. The Speech has been seen as part of a definite attempt to construct a new educational consensus around 'a more direct subordination of education to what were perceived to be the needs of the economy'.[37] In the process, the government could also show that it was seriously concerned to raise standards and improve pupils' life-chances, against a background of economic stringency. According to Bernard Donoughue, the basic principle of the Ruskin Speech was 'improving the quality as opposed to the quantity of education at a time when resources were constrained'.[38]

The Prime Minister's sentiments were echoed by his new Secretary of State, Shirley Williams,[39] in a speech at Rockingham College of Further Education on 22 October 1976:

> Among the splendours of the English [education] system are its flexibility, its imagination, and the freedom of the teacher in the classroom. No one wishes to jeopardise that. But the curriculum is a matter in which many people have a stake: parents, teachers, employers, trade unions, Parliament and, of course,

the Government itself. We have, through discussion and debate, to produce the most satisfactory curricula we can.[40]

Yet, despite the assurances of the Prime Minister and of the Secretary of State, a clear recognition of the perceived need to curtail 'teacher power' was inscribed in the very format of the Great Debate which followed the Ruskin Speech. As Inge Bates has observed:

> The Great Debate reflected a trend towards defining and limiting the boundaries of teacher autonomy. The very initiation of a public debate on education, involving the unprecedented consultation of industrial organizations and parents as well as educational organizations, served as an explicit reminder to the teaching profession ... that the curriculum was not solely their responsibility to determine ... Thus the Great Debate, irrespective of its content, simply as a *means* of intervening in education, helped to change the political context in which educational issues were discussed.[41]

It could be argued that the Great Debate began the process which ended with the National Curriculum proposals of 1987. 'Teacher power', if it ever existed, was to be first eroded, then destroyed – at least in theory.

Documents issued by the DES after 1976 emphasised both the new leadership role of the Secretary of State and the need to seek agreement with other interested parties. The Green Paper of July 1977, *Education in Schools: A Consultative Document*, summarised the position succinctly within the space of a single paragraph:

> It would not be compatible with the duty of the Secretaries of State to 'promote the education of the people of England and Wales', or with their accountability to Parliament, to abdicate from leadership on educational issues which have become a matter of lively public concern. The Secretaries of State will therefore seek to establish a broad agreement with their partners in the education service on a framework for the curriculum.[42]

Two years later, in *Local Authority Arrangements for the School Curriculum*, the DES expanded upon this theme:

> [The Secretaries of State] believe they should seek to give a lead in the process of reaching a national consensus on a desirable framework for the curriculum and consider the development of such a framework a priority for the education service ... This task cannot be undertaken from the Centre alone. The Government must bring together the partners in the education service and the interest of the community at large; and with them seek an agreed view of the school curriculum which would take account of the range of local needs and allow for local developments, drawing upon the varied skills and experience which all those concerned with the service can contribute.[43]

At this stage, the DES model was still one of partnership and shared objectives.

Between 1976 and 1981, a stream of documents on the curriculum flowed from the DES, those emanating from HMI advocating an 'areas of experience' approach and those representing the bureaucratic viewpoint arguing for a compulsory core consisting of a limited range of subjects. Then, suddenly, the DES bureaucrats seemed to tire of the politics of persuasion. It has been argued[44] that, having failed in their attempts to determine what was taught in schools through documents like *A Framework for the School Curriculum* (1980) and *The School Curriculum* (1981), they simply decided to try to achieve their aims by other means, notably the instigation of examination reforms. It is, of course, significant that the new CPVE (Certificate of Pre-Vocational Education) and the proposed AS (Advanced Supplementary) levels emanated from the Department, and criteria for the new GCSE (General Certificate of Secondary Education) are vetted there. This argument has certainly been supported by Sir James Hamilton. Looking back over his seven years at the DES, he argued at a conference organised by the Association for Science Education in 1983 that the Government had generally shown too much 'delicacy' about making its presence felt in the classroom:

> I believe we erred on the side of safety. I believe that we could, with benefit, have produced a more pungent, a more purposive analysis ... There is an argument for the DES acting more directly in certain limiting areas of the curriculum ... The present exercise of reforming examinations at sixteen-plus should be seen as part of this process of establishing greater central control.[45]

Other examples of the centralising process between 1981 and 1986 would include: the introduction of the Technical and Vocational Education Initiative (TVEI) funded by the Manpower Services Commission in 1983; the abolition of the Schools Council in January 1984; the control of teacher education through the introduction of the Council for the Accreditation of Teacher Education; and the control of in-service training for teachers by means of a specific grant, as outlined in the 1985 DES document *Better Schools*.[46]

[...] The Government appeared to embark on a change of direction after Kenneth Baker replaced Sir Keith Joseph as Education Secretary in May 1986. It could, of course, argue that its curriculum strategy was simply the logical outcome of events initiated in 1976. Yet the National Curriculum proposals have to be viewed in the context of the whole Baker Education Bill, some of which, and particularly the 'opting-out' clauses, could result in the disruption of the system that has existed since 1944.

There is evidence to suggest that current education policy owes much to the thinking of such organisations as the Institute of Economic Affairs, the Centre for Policy Studies and the Hillgate Group. These form part of what is often referred to as the 'New Right', and their views have acquired a certain respectability in recent years. At the apex of the Centre for Policy Studies, for example, are several former members of Mrs Thatcher's Policy Unit in Downing Street, with links to Professor Brian Griffiths, now head of that unit. Yet New Right philosophy is notable for its in-built contradictions,[47] and the National Curriculum is one issue where the prevailing attitude is decidedly ambivalent. For some of these right-wing Conservatives, a National Curriculum is both illogical and unnecessary since, in their view, the whole state system should be dismantled and handed over to market forces. Schools would then be free to devise a curriculum in line with the wishes of parents and local business interests. One of the paradoxes of the Education Bill is that it involves central control of the curriculum alongside a hierarchical system of schooling which will be subject to consumer demand. Yet for other adherents of New Right ideology, a centrally controlled curriculum has validity precisely because it facilitates the 'commodification' of education. As justification for a massive programme of testing at 7, 11, 14 and 16, a National Curriculum is clearly, in their view, compatible with market principles. A market system demands attainment targets, with, in addition, the publication of test scores. A market in education can work effectively only when there is maximum consumer information. Without national tests and test results, parents would have little hard information upon which to base their choices. The whole process of curriculum standardisation and testing can provide evidence to parents for the desirability or otherwise of individual schools.[48]

With these considerations in mind, one cannot help reflecting that, while the National Curriculum may have its roots in the Great Debate of 1976/77, its *raison d'être* has changed dramatically in the hands of the policy-makers of 1987/88.

NOTES

1 T. Raison (1976) *The Act and the Partnership: An Essay on Educational Administration in England*. London, p. 76.
2 K. Evans (1985) *The Development and Structure of the English School System*. Hodder & Stoughton: Sevenoaks, p. 109.
3 R. Aldrich and P. Leighton (1985) *Education: Time for a New Act?* University of London, Institute of Education: London, p. 73.
4 R. A. Butler had become President of the Board of Education in July 1941. He is closely identified with the 1944 Act, though his role in drawing up the legislation has been questioned by R. G. Wallace (1981) (in 'The Origins and Authorship of the 1944 Education Act', *History of Education*, 10(4), pp. 263–90). He was, of course, to become a prominent member of the various Conservative administrations between 1951 and 1964.
5 *Hansard*, House of Commons, 397, cols. 2363–4, 10 March 1944.
6 J. P. White (1975) 'The End of the Compulsory Curriculum', in *The Curriculum*. University of London, Institute of Education: London, the Doris Lee Lectures, pp. 22–39.
7 Ibid., 39.
8 Raison (1976), pp. 17, 43.
9 D. Lawton (1980) *The Politics of the School Curriculum*. Routledge & Kegan Paul: London, p. 22.
10 *Hansard*, House of Commons, 620, cols. 51–2, 21 March 1960.
11 R. A. Manzer (1970) *Teachers and Politics*. Manchester, p. 91.
12 See M. Kogan (1978) *The Politics of Educational Change*. London.
13 C. Hunter (1984) 'The Political Devaluation of Comprehensives: What of the Future?', in S. J. Ball (ed.), *Comprehensive Schooling: A Reader*. Falmer Press: Lewes, p. 274. Sir

Edward Boyle was Education Minister in 1962–4; Anthony Crosland was Education Secretary in 1965–7.

14 Lawton (1980), p. 67.
15 D. Lawton and P. Gordon (1987) *HMI*. Routledge: London, p. 24.
16 Department of Education and Science (DES) (1976) *School Education in England: Problems and Initiatives*. Yellow Book, p. 17.
17 Raison (1976), pp. 15, 42.
18 DES (1976), p. 17.
19 Title of Jackson Hall's 1985 article in *Forum*, 28(1).
20 Interview (1980) with Eric Hobsbawm, *Marxism Today*, October.
21 A. Gamble (1981, 1985) *Britain in Decline: Economic Policy, Political Strategy and the British State*. Macmillan: London, p. 6.
22 See D. Currie (1983) 'World Capitalism in Recession', in S. Hall and M. Jacques (eds), *The Politics of Thatcherism*. Lawrence & Wishart: London, p. 89.
23 G. Bernbaum (1979) Editorial Introduction to *Schooling in Decline*. London, p. 12.
24 It is commonplace to argue that the Yellow Book was compiled after a discussion between Prime Minister James Callaghan and the then Secretary of State for Education, Fred Mulley, in May 1976. I learn from Stewart Ranson, however, that in the course of his research into central-local relations in education, he was told by a DES official that work had actually begun on the document in 1974.
25 DES (1976), p. 11.
26 DES (1976), p. 22.
27 T. Wragg (1986) 'The Parliamentary Version of the Great Debate', in M. Golby (ed.), *Ruskin Plus Ten*. Exter University, Exeter, p. 11.
28 DES (1976), p. 25.
29 For further discussion of this point, see: C. Chitty (1988) 'Two Models of a National Curriculum: Origins and Interpretation', in D. Lawton and C. Chitty (eds), *The National Curriculum*. University of London, Institute of Education: London, pp. 34–48.
30 B. Donoughue (1987) *Prime Minister: The Conduct of Policy under Harold Wilson and James Callaghan*. Cape: London, p. 111.
31 *Times Educational Supplement* (1983), 24 April.
32 Quoted in K. Fenwick and P. McBride (1981) *The Government of Education*. Oxford University Press, Oxford, p. 220.
33 See Donoughue (1987), pp. 111–12, and J. Callaghan (1987) *Time and Chance*. Collins: London, p. 410.
34 The Ruskin College Speech is printed in full, under the title 'Towards a National Debate', in *Education* (1976), 22 October, pp. 332–3.
35 See, for example, Arnold Weinstock's (1976) article 'I blame the teachers' in the *Times Educational Supplement*, 23 January.
36 27 June 1977.
37 D. Finn (1987) *Training Without Jobs: New Deals and Broken Promises*. Macmillan: London, p. 105.
38 Donoughue (1987), p. 111.
39 Shirley Williams replaced Fred Mulley as Secretary of State for Education in September 1976.
40 Quoted in *Education: The Great Debate*. London, National Union of Teachers, p. 4.
41 I. Bates (1984) 'From Vocational Guidance to Life Skills: Historical Perspectives on Careers Education', in I. Bates *et al.* (eds), *Schooling for the Dole? The New Vocationalism*. London, p. 199.
42 DES (1977) *Education in Schools: A Consultative Document* (Green Paper), Cmnd 6869.

London, July, p. 12. The Secretaries of State referred to in this and the following document were the Secretary of State for Education and Science and the Secretary of State for Wales.

43 DES (1979) *Local Authority Arrangements for the School Curriculum: Report on the Circular 14/77 Review*. HMSO, London, pp. 2–3, 6–7.

44 See: J. Maw (1985) 'Curriculum Control and Cultural Norms: Change and Conflict in a British Context', *The New Era*, 66(4), pp. 95–8; D. L. Nuttall (1984) 'Doomsday or a New Dawn? The Prospects for a Common System of Examining at 16+', in P. Broadfoot (ed.), *Selection, Certification and Control: Social Issues in Educational Assessment*. Falmer: Lewes.

45 Reported in the *Times Educational Supplement* (1983), 1 July.

46 London, March, p. 54.

47 See: J. Quicke (1988) 'The "New Right" and Education', *British Journal of Educational Studies*, 36(1), pp. 5–20.

48 See: P. Cordingley and P. Wilby (1987) *Opting Out of Mr Baker's Proposals*. Local Education Authority Publications: London, pp. 7–8.

THE NEW RIGHT AND THE NATIONAL CURRICULUM: STATE CONTROL OR MARKET FORCES?[1]

1.2

GEOFF WHITTY

[...]

> I sometimes think that a study of the life and teachings of Adam Smith should be compulsory in all schools.
> Bob Dunn addressing the IEA in July 1988 (quoted in *Education* (1988), 8 July)

In one of the many consultation papers issued during the passage of the Education Reform Bill, the Government asserted that it was 'taking action to increase the autonomy of schools and their responsiveness to parental wishes' (DES, 1987). The provisions in the Education Reform Act on open enrolment, financial delegation, grant maintained schools and city technology colleges were all presented by the Government as consistent with this aim. They were presented as building upon the parental choice and accountability provisions of the 1980 Education Act and, more particularly, those of the 1986 Education (No. 2) Act, which enhanced the powers of governors and increased the influence on governing bodies of parents and members of the local business community. The Government claimed, for example, that grant maintained schools would 'add a new and powerful dimension to the ability of parents to exercise choice within the publicly provided sector of education' and that 'parents and local communities [would] have new opportunities to secure the development of their schools in ways appropriate to the needs of their children and in accordance with their wishes'. However, significantly, it added 'within the legal framework of the national curriculum' (DES, 1987).

Then, during the passage of the Bill in the House of Commons, Norman Tebbitt argued that 'This Bill extends choice and responsibility. Some will choose badly or irresponsibly, but that cannot and must not be used as an excuse to deny choice and responsibility to the great majority. Today, only the wealthy have choice in education and that must be changed' (quoted in the *Daily Telegraph* (1987), 2 December). Yet the exercise of choice and responsibility was to be denied to the majority of parents in the field of the curriculum, where (given the exclusion of independent schools from the legislative imposition of a National Curriculum and system of testing), only the wealthy would continue to have choice.

Source: G. Whitty (1989) 'The New Right and the National Curriculum: State Control or Market Forces?', *Journal of Educational Policy*, 4(4), pp. 329–41.

TENSIONS WITHIN THE EDUCATION REFORM ACT

As a result of this, many commentators suggested that there was something of a paradox or contradiction within an Act which increasingly gave market forces their head within whole areas of policy which had previously been subject to detailed regulation and planning by central and local government, yet suddenly introduced prescription into the one area of education where hitherto there had been autonomy, save in the case of RE, which was mandatory under the 1944 Education Act. Of course, that autonomy has essentially been professional autonomy rather than the autonomy of consumer choice; but why should consumer choice replace LEA and teacher judgement in most matters, but ministerial prescription take over from it in the area of curriculum decision-making? Given the tendency of most ministerial statements on the curriculum to portray the curriculum as a commodity, which presumably could be marketed just like other goods, the paradox seemed especially puzzling.

Some critics have resolved the paradox by suggesting that the devolution proposals are themselves as much about increasing central government control, at the expense of the teaching profession and local government, as they are about increasing the power of local communities, which are linked with parents in the Government's rhetoric (Demaine, 1988). Indeed, with the demise of any significant LEA function in relation to grant maintained schools, it can surely be argued that the role of the local people (except current parents) in relation to such schools is diminished rather than enhanced. Thus, the argument goes, the rhetoric of decentralisation is a cover for centralisation. The atomisation of decision-making and the removal or marginalisation of intervening arenas of political mobilisation, such as LEAs and trade unions, effectively removes any chance of a collective challenge to the government, thus enhancing its ascendant position. And this is then consistent with an enhanced central government role in the curriculum. But again the question remains – if that is the aim, why not employ a consistent strategy? Either go for direct government management of the whole enterprise, or let market forces decide the fate of everything including the curriculum.

Of course, while this paper is largely about the position of the New Right, it is also the case that, in government, the rhetoric of the New Right is tempered by other considerations (Demaine, 1988) – indeed other political forces have to be taken into account even by a Thatcher government, and I will return to this point later. But yet another way of resolving the paradox has been to see different factions within the so-called New Right itself as influencing different areas of policy. It has now become a commonplace to identify two main strands within New Right thinking – namely, neo-liberal and neo-conservative. Thus, Andrew Gamble, amongst others, argues that what is distinctive about Thatcherism as a force within British Conservatism is its capacity to link the neo-conservative emphasis on tradition, authority and national identity/security with an espousal of neo-liberal free market economics and the extension of its principles into whole new areas of social activity, including the provision of welfare (Gamble, 1983b; see also Levitas, 1986). In analysing education, Demaine's discussion of the New Right (Demaine, 1988) focuses mainly on its neo-liberal elements, while another recent paper that recognises this distinction places most of its emphasis on neo-conservative influences (Quicke, 1988).

New Right ideology is based on a blend of moral and economic, academic and philosophical doctrines, sometimes complementary, but sometimes in tension, particularly in its mediated political versions (see Edwards *et al.*, 1984; Whitty and Menter, 1989). It has also been pointed out that, provided the discourse of the New Right as political rhetoric strikes a chord and can command assent, its internal inconsistencies and its eclectic philosophical roots are something of an irrelevance (Ball, forthcoming). So greater consumer power over choice and management of schools, a neo-liberal response to criticisms of LEA bureaucracies, and a National Curriculum, a neo-conservative response to charges that trendy teachers are subverting traditional moral values and selling the nation short, may both resonate with popular experience and be electorally attractive, even if the whole package does not add up.

Various policies are at least broadly reconcilable. Gamble has suggested that the paradox of at one and the same time building a strong state through increased expenditure on the military and the apparatuses of law and order, while at the same time using state power to roll back state intervention from whole areas of social activity, does have a degree of consistency. This is because the state needs to protect the market from vested interests and restrictive practices and prevent the conditions in which it can flourish being subverted from either without or within (Gamble, 1983a). On this basis, the Government's curriculum policies may not necessarily be as much at variance with its policies on the structure of the education system as is sometimes suggested, even at the level of principle. The contrast between apparent centralisation in one sphere and apparent decentralisation in the other may not be the paradox it at first appears. Schools which are responsive to choices made by parents in the market are believed by the Government to be more likely than those administered by state bureaucrats to produce high levels of scholastic achievement, to the benefit of both individuals and the nation. The strength of the state therefore has to be used to remove anything that interferes with this process or with the development of an appropriate sense of self and nation on the part of citizens who will be making their choice in the market. Thus, not only does the traditional partnership with LEAs and teachers' unions need to be abandoned in favour of the discipline of the market, it also becomes imperative (at least in the short term) to police the curriculum to ensure that the pervasive collectivist and universalistic welfare ideology of the post-war era is restrained. In this way, support for the market, self-help, enterprise and the concept of the 'responsible' family and a common 'national identity' can be constructed. Hence, for example, whether or not Bob Dunn's intriguing suggestion that there should be compulsory teaching of free market economics was offered tongue in cheek, it may merely be an extreme example of a more general approach to the problem confronting the political project of Thatcherism within education (Hall, 1988). In other words, the overt ideology of the curriculum needs to be addressed directly before the ideology of the new structure is sufficiently developed to do its work. So, in this sense, there may actually be an ideological congruity rather than incongruity between the National Curriculum proposals and other aspects of the Education Reform Act.

NEO-LIBERAL AND NEO-CONSERVATIVE APPROACHES TO THE CURRICULUM

Although certainly in some respects rather too neat both theoretically and empirically, this reading does actually gain credence from a study of the internal debate going on between the various pressure groups associated with the New Right. The contribution of the Hillgate Group (1986, 1987), comprising Caroline Cox, Jessica Douglas-Home, John Marks, Laurie Norcross and Roger Scruton, is particularly significant here and the apparent contradictions within it more explicable than some commentators imply (Demaine, 1988; Ball, forthcoming). Rather than being the product purely of muddled thinking, these contradictions derive from an attempt to consider both short-term and long-term strategies, and this is what leads to their adoption of both neo-liberal and neo-conservative policies to achieve long-term ends that will be broadly acceptable to both. Heavily influenced by neo-conservative critiques of progressivism, members of the Hillgate Group are attracted by the idea of prescription at the level of the curriculum in order to defend traditional standards and values. However, they also see parents as a potent force against progressivism, and embrace – and indeed wish to extend – the Government's espousal of market forces in open enrolment, opting out and so on, as the best way of improving educational standards. But their political allies in the latter cause, including some of those closest to them, such as Keith Joseph, Stuart Sexton and Dennis O'Keeffe, have argued that if market forces are to be efficacious in these other areas, why not in determining the curriculum?

O'Keeffe, for example, in what he claims to be a libertarian view of government policy (O'Keeffe, 1988), says that open enrolment, opting out and financial delegation are all entirely to the good, and so is testing, in principle, providing it is conducted independently on behalf of the taxpayers and not controlled by the educational establishment. But a prescribed curriculum is both 'alien to the British tradition' (and hence presumably should be questioned by neo-conservatives as well as neo-liberals) and looks like being controlled via that 'network of in-house trading and special interest' which has controlled our quasi-syndicalised educational culture of recent years – and incidentally by the very same personnel who are especially culpable for pulling a fast one over the Government with the GCSE. This group is usually referred to disparagingly by the New Right as the 'liberal educational establishment', though they sometimes suggest that its members are 'socialist' (for example, O'Keeffe and Stoll, 1988). They fear that it could still subvert the new proposals from within, and O'Keeffe would presumably see the Mathematics, Science and English Working Group reports (DES, 1988a, 1988b, 1988c), as well as the reports of the Task Group on Assessment and Testing (TGAT, 1987, 1988), as vindicating this view.

Far better than anything prescribed by such groups, or even by ministers and civil servants, would be a 'free enterprise curriculum' – or that mixture of contents and styles that a 'free citizenry' plumps for. As O'Keeffe puts it himself, 'if you do not like the groceries at one supermarket, try another. The system which has utterly outperformed all others in history in the production of a wide range of goods and services needs trying out in the field of education too' (O'Keeffe, 1988, p. 19). (Incidentally, I would argue that the emphasis of the neo-liberals, like some sections of the New Left, on devising new ways of arriving at a curriculum model rather than providing an alternative blueprint is one of the reasons why, when it comes to concrete thinking about the curriculum, such as that demanded of the National Curriculum working groups, the educational establishment usually gets its way.)

Stuart Sexton, a former advisor to Keith Joseph and now Education Director of the Institute of Economic Affairs, places a particularly strong emphasis on finding an appropriate neo-liberal mechanism for determining the curriculum. Thus, he has argued a similar case to O'Keeffe's against a centralised and bureaucratically set 'nationalised curriculum', at the same time as regarding the main elements of the National Curriculum proposals as what most reasonable parents would actually want. But he points out that 'for the independent schools ... the "market" of parental demand dictates that they do provide such a "national curriculum"'. So if a more self-managing state sector emerges from the Government's other proposals, it too will 'have to respond to parental demand to provide an acceptable curriculum' (Sexton, 1988a). This would allow for choice, diversity and local variation, and remove the dangers of a Secretary of State imposing a straitjacket on enterprising schools on the say-so of the fifteen or so 'experts' on the National Curriculum Council (Sexton, 1988b). That is why Lord Joseph moved an amendment to make the whole National Curriculum discretionary rather than mandatory, and why when that failed there were attempts by Sexton and his colleagues to persuade the Government to make only the list of subjects mandatory and the programmes of study discretionary. One of the arguments Joseph used in the Lords' debate against a legislated and inflexible National Curriculum was that it might not meet the needs of either non-academic or gifted children (Blackburne, 1988). And Sexton has recently expressed concern that schools should remain free to teach Scottish examinations or the International Baccalaureate – or even a revived GCE 'O' level to able pupils if they wanted to and if boards wished to offer it – and he particularly deplores those parts of the Education Reform Act that will allow the Secretary of State, or effectively the School Examinations and Assessment Council, to determine what examination courses children in maintained schools can follow. He regards it as absurd that, while independent schools may teach non-GCSE courses if they and the parents want them to, state schools could be legally debarred from doing so whatever the parents might wish (Sexton, 1988b, 1988c).

Sexton (1988c) calls for 'more intellectually rigorous examinations', and his own preference for a return to GCE 'O' level is also something which the Hillgate Group and its close associates desire (Hillgate Group, 1987; North, 1987). However, because they are strongly linked to neo-conservative forces at the same time as having connections with advocates of a free market, they have rather more time than Sexton or O'Keeffe for the idea of government prescribing a National Curriculum in some way rather than leaving it to market forces. The Hillgate Group sympathise with the Government's proposals to control the curriculum, because the eternal vigilance of parents is neither to be expected nor desired, though in the long run they would prefer a proper system of examinations as a more appropriate and less contentious means of control than some of the detail of the present proposals. They firmly back the Government's desire to set attainment targets, though they are less convinced about its way of developing the detailed programmes of study. But given what has happened with GCSE, they are particularly supportive of the Government's specifying proper subjects as the basis of the curriculum, and not those which are either intellectually vacuous or a cover for political indoctrination or both. One of their central concerns in this field is, at the same time as giving members of minority groups opportunities to run their own schools, to integrate them fully into the national culture and ensure a common political loyalty – in other words, to provide a common framework of knowledge and values within which atomised decision-making can take place. There is therefore, for example, a need for attainment targets in history that 'ensure a solid foundation in British and European history and ... no concessions to the philosophy of the global curriculum currently advocated by the multi-culturalists' (Hillgate Group, 1987). So, although any actual programmes of study emerging from government will no doubt reflect other mediating influences, the neo-conservative strand of the New Right does clearly wish government curriculum policy to support a particular view of society and citizen. As Anne Sofer, until recently the education spokesperson of the Social and Liberal Democrats, has put it, the 'draconian control' now to be exercised over the curriculum by the Secretary of State as a result of the Education Reform Act has to be seen in a context where 'The prevailing philosophy is one that does get excited about Christianity being absolutely predominant in RE, about the need to make sure British history prevails over other sorts of history and to stamp on anything that has the label anti-racism attached to it' (quoted in *Education* (1988), 8 July). In the light of this comment, it is interesting to note that, in launching the National Curriculum Working Group on History, Kenneth Baker stated that 'the programmes of study should have at the core the history of Britain, the record of its past and, in particular, its political, constitutional and cultural heritage' (quoted in *The Times* (1989), 14 January).

The other major concern of the Hillgate Group, and associated groups such as the Campaign for Real Education (CRE), is to rid the system of the influence of the educational establishment which, of course, has traditionally regarded the curriculum as its own territory. They therefore want advisory bodies to include several members from outside the educational establishment (which they see as including DES officials and especially HMI). While they accept O'Keeffe's argument that curriculum prescription is alien to the British educational tradition, they believe that a National Curriculum is necessary so that the Government, on behalf of consumers, can rid us of the influence of the educational establishment 'which, prey to ideology and self-interest, is no longer in touch with the public'. It is 'time to set aside ... the professional educators and the majority of organized teacher unions (who rather than classroom teachers) are primarily responsible for the present state of Britain's schools' (Hillgate Group, 1987). Hence their broad support for a National Curriculum – though not necessarily the current Working Groups, which apparently contain 'the student radicals of the 1960s, who have marched through to leading positions in departments of education' (CRE, 1989) – at the same time as accepting with enthusiasm, though wanting to take further, all the other elements of government policy designed to devolve power to consumers. A prescribed curriculum can be used in the short term to re-educate consumers to use their newfound power responsibly and free them from dependency upon professional experts, while in the longer term the ideological changes in exercising their new responsibilities will ultimately produce changes in consciousness that will begin to render even the prescription of a National Curriculum unnecessary. [...]

NOTE

1 This paper was first presented at the International Sociology of Education conference at Newman College, Birmingham, 3–5 January 1989. Parts of the paper draw upon work carried out with Tony Edwards and John Fitz, in the context of our study of the Assisted Places Scheme (ESRC Award No. C00230036), and with Ian Menter, Nick Clough, Veronica Lee and Tony Trodd, my fellow members of the Bristol Polytechnic Education Study Group. However, none of these colleagues should be held responsible for the arguments put forward in this paper.

REFERENCES

Ball, S. (forthcoming) *Politics and Policy-making in Education*. London: Routledge.

Blackburne, L. (1988) 'Joseph's Curriculum Revolt Fails', *Times Educational Supplement*, 6 May.

Campaign for Real Education (1989) 'Cause for Concern?', *Newsletter*, 3(1).

Demaine, J. (1988) 'Teachers' Work, Curriculum and the New Right', *British Journal of Sociology of Education*, 9(3), pp. 247–64.

DES (Department of Education and Science) (1987) *Grant Maintained Schools: Consultation Paper*. London: Department of Education and Science.

DES (1988a) *Mathematics for Ages 5 to 16*. London: Department of Education and Science.

DES (1988b) *Science for Ages 5 to 16*. London: Department of Education and Science.

DES (1988c) *English for Ages 5 to 11*. London: Department of Education and Science.

Edwards, A., Fulbrook, M. and Whitty, G. (1984) 'The State and the Independent Sector:

Policies, Ideologies and Theories', in L. Barton and S. Walker (eds), *Social Crisis and Educational Research*. London: Croom Helm, pp. 118–50.

Gamble, A. (1983a) *Education under Monetarism*. London: World University Service.

Gamble, A. (1983b) 'Thatcherism and Conservative Politics', in S. Hall and M. Jacques (eds), *The Politics of Thatcherism*. London: Lawrence and Wishart, pp. 109–31.

Hall, S. (1988) *The Hard Road to Renewal: Thatcherism and the Crisis of the Left*. London: Verso.

Hillgate Group (1986) *Whose Schools? A Radical Manifesto*. London: Hillgate Group.

Hillgate Group (1987) *The Reform of British Education*. London: Claridge Press.

Levitas, R. (ed.) (1986) *The Ideology of the New Right*. Oxford: Polity Press.

North, J. (ed.) (1987) *The GCSE: An Examination*. London: Claridge Press.

O'Keeffe, D. (1988) 'A Critical Look at a National Curriculum and Testing: A Libertarian View', paper presented to American Educational Research Association, New Orleans, April.

O'Keeffe, D. and Stoll, P. (1988) 'Postscript' to S. Sexton (ed.) *GCSE: A Critical Analysis*. Croydon: IEA Education Unit.

Quicke, J. (1988) 'The "New Right" and Education', *British Journal of Educational Studies*, 26(1), pp. 5–20.

Sexton, S. (1988a) 'No Nationalization Curriculum', *The Times*, 8 May.

Sexton, S. (1988b) 'Squeezing Out Choice at the Grassroots', *Education*, 9 September.

Sexton, S. (ed.) (1988c) *GCSE: A Critical Analysis*. Croydon: IEA Education Unit.

TGAT (Task Group on Assessment and Testing) (1987) *A Report*. London: Department of Education and Science.

TGAT (1988) *Three Supplementary Reports*. London: Department of Education and Science.

Whitty, G. and Menter, I. (1989) 'Lessons of Thatcherism: Education Policy in England and Wales, 1979–88', *Journal of Law and Society*, 16(1), pp. 42–64.

'An Early Arrival of the Fascist Mentality': Robert Morant's Rise to Power

1.3

Tony Taylor

What is it about Robert Morant[1] that sets him apart from other educational administrators? After all, not many senior civil servants in the Board of Education have attracted the amount of fascination and attention that is devoted to the career of this extraordinarily talented and yet flawed man. There are two answers to the question. The first of these is that Morant had a particularly strong personality, an unsubtle blend of fawning charm towards his superiors and malevolent spite towards subordinates and others who dared to cross swords with this ambitious and unprincipled administrator.[2] The second answer is that Morant's rise to power was spectacularly swift. In January 1901, he was merely private secretary to Sir John Gorst, Vice President of the Board of Education. Although this was a reasonably satisfactory position to be in, it was still a modest and obscure appointment. By December of that year, however, Morant had become the *de facto* Chief of the Board of Education. He had leapfrogged thirty of his colleagues who had precedence and seniority, and in the following year he was appointed Acting Secretary of the department, an action that was confirmed by his being made first Permanent Secretary of the Board of Education in April 1903.

The start of this unusual story takes place in May 1895. Morant, having returned penniless and discredited from the internal politics of the Court of Siam,[3] presented himself for interview at the Parliament Street offices of the Education Department. The vacancy was for an assistant to the newly appointed Director of the Office of Special Inquiries, Michael Sadler. According to Sadler, who hired him, Morant appeared for the interview 'out at elbows, subdued and humble', but was 'fields better than any other candidate'.[4] Sadler took Morant under his personal as well as his professional sponsorship and thus began a familiar Morant technique, where the ambitious young civil servant sought out patrons, abandoned them abruptly when their usefulness was over and met any opposition to his progress with paranoid vindictiveness. It was this dynamic that led Sadler to describe his former friend as 'an early arrival of the fascist mentality',[5] for Morant became an authoritarian leader who believed in a monopoly of power and the effectiveness of charismatic leadership. Opposition

Source: A. Taylor (1985) 'An Early Arrival of the Fascist Mentality': Robert Morant's Rise to Power', *Journal of Educational Administration and History*, 17(2), pp. 48–62.

was smashed and any alternative proposal to Morant's own vision was regarded as an attack on Morant's personal capabilities.

In the Office of Special Inquiries, Morant, at first an assiduous worker, wrote to Sadler only a few months after his appointment, 'the day is never long enough . . . I must soak all the time in varied educational juices'.[6] After four years in Sadler's department, however, Morant realised that the Office of Special Inquiries was not the central policy-making organisation that he had hoped it would become. In 1899 he abandoned Sadler's patronage to become private secretary to Gorst, the Vice President. Within the year, Morant realised that he had made yet another career mistake. Gorst, a Tory maverick, was despised and disliked by Arthur Balfour, the Conservative leader in the House of Commons. Gorst's politics were sometimes even to the left of the Liberal party, a stance that annoyed Balfour, whose main concern was to keep the Unionist coalition on an even keel. As a patron, Morant had picked a loser and early in 1901 he began to cast around for a successor to the ineffectual Gorst. [. . .]

The breakthrough came in the spring of 1901, and it came not from the Board of Education but from an outsider, Edward Talbot, Bishop of Rochester.[7] Talbot, a close friend of Balfour's, had extensive contacts in the Church party, and to a certain extent was an episcopal representative of this political grouping. Not only that but Talbot enjoyed using his influence:

> It exhilarated him to be at the heart of national life and within reach of those chiefly concerned with its guidance. Talbot did not hesitate to use his personal friendship with Lord Salisbury and his sons, and with Mr Balfour, to ensure that the views he represented should be known at headquarters.[8]

It was Talbot's intention to push Balfour into action and the bishop, fully aware of the poor relationship that existed between Balfour and the Board of Education, chose to introduce the Tory leader to a junior official within that department. The junior official was, of course, Morant, and the occasion of the meeting was a Palm Sunday luncheon at the Bishop's Palace, Kennington.

The closeness of Talbot's relationship with Balfour was to a large extent the consequence of a personal tragedy in the life of the Commons leader. May Lyttleton, Talbot's sister-in-law, had once been on the point of becoming engaged to Balfour but had died prematurely before their relationship had been placed on a formal footing. Balfour, deeply affected by the event, came to Talbot's household for an annual memorial luncheon, on Palm Sunday. The depth of Talbot's desire to press Morant's ideas on to Balfour can be gauged from the fact that the same commemorative occasion was attended by this obscure official, a man known by Talbot to be sympathetic to the ideas of the Church party.

Why Talbot chose Morant then is fairly clear. At university, Morant had originally intended to join the Church of England, and according to his biographer, had had a very 'churchy' time at Oxford. His degree had included a first class in theology and it was at Oxford that he met Talbot, who was then the founding Warden of Keble College. In this pioneering institution, Talbot acquired a reputation for progressiveness and personal kindliness, adopting and sponsoring young undergraduates who often remained friendly with him long after leaving university. Morant and Talbot were still in touch in 1901 and their relationship, together with Talbot's desire for educational legislation, as well as Morant's knowledge of the Board of Education, combined to push the bishop into inviting Morant to this normally intimate occasion.[9]

At the meeting, Morant was allowed to make a case for his own belief in a strong centralised educational administration. In this desire he was at loggerheads with his political chief Gorst, who was in favour of devolved control, but Morant's opposition to Gorst's plans could only have been an advantage in Balfour's eyes. Allen's colourful prose points out the significance of the meeting:

> That moment was fraught with destiny for the future. For it marked the beginning of that mutual regard and confidence that was to keep these two master spirits side by side throughout the coming struggle.
>
> A few minutes later the First Lord of the Treasury was summoned away by an urgent political message and Morant left the Bishop's Palace with the feeling that his appeal had been made in vain. As a matter of fact, it had succeeded. A few days later, on the last day of the session, he received a friendly personal letter from Balfour, asking him to prepare the draft of a new Bill for the next session.[10]

Thus Balfour and Morant began their relationship. At first glance it was an unlikely combination. Balfour was the enigmatic aesthete, cool and distant, with a profound distaste for displays of emotion; next to him, Morant, a tall man, excitable, intense, was constantly alert against plots to thwart him. Balfour's daughter described the contrast: 'I recall Morant's arrival in lovely October weather, and a vision of the two walking about the garden, earnestly talking. Morant's personality impressed itself at once. He was a giant, with a large, pale, melancholy face, the eyes glowing out of deep black pits. Beside him Balfour, tall as he was, looked small in frame.'[11]

To a large extent, Morant shared Balfour's educational objectives. It was in Morant's interest to clear up the educational 'muddle', firstly because of Morant's liking for centralised administrative apparatus and secondly because any Permanent Secretary of the revamped Board of Education would be a much stronger and more powerful figure than had been the case before: that particular outcome would suit Morant's taste for power and authority.

Given the choice, however, Balfour would have plumped for gradual legislation. This would have meant dealing with the secondary schools issue in 1902 and following up by helping the denominational schools in a following session. Both Talbot and Morant objected to the piecemeal approach, mainly because there was no guarantee that promises made by Balfour in 1901 would be realised in 1903. After all, the Unionist government was fighting a difficult war. If the Boer campaign collapsed after some kind of military disaster, Salisbury's government could be thrown out of office. From the beginning of his relationship with Balfour, Morant made it plain that he, the official, was only interested in a single, large Bill that would encompass both elementary and secondary issues. In a crucial fourteen-page memorandum prepared for Balfour in the summer of 1901, Morant continued to argue strongly that the two issues were related and could not be dealt with separately.[12]

Balfour was impressed by Morant and, in the early stages at least of their relationship, trusted him. By the beginning of July 1901, Morant had been detached from Gorst's office to serve as a special advisor to Balfour. The real breakthrough for the ambitious civil servant came, however, in August of that year, when he was present at a meeting held in Balfour's room at the Commons. A small group of advisors had gathered with Balfour to examine the education question. Amongst its number was Morant, still officially only a Senior Examiner in the Board of Education. Absent were two of Morant's superiors, Bruce, the Assistant Secretary for Secondary Education, and Abney, Principal Assistant Secretary and Kekewich's deputy. Morant's presence, as well as the existence of his private memorandum to Balfour which preceded the meeting, are a telling indication of just how much progress he had made since his first meeting with Balfour at Kennington Palace on 31 March.

Balfour's problems had not disappeared, however, simply because he had acquired the services of a keen junior in the Board of Education. It is true that Morant shared both Balfour's views about the elitist nature of secondary schooling and a broad sympathy for the voluntary schools, but there still remained other officials, more senior than Morant, who did not share this conservative vision. Amongst these were George Kekewich, a lame duck Permanent Secretary, but still a powerful and influential civil servant. Another opponent to the Balfour–Morant nexus was Michael Sadler, angry and touchy about Morant's abandonment of the Office of Special Inquiries. It was certain that any major research for the new measure would emanate from Sadler's office, and much of it could be damaging to Morant's plans for a resolution of the education question. In order to accomplish this, Morant, a gifted polemicist, would seek to skate over difficulties, conceal conflicts and avoid honesty. Sadler's view was opposed to the Morant *modus operandi*:

> There was, behind and embodied in our way of working at the Office of Special Inquiries and Reports, the doctrine that the Office ought to tell the truth, disclose the strong and weak points of great educational policies, and behave with self-restraint but unshakeable honesty ... But Morant had no use for scientific impartiality.[13]

Sadler had been an Acland appointee, and, like Kekewich, still held the radical former Vice President in high regard. Indeed it had been Acland who had warned Sadler about Morant's behaviour as early as 1895, when he had written, 'Some of the language used by the man under you ... to others [is] in ignorance of how *very* careful Civil Servants ought to be.'[14] There was therefore no possibility that Morant could retrieve his relationship with Sadler in an effort to persuade the Director of the Special Inquiries Office to support any Balfour–Morant scheme for a large Bill and for a powerful, centralised administration.

The third official obstacle lay outside the Board of Education in the office of the

Parliamentary Counsel, Sir Courtney Ilbert. There was little room for doubt as to Ilbert's political sympathies. In the following year he was to write to James Bryce, the Liberal educationalist, that he hoped 'to see this Government out',[15] and from the beginning of his acquaintanceship with Balfour's educational schemes, Ilbert had expressed contempt for Balfour's capabilities as a legislator.[16]

Any one of these three officials could break Morant's plan for a single, large Bill, sympathetic to the voluntary schools and hostile to the school board influence in both elementary and secondary education. Morant was determined to get his measure through, and in order to make this possible he began a campaign to have his three civil service colleagues removed, either from office or from the central arena of educational debate, or, if possible, both.

The first signs of a Morant plot come in July 1901 when he warned Balfour about Kekewich. Balfour passed the news on to the Duke of Devonshire: 'I vent: to trouble you upon a matter wh. I quite admit does not immediately concern you ... I know from gossip. And tho' it be gossip is *I* am sure well informed that yr Permanent Sec nevr loves govt policy nor in anywise supports it.'[17]

Morant reiterated his feelings about Kekewich's untrustworthiness in September, as the pace of negotiation and manoeuvre began to gain speed. Rather foolishly, the Permanent Secretary, unaware of Morant's deviousness, confided in Morant:

> My view has always been that it is practically impossible for the Govt: to include elementary education in the same Bill as Secondary, & I think they will have to have two Bills, pass the Secondary next year, & the Elementary the next, if they can. I think there are elements of danger to the Government in any Elementary Bill of the character proposed.[18]

These views were of course not far removed from Balfour's original intentions, but Morant was determined to have the single, large Bill. He told Balfour about Kekewich's views, adding a few embellishments of his own:

> As to the question of including Elementary in next Sessions bill – Kekewich is, I find, most anxious that only Secondary shd be touched, & that Elementary shd be postponed till a session or two later – as he still hopes that ere long some turn of the Parliamentary wheel of fortune may bring to the top some authoritative voices more favourable to his friends the Schl Boards & N.U.T. than he finds at present!!
>
> The Duke however does not realise this, but only wonders how all the 'difficulties can ever be met'.[19]

Whether Kekewich was able to influence the Duke towards a more sympathetic approach to the school boards or not is uncertain but the consequences of Morant's carefully laid plans are much more clear: during that crucial autumn period when the 1902 measure was being drafted and redrafted, Kekewich was completely excluded from the process of drafting the Bill: instead he was given the task of dealing with the teacher supply problem in South Africa. By January 1902

Kekewich's isolation was so complete that he was forced to complain to Gorst, his companion in exile, that departmental business was passing him by,[20] and by the spring of 1902, Kekewich's plight had become the talking point of political gossips. Lord Robert Cecil wrote to his wife: 'The Education Office is in chaos! Neither the Permanent Head of the Office, one Kekewich, nor Gorst the House of Commons representative has ever seen the Education Bill till introduced!!'[21]

Morant's policy of isolating those likely to prove difficult during the negotiations preceding the 1902 Bill were not confined to Kekewich, however. Michael Sadler also found himself caught up, in another Morant conspiracy.

Sadler, increasingly unhappy with Morant's behaviour in the Board of Education and no supporter of Unionist politics, was anyway drifting further and further from the atmosphere of intrigue at the Parliament Street offices, preferring the calmer, more professional and methodical atmosphere of his own office, now in South Kensington. Morant undoubtedly attempted to speed up the process of separation by ensuring that Sadler could play no significant part in forthcoming discussions.

The first sign that Sadler was in danger of being removed came in November 1901, when he was unexpectedly offered the post of Director of Education in India. This post was the gift of the India Office, then commanded by Lord George Hamilton, an old Church party member and former Chairman of the London School Board (in the Conservative or Moderate interest). Sadler became agitated at the offer and consulted his friend Courtney Ilbert, who conferred with other officials on the wisdom of taking up the offer. Ilbert obviously heard something that persuaded him to advise Sadler to remain in his post, 'Saw Godley about the offer of India Directorship of Education to Sadler. Afterwards saw Sadler & advised him not to accept office of Director General.'[22]

Sadler would not move. Therefore another scheme had to be devised. In the end, the Office of Special Inquiries was given the time-consuming task of examining the religious difficulty in European schools. Sadler, in his customarily zealous fashion, was soon bogged down in overwork. Early in the new year of 1902, he pleaded with Kekewich for more assistance, a request which in turn led to a similar plea from Kekewich to Gorst. Kekewich grumbled 'I presume that this Memorandum [on European schools] was asked for by Mr Morant for your use, though his letter did not say so, nor was the demand for it made through me.'[23] The European schools project does not seem to have figured large in discussion of the Cabinet Committee during the framing of the 1902 Bill, and Sadler's makework assignment was successful in keeping him away from the Balfour–Morant deliberations.

As for Ilbert, Morant was faced with a problem. Courtney Ilbert was a strong character with a powerful reputation and some powerful friends. Not only that, but as Parliamentary Counsel he was theoretically immune from Morant's machiavellian tendencies. This immunity was only a temporary obstacle to Morant's plans, however, for, by Christmas 1901, Ilbert had been taken off the preparation of the Bill, sacked by Balfour, at Morant's instigation.

From the very beginning, Ilbert had been hostile to Balfour and Morant's ideas, for professional and ideological reasons. Morant very quickly picked up Ilbert's emanations of hostility and briefed Balfour on Ilbert's closeness to an untrustworthy junior official in the Board of Education, one Francis Acland, son of the former Vice President:

> The last letter that I saw from Ilbert was dated from the same country house as was a note I received the same day, on office matters, from young Acland!! So that no doubt, there is as usual a happy 'collaboration' going on, of which the poor old Duke is blissfully unconscious but unhappily the victim.[24]

Morant informed on Ilbert again in November when he wrote to Balfour that the Parliamentary Counsel 'still drafts the Bill in a highly hostile spirit'.[25] By December, Ilbert's position had become too much for Balfour. Five days before Christmas, Ilbert was visited by Sir Francis Mowatt, Permanent Secretary to the Treasury and the leading civil servant in Whitehall.

> Had a visit from Mowatt who was sent by Balfour to explain that he though the drafting of the Education Bill had better pass into other hands. I said, I should be glad to be freed from a disagreeable task which had been attempted under impossible conditions but I must have an assurance that the change implied no reflection on me. Wrote Balfour accordingly.[26]

The following day Ilbert received a letter of explanation from Balfour:

> It is an attempt to re-organise our Education System on lines which you heartily dislike, and which you think are unlikely to pass the House of Commons, or if it did pass, to work satisfactorily in the country. If I were in your place, and felt as you do about the Bill, I know that I could not do it as well as one in which I believed.[27]

On the same day that Balfour wrote to Ilbert about his dismissal, the Commons leader gave instructions to Morant alone to draft the next version of the Education Bill.[28]

Thus within the space of three months, Morant had been instrumental in the isolation of Kekewich, the neutralisation of Sadler and the dismissal of Ilbert, who was put on to less controversial legislation and replaced by a 'safe' junior, Thring.[29] [...]

Morant had won. His sophistry, his guile and his unscrupulousness had triumphed over the professionalism and limited muscle of three of his superiors. Morant's first aim, a special vision of the secondary education system, was also victorious. The 1902 Act, in its final form, did not instruct local authorities on the form of education to be followed, but it was Morant, as Permanent Secretary, who, by administrative decrees, laid down certain formulae which would guarantee the establishment of new secondary schools, at a clear remove from elementary schools. Thus the public-school traditions of nineteenth-century England, as adhered to by Morant, were influential in establishing the kind of education to be received by the consumers of mass secondary schooling, the new grammar school pupils. Not that Morant represented an unorthodox vision in pushing for an elitist form of secondary schooling. In this he was joined by Conservatives and Liberals alike, but in allowing the great School Boards to be disbanded and in formulating a kind of secondary education based on 'exceptional ability' Morant was pandering to the embryonic notions of meritocracy that were abroad at the turn of the century. It had been the School Boards that had represented a devolved and democratic form of education, more akin to the American system. Had they been allowed to develop, it is possible that they might have established a capacity for mass secondary education without that sudden break at early adolescence, a break that was to prove a barrier for many pupils who might otherwise have benefited from some form of advanced education. [. . .]

Morant's final but overriding ambition, control of the Board of Education, had also been accomplished as a consequence of his activities in 1901–2, but his success was not a prolonged one. In 1911 Morant was allowed to resign from the Board of Education after the publication of a damaging internal memorandum. At the time, there was a certain amount of speculation as to why the Liberal government did not do more to protect Morant. In the light of the evidence, it may be suggested that the Liberal government were only too glad to see Morant go.

Did Morant have, in Sadler's phrase, a 'fascist mentality'? It has to be remembered that Sadler was writing in 1941, at a time when fascism had a very powerful meaning, and Sadler was not one to use words carelessly or lightly. Morant was certainly authoritarian. He had a vision and it had to be implemented: to bring it about, opposition was eradicated by fair means or foul. Morant, like many authoritarian personalities, was also paranoid, equating opposition with enmity, and his reaction was to harass or persecute any who gainsaid him and to vilify others who might be able to block him.

Morant was also a man of action. He was good at initiating schemes and convincing others of their value, but less good at reflection and implementation. Forcing through was Morant's forte. If Morant could be convinced that a course of action had merit, then he would take personal responsibility and push it through to some form of conclusion.

In those senses he had a 'fascist mentality': he was authoritarian, paranoid and a believer in action before reflection. In another sense too he was 'fascist': Morant was totally unscrupulous. Michael Sadler should have the last word: 'The technique of these seven years of adroit and shameless self-aggrandisement might serve as a model to any aspiring bureaucrat, blessed with the lack of scruple, the timing and the nerve of Robert Morant. The man had genius, but it was genius *détraqué*.'[30]

NOTES

1 Sir Robert Morant (1863–1920). Winchester and New College Oxford. Assistant Director in Office of Special Inquiries, Education Department 1895–99. Private

Secretary to Sir John Gorst (Vice President of Education Department) 1899–1902. Acting Secretary of Board of Education 1902. Permanent Secretary of Board of Education 1903–11. Chairman of National Health Insurance Commission 1911–20. Knighted 1907. See B. Allen (1934) *Sir Robert Morant*.

2 One education delegate outlined his reaction to Morant's negotiating technique in these terms: 'I left my youth behind in the Conference Room at the Board of Education.' Cited E. Eaglesham (1963–4) 'The Centenary of Sir Robert Morant', *British Journal of Educational Studies* xii, p. 15. Michael Sadler, not a friendly witness, tells of the experiences of Herbert Trench: 'Trench had Morant very much on his mind. He told us how badly Morant treated him when he was in the Office, making his position absolutely untenable.' Cited M. Sadleir (1949) *Michael Ernest Sadler*, pp. 192–3. A Thai official who had been involved in Morant's expulsion from Bangkok referred to the future Secretary of the Board of Education as 'the disease': Thai National Archives R5, 28 Devawongse to Rolin-Jaequemyns, 15 January 1894. (I am indebted to Dr Neil Daglish of the Victoria University of Wellington for this quotation.)

3 See N. Daglish (1983) 'The Morant–Chulalongkorn Affair of 1893–4', *Journal of Educational Administration and History*, xv (2).

4 Sadleir (1949), p. 194.

5 Ibid., p. 195.

6 Cited M. J. Wilkinson (1979) 'The Office of Special Inquiries and Reports', *History of Education*, 8, p. 277.

7 Edward Stuart Talbot (1844–1934), Charterhouse and Christ Church Oxford. Younger brother of John Gilbert Talbot (1835–1910), Tory MP for Oxford University and leading light of the Church party.

8 G. Stephenson (Talbot's daughter) (1936) *Edward Stuart Talbot*, p. 125.

9 For details of Morant's career at Oxford see Allen (1934), pp. 16–39. According to Allen, Morant ceased to believe in 'Revealed Religion' after the Siamese *débâcle* but he was far from the agnostic that others make out (J. R. Fairhurst (1974) 'Some Aspects of the Relationship between Education, Politics and Religion from 1895–1906', unpublished D. Phil. thesis, University of Oxford, p. 197), since he worked at Toynbee Hall on his return from Siam and was recommended to Michael Sadler by Canon Sam Barnett. The final word has to be Morant's funeral service in the very denominational setting of St Martin-in-the-Fields, with all the trimmings of a High Church service (*The Times* (1920), 18 March).

10 Allen (1934), pp. 155–6. Other sources, including Allen (1934) and Fairhurst (1974), place the first meeting of Balfour and Morant later in the year, probably at the beginning of August. Morant, however, referred to the day of that critical conference in a letter to Talbot: 'I have always treasured the memory of many talks at Kennington and in particular on that first Palm Sunday, when you opened everything for me': cited G. Stephenson (n.d. but probably c. 1911), p. 142. Palm Sunday in 1901 was 31 March, the day before the Master of the Rolls delivered what was to be the final judgement on the Cockerton case. Balfour was summoned to Buckingham Palace to see the King (*The Times* (1901), 1 April) for an afternoon discussion of the previous Friday's Cabinet meeting (see Balfour to the King, 29 March 1901, PRO CAB/41/26/7). Balfour then stayed for dinner at the Palace. Morant may indeed have received a letter a few days later 'on the last day of the session', but Allen has confused the Easter adjournment of 2 April 1901 with the end of the session on 17 August 1901.

11 The occasion was Morant's visit to Whittingehame, Balfour's home in Scotland, in the autumn of that year. *Quarterly Review* (1933), 260, p. 154.

12 Memorandum PRO, Ed. 24/14/13a, 'Some questions to be considered before the

drafting of the Education Bill for 1902.' The provenance of the memorandum 'Some questions' is vital to any examination of Morant's role in the events of 1901–2. Allen, Fairhurst and others assert that the memorandum was a general document for the August meeting, but the language used by Morant dispels this notion. The references to 'The Duke's House of Lords Bill' (p. 2), 'Sir John Gorst's idea' (p. 8) and 'Our friends' (p. 8) indicate that this was a private memorandum to Balfour. In an official memorandum prepared for a meeting where the Duke of Devonshire and Gorst were likely to be present, Morant would have used formal titles or the correct style of address and would scarcely have referred to the Church party as 'Our friends'. Furthermore, if Morant had been commissioned to prepare this memorandum for the 8 August meeting, there is little evidence from either Morant's notes of the occasion or Ilbert's notes and references that any memorandum was used as a basis for discussion. See PRO, Ed. 24/16/79 and Ed. 24/16/81.

13 Cited Sadleir (1949), pp. 194–5. Sadler was strongly opposed to over-centralisation in a national education system.

14 Cited Wilkinson (1979), pp. 280–1.

15 Bodleian Library, Bryce MSS., vol. xiii, ff. 99–101.

16 'Long discussion . . . He [Balfour] has prepared for Cabinet a memorandum of his own, . . . containing many wild & unusual suggestions': Ilbert's political diary, House of Lords Library, 15 December 1899.

17 Balfour to Devonshire, 25 July 1901: rought draft in Sandars MSS., Bodleian, MS. Eng. hist. c. 737.

18 Kekewich to Morant, 9 September 1901: PRO, Ed. 24/16/79 e.

19 Morant to Balfour, 14 September 1901: BL, Add. MS. 49787, ff. 20–1.

20 Kekewich to Gorst, 1 January 1902: PRO, Ed. 24/18/144.

21 R. Cecil to E. Cecil, 13 April 1902: Chelwood MSS., Hatfield House, CHE 3/139.

22 Ilbert's political diary, 4 November 1901. Godley was the influential Permanent Secretary at the India Office.

23 Kekewich to Gorst, 9 January 1902: PRO, Ed. 24/18/144.

24 Morant to Balfour, 14 September 1901: BL Add. MS. 49787, ff. 20–1. It is clear from this and other exchanges that Morant is attempting to establish the notion that Devonshire was being tricked by Kekewich into taking a line hostile to the Balfour–Morant position. Nothing could have been further from the truth. Devonshire may have been lethargic but he was far from gullible. This is merely Morant's attempt to blacken Kekewich's name.

25 Morant to Balfour, 1 November 1901: BL, Add. MS. 49787, ff. 33–4.

26 Ilbert's political diary, 20 December 1901. Ilbert was head of the Office of the Parliamentary Counsel. This dismissal was quite a humiliation.

27 Balfour to Ilbert, 20 December 1901: BL, Add. MS. 49854, ff. 220–1.

28 Balfour to Morant, 20 December 1901: BL, Add. MS. 49787, f. 51: marked 'Confidential Mr Balfour's instructions to me December 20, 1901, as to lines of Education Bill'.

29 Thring, Ilbert's deputy, was politically reliable as far as the Unionist administration was concerned. Sandars wrote that Thring 'did good work': Sandars (Balfour's Private Secretary) memorial on Balfour, copy in Chandos MSS., Churchill College Cambridge, Chan. 1 3/6. No date but written c. 1911.

30 Sadleir (1949), p. 182.

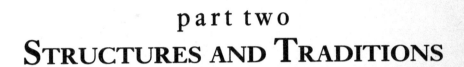

part two
STRUCTURES AND TRADITIONS

Two National Curricula – Baker's and Stalin's. Towards a Liberal Alternative

2.1

JOHN WHITE

A NATIONAL CURRICULUM

There is no virtue in a national curriculum as such. Hitler had a national curriculum and so did Stalin. The basic issue is: what *kind* of national curriculum is Mr Baker giving us?

Stalin's curriculum is especially instructive. Leaving out tiny inputs on the USSR Constitution, astronomy and psychology, it consisted of: language and literature, mathematics, history, geography, the sciences of biology, physics and chemistry, a foreign language, physical education, drawing, singing and practical work in agriculture or industry. The list is almost identical to Mr Baker's ten foundation subjects. Not only that: three of Stalin's items were classified as 'important subjects' – language, mathematics and science. Today we call these 'core subjects'. Detailed syllabuses for every subject mentioned, covering the ten years of compulsory education, were laid down rigidly from the centre.

None of this implies that our government's policy is Stalinist or that there is an affinity between Russia's Man of Steel and our own Iron Lady. But it does prompt the question: in the light of the surprising similarities between the two curricula, what differentiates them?

The obvious first move is to look at their underlying rationale, the aims and ideals which underpin them – taking care to distinguish publicly avowed from covert intentions. In Stalin's case the task is pretty easy. Behind the Marxist-Leninist rhetoric about the making of the New Soviet Man lay Stalin's desire to harness the school system to the demands of his police-state autocracy. What about Mr Baker?

His consultation document on the National Curriculum contains just three pages of rationale. Most of it Stalin could have accepted. To equip pupils 'for the responsibilities of citizenship and for the challenges of employment in tomorrow's world'. No problem. To ensure that all pupils 'study a broad and balanced range of

Source: J. White (1988) 'Two National Curricula – Baker's and Stalin's. Towards a Liberal Alternative', *British Journal of Educational Studies*, 36(3), pp. 218–31.

subjects throughout their compulsory education'. Ditto. To ensure that 'all pupils, regardless of sex, ethnic origin and geographical location, have access to the same good and relevant curriculum'. Ditto! To 'check on progress towards objectives at different stages'; to 'enable schools to be more accountable'. Ditto again!

The only hint of distinctiveness comes not in the document itself but in its reference to the White Paper *Better Schools* (1985). This gave us a very brief list of aims, including such things as helping pupils to develop lively, enquiring minds and the ability to question and argue rationally; to acquire knowledge relevant to adult life and employment; to use language and numbers effectively; to develop personal moral values and acquire respect for religious values and tolerance of other races and ways of life; to understand the world in which they live; to appreciate human achievements.

Apart from the references to personal moral values, religion, tolerance of other ways of life and the ability to question, there is again nothing here to which Stalin need have objected. Agreed, though, these do give us something.

But how much? Three lines of text scarcely provide a fully worked out underpinning for a non-Stalinist national curriculum. They are capable of innumerable interpretations. Not only this: we are not told how they are supposed to map on to the curriculum subjects. The most puzzling thing about this National Curriculum is that it includes no obvious vehicle whereby to develop personal values, including tolerance of other races and ways of life. True, some of the foundation subjects, especially English, history and geography, can play a part – not that the Baker curriculum says they should. But there is in any case only a limited amount that *academic subjects* can do to promote these aims – as compared, say, with whole school policies on respect and tolerance within the classroom, the pastoral curriculum and non-authoritarian forms of school organisation.

Mr Baker fails to explain why he says nothing about other means of realising aims than traditional subjects. But this is only one instance of his more general reluctance to give us more than the glimmerings of a rationale. We simply don't know, on the information given so far, how un-Stalinesque the National Curriculum will turn out to be. Part of the problem is that the Bill gives ministers very wide powers to determine the details of curricular programmes, all these being as yet unspecified. Since public statements about underlying aims are so meagre, the way is left open for Mr Baker and his successors to gear the syllabuses in different areas to virtually whatever purposes they think fit.

One should not confuse favouring the principle of a national curriculum with favouring *this* National Curriculum. The main argument for shifting from professional to political control of the broad framework of the curriculum is that questions about the aims and content of education are intimately connected with views about the kind of society we wish to live in. They are as much political questions as are issues of taxation policy or defence. Every citizen in a democracy – as we, but not Stalinists, understand these terms – should have an equal right to participate in the control or exercise of political power in these and other areas. The problem with leaving curricula in the hands of the teaching profession is that it is, after all, only one section of the citizenry and there is no reason why its opinions should be privileged over other people's.

The only defensible form of national curriculum is one that is genuinely committed to democratic principles, not least equality of political power. A minimum test of its commitment is whether it includes among its goals preparing all young people to become equal citizens of a democracy. There is nothing in the Baker curriculum about this – nothing about the prerequisite understanding of the socio-economic structure or the principles of democracy, about fostering the virtues necessary in democratic citizens, about equipping people for critical reflection on the status quo, or about building the imperfect democratic structures we have now into something more adequate.

All of which raises again the question: in what way does Mr Baker's National Curriculum diverge from Stalin's? If it does nothing to celebrate and nurture our democratic values, wherein lies the difference?

NEUTRALISM IN POLITICS

While I believe the argument in the last few paragraphs – about the desirability of political control – to be substantially correct, it is too quick as it stands and needs further filling out.

Just to remind you of the central feature of the argument: questions about the aims and broad content of education are intimately connected with views about the kind of society we wish to live in: they are therefore political questions, to be resolved by the citizenry as a whole, not a sectional group within it.

There are two ways in which this argument is too quick. First, its conclusion is only that there should be political control. It does not say anything about the level at which that political control should operate. So a further argument has to be brought in to show that there should be *national*, as distinct from local, control.

The second way in which the argument is too quick is this. It seems to assume that democratic political control is in order whenever decisions are made which imply views about the general shape of society. But this is questionable. Suppose a democratically elected government decided to shape its educational and other institutions so as to promote a certain view of what human well-being consisted in and to discourage rival views. Suppose, for instance, it sought to set up some kind of theocracy in which the good life for the individual was premised on the love of God and obedience to His will. We can have in mind, perhaps, the religious communities of seventeenth-century New England for a partial parallel.

All of us, I would imagine, would reject such a polity. If we did so, we would be appealing, I suggest, to something like the principle that, in a *liberal* democracy, governments should not steer people towards determinate ideals of human well-being. Insofar as we accepted something like this principle, we would be implicitly accepting that it is not enough for a government to be democratically elected to be justified in imposing a national curriculum. That curriculum must also conform to this basic liberal principle: the government would be exceeding its powers if it steered pupils towards determinate pictures of the good life. These need not, of course, be religious.

It is important, I think, to look further into how we should formulate this basic liberal principle, of which we all have, I suggest, a rough intuitive idea.

A common way of expressing it among philosophers of liberalism is in terms of *neutrality*. They hold that government ought to be neutral with regard to different conceptions of the good life. Dworkin, for instance, takes off from the claim that

> Each person follows a more-or-less articulate conception of what gives value to life. The scholar who values a life of contemplation has such a conception; so also does the television-watching, beer-drinking citizen who is fond of saying 'This is the life', though he has thought less about the issue and is less able to describe or defend his conception.[1]

Dworkin argues that if government is to treat its citizens equally it has not to prefer one conception of the good life to another. Rawls and Nozick, who differ radically in other ways about the proper sphere of government, nevertheless agree with Dworkin that conceptions of the good are not for government to promote.

If one accepts this, then how is the proper sphere of government to be delimited? One argument might be that government should have a hand in trying to ensure that the necessary conditions are provided for everyone to lead his or her preferred way of life. These necessary conditions may take different forms.

There is first of all what we might call the 'moral framework' of the society. This is a set of rules which protects or promotes the actions of individuals in pursuit of their own well-being. Examples might be prohibitions against murder, physical injury, stealing, breach of contract, lying, as well, perhaps, as positive injunctions like that of helping those in distress. It is generally accepted that part of government's task is to try to secure compliance to at least some of such rules. The chief way in which it does this is by a system of laws against murder, stealing, bodily harm etc. The moral framework, however, goes beyond the framework of law. Lying and promise-breaking are not always, or typically, legal offences, but moral prohibitions against them are still basic to personal well-being.

Government may also have a role in helping to provide other necessary conditions of the good life which we may label 'welfare'. Whatever one's particular view of the good life, one will need, among other things, food, clothing, shelter, good health, a secure and predictable environment, an income and freedom from interference. (The list is not intended to be complete.) Government can play a part in providing these goods, although people will differ about how far its powers should extend. Whatever its political complexion, it will deal with defence against external aggression and with policing; it may well also have to do with housing, health, food regulation, as well as with laws protecting various liberties. Even though it is only in fully socialist economies that it engages directly in the production of food, clothing and other basic necessities, in any nonsocialist modern society, government will promote such economic objectives in all kinds of other ways.

EDUCATIONAL IMPLICATIONS

While it may be true, then, that educational aims carry with them some picture of the good society, it does not follow that government must have a hand in determining them. On the neutralist liberal theory of politics just outlined, government would be debarred from laying down any aims which encapsulated a view of the good life.

If it is the case that all acounts of educational aims must encapsulate such a view, then on the liberal view the determination of aims should lie entirely outside the province of government. It might well seem that any reasonably comprehensive account of aims must say something about the constituents of personal well-being. Perhaps this thought has lain behind the belief, virtually unchallenged in Britain before its recent shift towards governmental control of school curricula, that aims should be left to the teaching profession.

On the other hand, it might be possible to distinguish among aims between those which carry with them a picture of the good life and those which have to do with necessary conditions for leading the good life, however that be conceived. If government can legitimately be concerned with helping to supply those necessary conditions, then it could legitimately help to determine aims falling in this category.

Following the distinction made above, it could be involved in aims to do with the moral framework or aims to do with welfare.

This still leaves it a broad territory. As to the moral framework, it might lay down aims to do with law, or aims about that part of morality not enshrined in law. It could, for instance, insist that everyone is brought up with some knowledge of what law is in general and its function in promoting individual well-being. To that aim it might add an acquaintance with major particular laws currently in force. Again, it might also think it important to build up dispositions in children not to want to break these laws and, more widely, dispositions to conform to moral rules that lie outside the legal framework. Some people would want government prescription under this heading to go still further – beyond law and order and conventional morality. Part of the moral framework within which we live is our democratic constitution. It would be possible to argue on neutralist grounds that governments should develop in future citizens the understandings and attitudes necessary to making democracy work. One might also want to argue that governments should promote not only conformity with moral rules but also a reflective attitude towards them. Here I simply list the various things which might fall under 'moral education' aims of government, without arguing their various pros and cons.

Welfare aims might also be various. The government could lay down, for instance, that children are acquainted with the different forms of welfare and their contribution to individual well-being: this might cover work on such things as peace, the police, health, the social services, the economy. Preparation for roles within the economy might also fall under this heading: it might range from equipping pupils with useful general skills and knowledge, in the areas of science and technology, for instance, to more specific training for particular types of job.

It is not difficult to find examples of governmental determination of moral and welfare aims in the recent history of education in Britain:

1   Before the recent shift away from professional and towards political control of aims and curricula, the only compulsory curriculum subject in state schools was religious education. One of the reasons why this was included in the 1944 Education Act was that it was felt that it would help to shore up moral values in the post-war period.
2   More recently, since the Great Debate of 1975–6, and more particularly since the Thatcher government of 1979 to date, we have seen a marked emphasis on economically orientated aims.

As far as I am aware the Thatcher moves towards a national curriculum owe no explicit allegiance to neutralist liberal principles. I leave on one side Conservative onslaughts on peace education. Since security against external attack is one of the deepest foundations on which personal well-being is built, it would be entirely consonant with the welfare aims permitted by neutralism to urge that government should include work on this topic in its national curriculum proposals.

I would suggest that present Conservative thinking about education is *not* based on liberal principles at all but has quite another basis. At present there are two strands in Conservative thinking – the 'Scrutonian' strand which emphasises traditional academic subjects, and the 'Keith Joseph' strand which stresses the needs of the economy. What both views have in common is elitism. The first group would like the country to be run by an intellectual elite, the second by businessmen. Elitism of these sorts or any other sort offends against liberalism in privileging a certain view of the good life over others – namely the conception of the good life favoured by the elite.

In this connection, the argument that a national curriculum is desirable because it can increase 'equality of access' is not necessarily a liberal argument. For it, too, can be interpreted in such a way as to presuppose the existence of an elite. If there is no elite, then to what is the 'access'?

Let us come back to more general considerations. Suppose a government restricted itself to moral framework and/or welfare aims, who would be responsible for aims to do with the good life? Could these be justifiably left to the schools and/or parents? A difficulty is that if those educators steered pupils towards some ways of life rather than others, they would be in the same position as a non-neutralist government, and neutralist objections to the latter would also seem to apply to them. One alternative would be to exclude life-ideals from educational aims altogether. But this would seem to leave children without any guidance, except what they might pick up incidentally, about what goals in life they should follow, and this is especially hard to defend.

But is it clear, in any case, that a neutralist government must restrict itself to aims to do with the moral framework and welfare? For there is one further way in which it can help to provide the necessary conditions of the good life without favouring a particular version of the latter. It could aim at acquainting pupils impartially with a whole range of different ideals of the good life, without steering them towards any in particular. I had this principle very much in mind in writing *Towards a Compulsory Curriculum.*[2]

CRITIQUE OF NEUTRALISM

There is one major problem with this line of thought. Is it true, in fact, that being acquainted with different ideals of life is a necessary condition of personal well-being? A positive answer here presumably takes for granted that this knowledge is indispensable for *choice* of a way of life. But this itself embodies a particular view of the good life, namely, as one in which the individual chooses his or her way of life, rather than having this determined by others. Because this conception is so much a part of our cultural background, it is often difficult for us to see it for what it is. But it should be clear enough on reflection that the autonomous life, as just described, is not without its competitors. In more traditional societies than our own there are many other versions of the good life which do not embrace personal autonomy: societies, for instance, in which life-goals are determined by caste, by gender, by fortune-telling or magic, by parental profession, by religious doctrine or by various combinations of these. In supporting autonomy, a government would be abandoning neutralism, since it would be favouring one particular version of the good life.

This means that a neutralist government cannot consistently lay down aims to do with acquainting pupils with different life-ideals. It also brings us back to the problem of what guidance any pupil can expect, on neutralist principles, about what kind of life he or she should lead. Nothing now seems to be available.

But this in its turn provokes further questions about the role of a neutralist government in laying down aims to do with the moral framework and/or welfare. For the reason for doing this is to help to provide necessary conditions for people to lead a life of well-being. Yet if no guidance can be given on what such a life might consist in, one wonders what is the point of building a substructure if there is no superstructure to support.

The truth is, however, that there *is* a superstructure, after all. In the kind of society in which we live, that is a liberal democracy built around an advanced industrial economy, welfare provision and a moral framework only make sense if seen as necessary conditions for an autonomous way of life.

It is true that some version of a moral framework and some version of welfare will be necessary for *any* type of society, including those resting on non-autonomous forms of life. Every society will need prohibitions on murder, bodily injury, stealing, lying and promise-breaking; and in every society people will need food, clothing and shelter. But in our kind of society more is included under our two headings than these very basic requirements. In particular we see it as a vital function of government to protect various individual liberties: there are, for instance, legal or moral prohibitions on interference with freedom of expression, freedom of movement, freedom from indoctrination or manipulation, freedom from intrusion into one's private affairs.

Why do we consider personal liberty important? One could take the view that this is an ultimate value, which cannot be supported by reference to anything more basic. But such a position would be hard to maintain. If it were true, then *any* form of liberty would be seen as valuable. But it is noteworthy that the liberties we see as requiring protection, like those mentioned above, are of a particular kind. Charles Taylor[3] has recently pointed out that although there are far fewer traffic lights per kilometre in the streets of the capital of Albania, Tirana, than in, say, London, we would not call the Albanians freer than the British because they are less constrained in this way. A liberal's attachment to negative liberty, that is freedom from interference in doing what one wants, has to do with forms of interference which most seriously impede the kind of life one chooses to lead. Impediments to the realisation of one's most important desires are of more moment than others. It is because people's desires to practise their religion, to express their ideas, to control their own lives, to determine where they will live and what kind of work they will do are seen as more important to them than the desire to drive unimpeded through city streets, that political liberty has to do with the former rather than the latter. If this is right, then negative liberty is desirable not in itself, but as a requirement of positive liberty, that is of one's leading a life which one has autonomously chosen to lead.

All this means that neutralism is an untenable position: in refusing preference to some ideals of life over others, it overlooks the fact that it is tacitly presupposing the value of personal autonomy.[4] This comes out not only in its commitment to negative liberty, but also in the underlying reasons for advocating neutralism in the first place. Why, after all, should it be thought desirable to avoid entanglement in different conceptions of the good? Why should one try to ensure that one conception is not favoured over another? The root anxiety here seems to be that non-neutrality brings with it the danger of *imposing* one way of life rather than another. But this is only an anxiety for someone who is already wedded to the view that individuals should freely determine their own way of life, that is for someone who already places a high value on autonomy.

But if the so-called neutralist turns out to value autonomy, can he or she avoid the charge of imposing *this* value? To tackle this, we need, I think, to distinguish between acceptable and unacceptable imposition, not assuming from the start, as the neutralist appears to do, that every form of imposition is reprehensible. Imposing a *determinate* way of life is seen as undesirable, by neutralists and others, because it prevents one from choosing one's own way. The opposition to imposition stems from a commitment to autonomy. But the imposition of autonomy cannot be objected to for the same reason, for it is *in line with* this commitment and not opposed to it. If a government's institutions and policies are all autonomy-supporting, and if its educational policy is directed towards the cultivation of autonomy in its citizens, there can be nothing reprehensible about that for anyone who holds that autonomy is a good thing. And that, as we now see, includes the would-be neutralist. More than that: it is only rational for adherents of autonomy, not merely to condone, but also positively to welcome, any such autonomy-bolstering activities on the government's part.

GOVERNMENT, EDUCATION AND AUTONOMY

All this has important implications for the conduct of government in a liberal democracy like our own. Political battle lines tend to be drawn between those on the Right, who advocate freedom from state control in sphere after sphere, and Left-wingers, who call for an extension of state welfare provision. Insofar as negative freedom derives its value from positive freedom, or autonomy, and insofar as welfare provision likewise subserves autonomy, then Left and Right could well be united in a common goal: the promotion of general autonomy.

In practice things are not as simple as this. There may be other motives for non-interventionist policies than the furtherance of general autonomy. Reductions in income tax, or the removal of parts of industry, education, health and other services from state control, can be undertaken so as to shift wealth and income further towards the rich. They may give greater autonomy to those who are already highly autonomous, at least in many dimensions, but they may also make it harder for many other people to become autonomous, in depriving them of the welfare services they need. This raises questions about justice. If autonomy is important, then why does the autonomy of one group weigh more in the balance than that of another?

I shall take it henceforth that a *justifiable* government policy is one which seeks to promote the autonomy of all its citizens and does not favour some at the expense of others.

This is a difficult position to argue against and it is noteworthy that no mainstream political party would overtly resist it. However much it was actually in favour of greater autonomy for the rich rather than for the poor, for the managers rather than for the managed, for the white majority than for the black minority, it could not publicly declare this without contravening the Kantian principle that everybody is equally worthy of respect as an end in himself or herself, which is so centrally enshrined within our public culture, although deviations from it in practice are very common.

How does education fit into this picture? We have seen that the autonomous life has many prerequisites, covering both what we have called the 'moral framework' and 'welfare'. Government has a role in both areas. Some of its work has to do with trying to ensure that its citizens' autonomy can be *exercised*. To this end it maintains a framework of protective laws, provides internal and external peace, health and other social services etc. But one cannot talk about individuals' exercising their autonomy unless they have become autonomous in the first place. Government can help in this task, too. Of course, many of the institutions needed in order to protect the exercise of autonomy are also necessary for its formation: if children were brought up without health care, or in a society in which law and order had broken down completely, then their chances of growing into self-determining adults would be severely reduced. But other policies and institutions are needed, too. In order to become autonomous, there has to exist a range of options from which one can choose preferred alternatives. How extensive this range should be is a further question, but, whatever its extent, government can and should have some hand in seeing that it exists. There must be, for instance, a sufficiently wide range of occupations, open, moreover, to the population at large.

But it is not enough that a wide range of options *exists*. Those who are to choose them must *know* that they exist. This is where education begins to enter the picture. More generally, in order to become autonomous one needs to have acquired various capacities, dispositions, and types of understanding. If a government is committed to the promotion of autonomy for everyone, it must try to bring it about that everyone has been educated so as to exercise it. A full account both of what autonomy is and what is educationally necessary for it cannot be given here, but for the moment it will be enough to bring out the following points. To become self-determined one needs, as we have seen, an understanding of the various options open to one. Some choices that one faces are more important than others. Knowing the differences between the types of socks, or baked beans or television sets from which one can choose is less important than understanding what differentiates the life of a religious believer from that of a sceptic, or being a trade union official from being a manager, or voting for the policies of one political party over another. Behind such more specific knowledge will be knowledge of a more general sort – about religion, for instance, the structure of one's society, the physical sciences. But autonomous persons need more than knowledge or understanding. They also have to have certain dispositions of character. If they are to withstand possible manipulation or coercion by others they need independence of mind, resoluteness, courage. If they are to be free from obstacles arising from their own psyche, they need to be clear on where their major priorities lie and firmly committed to those priorities over values of lesser importance. There is much more to add later about the virtues necessary for autonomy. In particular, nothing has yet been said about attitudes towards other people. But even this brief introduction should be enough to underline the point that a government committed to autonomy must see to it that certain educational aims are met which go beyond those to do with welfare and with the moral framework that we earlier described. To the latter, which are concerned with knowledge and dispositions pertaining to the necessary conditions of personal well-being, are now added aims to do with the nature of that well-being itself. How all these various aims are to be related each to the other is again a further question. The main conclusion at this point is the extensive responsibility that liberal democratic governments should have for laying down educational aims which prepare their citizens for autonomy.

GOVERNMENT AND THE AIMS OF EDUCATION: THE IDEAL AND THE PRACTICABLE

Where does all this leave us in the debate, currently still unresolved in Britain, about whether government should have any role in laying down educational aims – aims which will steer and constrain the work of schools and other institutions? In theory, there is a strong case for government control. There are no grounds for allowing any *section* of the population to determine aims, since any serious account of the latter will bring with it some picture of how society is to be, and since this picture is no private and fleeting vision, but is intended to inform the workings of public institutions, *every* citizen, and not only a sectional group, has an interest in the subject. There is thus no reason why teachers should have any privileged voice; or parents; or teachers and parents together.

Aims, then, must be publicly determined. But it is not open to government to lay down just *any* aims. Those it favours must be related to its role. In a liberal-democratic society the proper task of government is to promote the well-being of all citizens by equipping them with the necessary conditions of an autonomous life. Educationally, this means helping to build up in them those dispositions and forms of understanding which are required for autonomy.

It does not follow from this that the wisest policy in any liberal democracy is to put the aims of education under government control. For actual governments may not be motivated by the desire to help everyone to become autonomous. What goes for a liberal democracy outlined in the abstract may not go for an imperfect liberal democracy in which ideal motivations are sometimes lacking.

Whether or not aims should be left to government cannot be laid down by a formula. Everything depends on local considerations.[5] If there has been a long tradition of benign – that is autonomy-supporting – action on the part of successive governments, then it might be safe to put aims under state control. Where a government is likely to misuse its power, to mouth autonomy for all, for instance, but in reality to encourage autonomy for a few and structure the educational system so that the many become their servants, then such a move would be unwise.

What alternative could there be, however, to government control? Since sectional interests have already been ruled out, what is there left? The dangers with leaving aims to sectional groups are that they may skew these towards their own interests, or towards doctrines to which they are attached, or leave them to the play of chance or the strongest pressure group. Those who put aims into practice – teachers and parents, and perhaps those working in the media, too – are susceptible to these faults along with everybody else. But again, the likelihood of this will vary from situation to situation, from one society to another and from one time to another. It might be the case in a particular situation that teachers and parents taken together are more likely to favour autonomy-supporting aims than the government is. Here there might be good grounds for leaving aims under professional rather than political control, if this were possible. But this would depend on teachers' and parents' and perhaps the media's working together on the basis of a good understanding of the issues at stake – such as those we have been examining in this paper, for instance. They will have to see themselves as acting as proxy for a more ideal government than the one they have.

The problems of co-ordinating an enterprise as large as this may make this solution impracticable. Others may be better. To reduce the danger of corruption or other mishandling on the part of future governments, all parties might agree to set up some quasi-independent public body to determine aims and oversee their translation into more specific objectives. This could include representatives both of government and of professional educators and, if possible, be protected by a code of educational principles premised on the promotion of autonomy for all and written into the constitution of the state.

Notes

1 R. Dworkin (1985) 'Liberalism', in S. Hampshire (ed.), *Public and Private Morality*. Cambridge: Cambridge University Press.
2 J. White (1973) *Towards a Compulsory Curriculum*. London: Routledge & Kegan Paul.
3 C. Taylor (1985) 'What's Wrong with Negative Liberty?', in his *Philosophical Papers*, Vol. 2. Cambridge: Cambridge University Press.
4 J. Ray (1986) *The Morality of Freedom*. Oxford: Oxford University Press, chapters 5 and 6.
5 Ray (1986), pp. 427–9.

CURRICULUM REFORM AND CURRICULUM THEORY: A CASE OF
2.2 HISTORICAL AMNESIA

IVOR GOODSON

The school curriculum is a social artefact, conceived of and made for deliberate human purposes. It is therefore a supreme paradox that in many accounts of schooling, the written curriculum, this most manifest of social constructions, has been treated as a given. Moreover, the problem has been compounded by the fact that it has often been treated as a *neutral* given embedded in an otherwise meaningful and complex situation. Yet in our own schooling we know very well that while we loved some subjects, topics or lessons, we hated others. Some we learnt easily and willingly, others we rejected whole-heartedly. Sometimes the variable was the teacher, or the time, or the room, or us, but often it was the form or content of the curriculum itself. Of course, beyond such individualistic responses there were, and are, significant collective responses to curriculum, and again when patterns can be discerned it suggests this is far from a 'neutral' factor.

Why, then, has so little attention been given to the making of curriculum? We have a social construction which sits at the heart of the process by which we educate our children. Yet in spite of the patchy exhortations of sociologists, sociologists of knowledge in particular, one looks in vain for serious study of the process of social construction which emanates as curriculum.

The reasons for this lacuna in our educational studies can be focused on two specific aspects: first, the nature of curriculum as a *source* for study, and secondly, associated with this, questions relating to the *methods* we employ in approaching the study of curriculum.

In this article I shall deal with some of the problems involved in employing curriculum as a source. Part of the problem has already been mentioned: namely that many accounts of schooling accept the curriculum as a given, an inevitable and essentially unimportant variable. Of course, some important work in the fields of curriculum studies and sociology of knowledge have provided a continuing challenge to this kind of curriculum myopia.

But once it is accepted that the curriculum itself is an important source for study, a number of further problems surface. For 'the curriculum' is a perennially elusive and multi-faceted concept. The curriculum is such a slippery concept because it is defined, redefined and negotiated at a number of levels and in a

Source: I. Goodson (1989) 'Curriculum Reform and Curriculum Theory: A Case of Historical Amnesia', *Cambridge Journal of Education*, 19(2), pp. 131–41.

number of arenas. It would be impossible to arbitrate over which points in the ongoing negotiations were critical. In addition, the terrain differs substantially according to local or national structures and patterns. In such a shifting and unfocused terrain it is plainly problematic to try to define common ground for our study. After all, if there is a lacuna in our study it is likely to be for good reasons.

The substantial difficulties do not, however, mean, as has often been the case to date, that we should ignore the area of curriculum completely or focus on 'minute particulars' that are amenable to focused study. Part of the problem is, I believe, resolvable. This resolution turns on identifying common ground or, conceptualised another way, some areas of stability within the apparent fluidity and flux of curriculum.

We should remember that a great deal of the most important scholarship on curriculum, certainly on curriculum as a social construction, took place in the 1960s and early 1970s. This was, however, a period of unusual change and flux everywhere in the Western world: and nowhere more so than in the world of schooling in general and curriculum in particular. For such a burgeoning of critical curriculum scholarship to happen during such times was both encouraging and, in a sense, symptomatic. The emergence of a field of study of curriculum as social construction was an important new direction. But, while itself symptomatic of a period of social questioning and criticism, this burgeoning of critical scholarship was not without its down-side.

I believe that down-side has two aspects which are important as we begin to reconstitute our study of schooling and curriculum. First, influential scholars in the field often took a value position which assumed that schooling should be reformed, root and branch 'revolutionised', the 'maps of learning redrawn'. Secondly, this scholarship took place at a time when a wide range of curriculum reform movements were seeking to do precisely this, 'to revolutionise school curricula' on both grounds. Therefore it was unlikely that such scholars would wish to focus upon, let alone concede, the areas of stability, of unchallengeable 'high ground' that may have existed within the school curriculum.

In the 1960s one might characterise curriculum reform as a sort of 'tidal wave'. Everywhere the waves created turbulence and activity, but they only actually engulfed a few small islands; more substantial land masses were hardly affected at all, and on dry land the mountains and high ground remained completely untouched. As the tide now rapidly recedes the high ground can be seen in stark silhouette. If nothing else, our scrutiny of the curriculum reform should allow recognition that there is not only high ground but common ground in the world of curriculum.

Standing out more clearly than ever on the new horizon are the school subjects, the 'basic' or 'traditional' subjects. Throughout the Western world there is exhortation but also evidence about a 'return to basics', a re-embrace of 'traditional subjects'. In England, for instance, the new National Curriculum defines a range of subjects to be taught as a 'core' curriculum in all schools. The subjects thereby instated bear an uncanny resemblance to the list which generally defined secondary school subjects in the 1904 Regulations. The *Times Educational Supplement* commented about this reassertion of traditional subject dominance:

'The first thing to say about this whole exercise is that it unwinds 80 years of English (and Welsh) educational history. It is a case of go back to go.' In the early years of the nineteenth century the first state secondary schools were organised. Their curriculum was presented by the National Board of Education under the detailed guidance of Sir Robert Morant:

> The course should provide for instruction in the English Language and Literature, at least one Language other than English, Geography, History, Mathematics, Science and Drawing, with due provision for Manual Work and Physical Exercises, and in a girls' school for Housewifery. Not less than 4½ hours per week must be allotted to English, Geography and History; not less than 3½ hours to the Language where one is taken or less than 6 hours where two are taken; and not less than 7½ hours to Science and Mathematics, of which at least 3 must be for Science.

But in looking at the new 1987 National Curricula, we find that 'The 8–10 Subject timetable which the discussion paper draws up has as academic a look to it as anything Sir Robert Morant could have dreamed up.'[1] Likewise, in scrutinising curriculum history in the US high school, Kliebard has pointed to the saliency of the 'traditional' school subjects in the face of waves of curriculum reform initiatives from earlier decades. He characterises the school subject within the US high school curriculum as 'The Impregnable Fortress'.[2]

But let us return to the conceptualisation of curriculum as our source of study, for it remains elusive and slippery, even in these times of centrality and tradition where we return to basics. In the 1960s and 1970s critical studies of curriculum as social construction pointed to the school classroom as the site wherein the curriculum was negotiated and realised. The classroom was the 'centre of action', 'the arena of resistance'. By this view what went on in the classroom *was* the curriculum. The definition of curriculum – the view from the 'high ground' and the mountains – was, it was thought, not just subject to redefinition at classroom level but quite simply irrelevant. Such a view, and such a standpoint from which to begin to study curriculum, is, I think, now unsustainable. Certainly the high ground of the written curriculum is subject to renegotiation at lower levels, notably the classroom. But the view, common in the 1960s, that it is therefore irrelevant is, I think, less common nowadays. Once again, I would suspect the view is gaining currency that the high ground, our common ground in this article, is of importance. In the high ground what is to be 'basic' and 'traditional' is reconstituted and reinvented. The 'given' status of school subject knowledge is therein reinvented and reasserted. But this is more than political manoeuvring or rhetoric: such reassertion affects the discourse about schooling and relates to the 'parameters to practice'. In the 1980s it would, I think, be folly to ignore the central importance of the redefinition of the written curriculum. In a significant sense the written curriculum is the visible and public testimony of selected rationales and legitimating rhetoric for schooling. In England and Wales I have argued elsewhere that the written curriculum both promulgates and underpins certain basic intentions of schooling as they are operationalized in structures and institutions. To take a common convention in preactive curriculum, the school subject: while the written curriculum defines the rationales and rhetoric of the subject, this is the only tangible aspect of a patterning of resources, finances and examinations and associated material and career interests. In this symbiosis, it is as though the written curriculum provides a guide to the legitimating rhetoric of schooling as they are promoted through patterns of resource allocation, status attribution and career distribution. In short, the written curriculum provides us with a testimony, a documentary source, a changing map of the terrain: it is also one of the best official guide books to the institutionalized structure of schooling.[3]

What is most important to stress is that the written curriculum, notably the convention of the school subject, has, in this instance, both symbolic and also practical significance. Symbolic – in that certain intentions for schooling are thereby publicly signified and legitimated; practical – in that these written conventions are rewarded with finance and with the associated work and career benefits.

Our study of the written curriculum should afford a range of insights into schooling. But it is important to stress that such study must be allied to other kinds of study – in particular studies of school process, of school texts and of the history of pedagogy. For schooling is comprised of the interlinked matrix of these, and indeed, other vital ingredients. With regard to schooling and to curriculum in particular, the final question is 'Who gets what and what do they do with it?'

The definition of written curriculum is part of this story. And that is not the same as asserting a direct or easily discernable relationship between the practical definition of written curriculum and its interactive realisation in classrooms. It is, however, to assert that the written curriculum most often sets important parameters for classroom practice (not always, not at all times, not in all classrooms, but 'most often'). The study of written curriculum will first increase our understanding of the influences and interests active at the preactive level. Secondly, this understanding will further our knowledge of the values and purposes represented in schooling and the manner in which preactive definition, notwithstanding individual and local variations, may set parameters for interactive realisation and negotiation in the classroom and school.

Studies of the preactive in relationship to the interactive are, then, where we should end. But for the moment, so neglected is the study of the preactive definition of written curriculum that no such marriage of methodologies could be consummated. The first step is plainly to undertake a range of studies of the definitions of written curriculum and, in particular, to focus on the 'impregnable fortress' of the school subject.

RECONSTITUTING SCHOOL SUBJECTS: THE EXAMPLE OF ENGLAND AND WALES IN THE 1980s

Traditionally in England and Wales those stressing 'the basics' have referred to the three Rs – reading, writing and arithmetic. In the 1980s it would be fair to say that those with curriculum power have been following a new version of the three Rs – rehabilitation, reinvention and reconstitution. Often the rehabilitation strategy for school subjects in the 1980s takes the form of arguing that good teaching is in fact good *subject* teaching. This is to seek to draw a veil over the whole experience of the 1960s, to seek to forget why many curriculum reforms were developed to try to provide antidotes to the perceived failures and inadequacies of conventional subject teaching. The rehabilitation strategy is itself in this sense quintessentially ahistorical, but paradoxically it is also a reminder of the power of 'vestiges of the past' to survive, revive and reproduce.

In England the 'reinvention' of 'traditional' subjects began in 1969 with the issue of the first collection of Black Papers.[4] The writers in this collection argued that teachers had been too greatly influenced by progressive theories of education like the integration of subjects, mixed ability teaching, enquiry and discovery teaching. This resulted in neglect of subject and basic skill teaching and led to reduced standards of pupil achievement and school discipline; the traditional subject was thereby equated with social and moral discipline. The rehabilitation of the traditional subject promised the re-establishment of discipline in both these cases. The Black Papers were taken up by politicians and in 1976 the Labour Prime Minister, James Callaghan, embraced many of their themes in his Ruskin Speech. Specific recommendations soon followed. In 1979, for instance, following a survey of secondary schools in England and Wales, Her Majesty's Inspectorate (HMI) drew attention to what they judged to be evidence of an insufficient match in many schools between the qualifications and experience of teachers and the work they were undertaking: later in a survey of middle schools they found that when they examined 'the proportion of teaching which was undertaken by teachers who had studied the subjects they taught as main subjects in initial training . . . higher standards of work overall were associated with a greater degree of use of subject teachers'.[5]

These perceptions provided a background to the Department of Education pamphlet *Teaching Quality*. The Secretary of State for Education listed the criteria for initial teacher training courses. The first criteria imposed the following requirement: 'That the higher education and initial training of all qualified teachers should include at least two full years' course time devoted to subject studies at a level appropriate to higher education.' This requirement therefore 'would recognize teachers' needs for subject expertise if they are to have the confidence and ability to enthuse pupils and respond to their curiosity in their chosen subject fields'.[6]

This final sentence is curiously circular. Obviously if the pupils choose subjects then it is probable that teachers will require subject expertise. But this is to foreclose a whole debate about *whether* they should choose subjects as an educational vehicle. Instead, we have a practical *fait accompli* presented as choice. In fact the students have no choice except to embrace 'their chosen subject fields'. The political rehabilitation of subjects by political diktat is presented as pupil choice.

In *Teaching Quality*, the issue of the match between the teachers' qualifications and their work with pupils, first raised in the 1979 HMI document, is again employed. We learn that 'the Government attach high priority to improving the fit between teachers' qualifications and their tasks as one means of improving the quality of education'. The criterion for such a fit is based on a clear belief in the sequential and hierarchical pattern of subject learning.

All specialist subject teaching during the secondary phase requires teachers whose study of the subject concerned is at a level appropriate to higher education, represents a substantial part of the higher education and training period, and is built on a suitable 'A' level basis.

The beginning of subject specialisation is best evidenced where the issue of non-subject based work in schools is scrutinised. Many aspects of school work take place outside (or beside) subject work – studies of school process have indeed shown how integrated pastoral and remedial work originates because pupils for one reason or another do not achieve in traditional subjects. Far from accepting the subject as an educational vehicle with severe limits if the intention is to educate all pupils, the document seeks to rehabilitate subjects even in those domains which often originate from subject 'fall-out':

> Secondary teaching is not all subject based, and initial training and qualifications cannot provide an adequate preparation for the whole range of secondary school work. For example, teachers engaged in careers or remedial work or in providing group courses of vocational preparation, and those given the responsibility for meeting 'special needs' in ordinary schools, need to undertake these tasks not only on the basis of initial qualifications but after experience of teaching a specialist subject and preferably after appropriate post-experience training. Work of this kind and the teaching of interdisciplinary studies are normally best shared among teachers with varied and appropriate specialist qualifications and expertise.[7]

The rehabilitation of school subjects has become the mainstay of government thinking about the school curriculum. In many ways the governmental and structural support offered to school subjects as the organising device for secondary schooling is reaching unprecedented levels. Hargreaves has judged that 'more than at any time previously, it seems, the subject is to take an overriding importance in the background preparation and curricular responsibility of secondary school teachers'. But the preferred policy sits alongside a major change in the style of governance of education, for Hargreaves argues that, nor does that intention on the part of HMI and DES amount to just a dishing out of vague advice. Rather, in a style of centralized policy intervention and review with which we in Britain are becoming increasingly familiar in the 1980s, it is supported by strong and clear declarations of intent to build the achievement of subject match into the criteria for approval (or not) of teacher training courses, and to undertake five-yearly reviews of selected secondary schools to ensure that subject match is being improved within them and is being reflected in the pattern of teacher appointments.[8]

The associated issue of increasingly centralised control is also raised in a recent DES publication on *Education 8 to 12 in Combined and Middle Schools*.[9] Again, the rehabilitation of school subjects is rehearsed in a section on the need to 'extend teachers' subject knowledge'. Rowland has seen the document as 'part of an attempt to bring a degree of centralized control over education'. He states that '*Education 8 to 12* may well be interpreted by teachers and others as recommending yet another means in the trend towards a more schematicized approach to learning in which the focus is placed even more firmly on the subject matter rather than the child.' He adds cryptically that 'the evidence it produces, however, points to the need to move in quite the opposite direction'.[10] His reservations about the effects of rehabilitating school subjects are widely shared. Another scholar has noted that one effect of the strategy 'will be to reinforce the existing culture of secondary teaching and thereby inhibit curricular and pedagogic innovation on a school-wide front'.[11]

The various government initiatives and reports since 1976 have shown a consistent tendency to return to 'basics', to re-embrace 'traditional' subjects. This government project, which spans both Labour and Conservative administrations, has culminated in the 'new' National Curriculum. The curriculum was defined in a consultation document, *The National Curriculum 5–16*. This was rapidly followed in the wake of the Conservatives' third election victory in succession by the introduction of the Education Reform Bill into the House of Commons in November 1987. The Bill defines certain common curricular elements which are to be offered to pupils of compulsory school age, which will be known as 'the National Curriculum'.

Whilst presented as a striking new political initiative, comparison with the 1904 Regulations shows a remarkable degree of historical continuity. The National Curriculum comprises

- the 'core' subjects of mathematics, English and science,
- the 'foundation' subjects of history, geography, technology, music, art, physical education and (for secondary pupils) a modern foreign language.[12]

Historical amnesia allows curriculum reconstruction to be presented as curriculum revolution; as Orwell noted, he (or in this case she) 'who controls the past, controls the future'.

DEVELOPING HISTORICAL PERSPECTIVES

In this article, I have argued that, following the frustrating results of curriculum reform efforts in the 1960s and their substantial dismantling and reversal in the 1980s, the arguments for historical study are now considerable indeed. The contemporary power of those 'vestiges of the past', traditional school subjects, has been evidenced at some length with instances drawn from Great Britain. To argue for curricular change strategies which ignored history would surely be improbable, if not impossible, in the current situation. Yet as we have seen, this has been the dominant posture of curricular activists and theorists in the twentieth century. It is time to place historical study at the centre of the curriculum enterprise, to exhume the early work on curricular history, and the spasmodic subsequent work, and to rehabilitate systematically the historical study of school subjects. [...]

Histories of the symbolic drift of school knowledge raise questions about the patterns of evolution through which subjects pass. There is a growing body of work on the history of school subjects. In *School Subjects and Curriculum Change*,[13] I have looked at geography, biology and environmental studies, but other monographs in the series of books *Studies in Curriculum History* have looked at science and technology (McCulloch *et al.*, 1985), mathematics (Cooper, 1985; Moon, 1985) and physics (Woolnough, 1987).[14] In *Social Histories of the Secondary Curriculum*,[15] work is collected together on a wide range of other subjects, classics (Stray), English (Ball), science (Waring, who had written an earlier seminal study on Nuffield science), domestic subjects (Purvis), religious education (Bell), social studies (Franklin and Whitty) and modern languages (Radford). These studies reflect a growing interest in the history of curriculum and besides elucidating the symbolic drift of school knowledge raise central questions about past and current 'explanations' of school subjects, whether they be sociological or philosophical.

Above all, these studies begin to illustrate the historical emergence and construction of the political economy of curriculum. The structuring of resources and finance, the attribution of status and careers are linked to a system that has developed since the foundation of state schooling, and in particular since the establishment of secondary schooling regulations in the early years of this century. This structure impinges on both individual intentions and collective aspirations. By focusing our studies on the historical emergence and evolution of structures and the ongoing activities of individuals and groups we would begin to alleviate our current amnesia.

NOTES

1 '1904 and All That', *Times Educational Supplement* (1987), 31 July, p. 2.
2 H. Kliebard (1986) *The Struggle for the American Curriculum 1893–1958*. New York: Routledge & Kegan Paul, p. 269.
3 I. F. Goodson (1988) *The Making of Curriculum – Collected Essays*. Lewes: Falmer Press, p. 16.
4 C. B. Cox and A. E. Dyson (eds) (1969) *Fight for Education: A Black Paper*. London: The Critical Quarterly Society. Followed by C. B. Cox and R. Boyson (eds) (1975) *The Black Paper 1975*. London: Dent.
5 Her Majesty's Inspectorate (HMI) (1983), para. 3.19.
6 Department of Education and Science (DES) (1983) *Teaching Quality*. London: HMSO.
7 HMI, para. 3.40.
8 A. Hargreaves (1984) 'Curricular Policy and the Culture of Teaching: Some Prospects for the Future' (mimeograph).
9 DES (1985) *Education 8 to 12 in Combined and Middle Schools: An HMI Survey*. London: HMSO.
10 S. Rowland (1987) 'Where is Primary Education Going?', *Journal of Curricular Studies*, 19(1), January, February, p. 90.
11 Hargreaves (1984).
12 DES (1987) *The National Curriculum 5–16*. London: HMSO.
13 I. F. Goodson (1987) *School Subjects and Curriculum Change: Studies in Curriculum History*. London: Falmer Press.
14 *Studies in Curriculum History* (Falmer Press) comprises:
I. F. Goodson (ed.) (1985) *Social Histories of the Secondary Curriculum: Subjects for Study*.
G. McCulloch, E. Jenkins and D. Layton (1985) *Technological Revolution? The Politics of School Science and Technology in England and Wales Since 1945*.
B. Cooper (1985) *Renegotiating Secondary School Mathematics: A Study of Curriculum Change and Stability*.
B. Franklin *Building the American Community: Social Control and Curriculum*.
B. Moon (1986) *The 'New Maths' Curriculum Controversy: An International Story*.
I. F. Goodson (1987) *School Subjects and Curriculum Change*.
T. S. Popkewitz (ed.) *The Formation of School Subjects: The Struggle for Creating an American Institution*.
B. E. Woolnough (1987) *Physics Teaching in Schools 1960–85: Of People, Policy and Power*.
I. F. Goodson *The Making of Curriculum: Collected Essays*.
15 Goodson (1985).

BEYOND VOCATIONALISM: A NEW PERSPECTIVE ON THE RELATIONSHIP BETWEEN WORK AND EDUCATION[1]

2.3

KEN SPOURS AND MICHAEL YOUNG

[...]

INTRODUCTION

We are aware that the issue of work and education is highly contentious in a number of ways. Not only can it appear that we are following a currently fashionable and politically acceptable course, but it is all too easy to slip into a concept of work that sustains rather than challenges existing divisions, particularly those of gender. For some the whole idea of work as an educational principle, regardless of its definition, speaks to the past rather than to the future. It is our view, and it is implicit in the paper, that work (or productive life), provided that it is not equated solely with manufacturing or paid employment, is a potentially progressive principle for curricula and their possibilities.

To refer to the issue of work and the curriculum in its broadest sense raises some of the most fundamental educational issues. However, the historical separation of educational research from concrete economic, as well as many wider social questions, means that there is much theoretical development needed. This paper is therefore very much only a beginning.

The issue, however, is one of more than philosophical or theoretical interest. The more that we talk to academic subject teachers and to those involved in pre-vocational courses, the more the problems of student progression and continuity of learning in the 14–19 curriculum are raised. In our work on Progression it is argued that the root of the problems, at least in education, is in the division between academic and vocational courses and the way it limits the possibilities for students and the potential of teachers to transform the curriculum creatively. This paper is our initial attempt to develop a proposal to overcome this division by integrating the experience and understanding of work into the curriculum of all pupils. It sets out a new agenda for academic subject teachers,

Source: K. Spours and M. Young (1988) 'Beyond Vocationalism: A New Perspective on the Relationship Between Work and Education', *British Journal of Education and Work*, 2(2), pp. 5–14.

and gives them 'a crucial but no longer protected role'. Above all it is an attempt to outline an alternative approach, anticipating the needs of a modernising society rather than simply responding to the highly polarised perspectives of the New Vocationalism or the existing liberal curriculum. This is why it is entitled 'Beyond Vocationalism'.

Addressed initially to history teachers, the paper is designed to open discussions with as wide a range of practitioners as possible. If our proposals are to have any practical value, it will be through the curricular initiatives of a whole variety of groups of teachers. We underline our invitation to you to respond to this paper as part of a discussion of alternatives to a divided curriculum.

THE NATIONAL CURRICULUM AND CONFLICTING TENDENCIES WITHIN THE LATE SECONDARY CURRICULUM

Two major criticisms of the secondary curriculum have been articulated by the Government in justifying their proposals for educational reform. They argue, first, that the curriculum does not have a sufficiently close relationship with industry and commerce, and second, that the unevenness allowed under the present system is itself a major cause of low levels of achievement. These criticisms in themselves are not new or the exclusive property of Conservative Governments. However, within the context of the rest of the 1988 Reform Bill, and particularly its plans to enable schools to opt out of LEA control and to support the establishment of privately managed CTCs, their proposals represent a new level of political intervention into the curriculum.

The Government's proposals are aimed primarily at the public anxieties about pupil failure. Such anxieties are made sharper by the continuing high rates of unemployment and concern about economic performance and competition with other advanced industrial economies. They are also a commentary on the continued and deepening crisis of the liberal curriculum that has been such a distinctive feature of English secondary schooling since the late nineteenth century. The economic aspect of this 'crisis' is of long standing but has taken on a more acute form in the last two decades. It is now expressed in a highly selective enthusiasm for incorporating ideas from Japan and West Germany, reflected by the recent prominence given to Richard Lynne's work on the Japanese curriculum (Lynne, 1987) and studies such as the HMI Report 'Education in the Federal Republic of Germany: Aspects of Curriculum and Assessment'.[2]

Two separate and seemingly contradictory responses have emerged from these criticisms and comparisons. From 1981 onwards, and inheriting tendencies from the previous Labour Government, there has been a process of what has been termed the 'vocationalisation' of the curriculum. This is exemplified by TVEI, the Joint Unit Foundation Programmes (14–16), CPVE and new first level BTEC awards at 16+. The early phase of vocationalisation saw the MSC (now Training Agency) in the ascendancy. The second response dates from the appointment of Mr Baker as Secretary of State for Education and the introduction of proposals for a National Curriculum in the Conservative manifesto for the 1987 General Election. There is now a new emphasis upon traditional subject teaching, led by testing at 7, 11, 14 and 16, and this is expressed in a reassertion of leadership by the DES.

The rapid growth in pre-vocational courses – CPVE, 14–16 foundation programmes and the lower level BTEC courses – and the very different pressures expected from the National Curriculum guidelines pose serious dilemmas for teachers, particularly those specialising in the currently unfashionable 'humanities'. The success, at least in terms of pupil motivation and attendance, of the new style courses has encouraged some academic subject teachers, physicists and linguists, as well as historians and social scientists, to place less emphasis on developing their subject teaching and to join colleagues in developing the new 'vocational' modules, with their emphasis on skills and experience.

Countering this trend are the National Curriculum proposals, which are designed to maintain traditional subject teaching. One of the objectives of the proposals is to limit the freedom of classroom teachers to develop their subjects, something that applies particularly to the case of history. Inevitably they also involve promoting certain subjects and excluding others, of which social studies is the most striking example. This narrowing of the academic curriculum, particularly in the humanities, by centralised testing is not, however, inconsistent with a particular form of vocationalisation. In fact the National Curriculum itself can be seen as a form of vocationalisation. Though not related directly to particular jobs, it does very much reflect the kind of response given by employers when asked their views about education. With an emphasis upon standards and discipline, it is clearly concerned with the kind of model citizen envisaged by many employers. There are parallels with many pre-vocational courses, which stress the attitudes and dispositions associated with 'employability' rather than specific skills. It undoubtedly resonates with sections of the public, and it has received widespread support from the Opposition in the House of Commons. By professionals, however, it is seen as thoroughly inconsistent with the more innovative forms of vocationalisation promoted by TVEI – learning outside formal schooling, activity based methods, modularisation etc.

These disparate responses to the crisis of the liberal curriculum nevertheless have serious shortcomings. The National Curriculum, in underwriting the separation of school knowledge from society and the economy in increasingly restrictive ways, can only add to the crisis. The vocationalisation of the curriculum, designed specifically to encourage the low achiever with its emphasis upon activities and 'real-life situations', has become part of new divisions of certification. This is a point that we shall return to.

A THIRD WAY: TOWARDS A VOCATIONAL MODEL OF GENERAL EDUCATION

The VAAL (Vocational Aspects of Academic Learning) perspective which we outline in this article is offered both as a basis for challenging the developments we have referred to and as a positive framework for developing a truly comprehensive curriculum from 14+. The proposal for linking academic subjects to working life is not in itself entirely new. However, our emphasis upon a clear and critical relationship between the academic curriculum and changes in the economy, work and technology is a new perspective within the current debates about vocationalisation and the National Curriculum. We want to bring out five principles in what we refer to as the VAAL perspective:

1 Instead of starting with academic subjects and vocational programmes, it proposes a critical relationship between academic subjects and the changing nature of the world of work. This is in contrast to a vocationalised experientialism in which there is no concept of knowledge, and to the academic subjects of the National Curriculum, ossified by a renewed emphasis upon testing.[3]
2 It recognises the central role of economic and technological understanding in the curriculum for all school students from 14+.
3 It is a proposal for a general and vocational education for all pupils and not just underachievers. It is therefore a new basis for a common secondary curriculum.
4 It is a perspective which encourages the development and renewal of existing academic subjects and their relationship to pupil experience, as well as the development of new specialisations.
5 It is a perspective that incorporates a concept of the future into its definitions of school knowledge, work and skill.

As a perspective on the relationship between education and work, it is distinctive insofar as it is based upon the understanding that fundamental changes are taking place in the economies of Western capitalist nations (often referred to as Post-Fordism), which have clear educational implications. Post-Fordism refers to a series of historic changes in the nature of advanced economies since the dominance of the assembly line methods first used in the manufacture of Ford cars in the 1920s. The main trends are: the declining role of mass production in society due to new technological developments, the declining role of industry and the growth of the service sector, the breaking down of old skill barriers in the workforce and the creation of new divisions (core and peripheral workers), and not least, the new levels of capitalist integration in what is seen as the 'global economy'. Such changes call for a new and flexible relationship between education and work; a relationship more profound than the 'occupationalist training perspective' that characterises the New Vocationalism,[4] or the simple rigours of subject-based testing.

Current changes in economic relations appear to make contradictory demands. They open up new possibilities and present new problems. At one level, there is an increasing recognition, particularly within large technologically based corporations, of the need for a more educated and flexible workforce.[5] At the same time, however, these developments in Western economies are creating new demands for low-paid service jobs which require little prior training. These processes of technological and economic modernisation, though not inherently divisive, inevitably have that potential. It is imperative therefore that one of our educational objectives should be to produce a greater level of understanding of these changes in the organisation of work, in order that all students/trainees are in a stronger position to participate in economic life and are better informed about its possibilities.

At a more immediate level, the VAAL perspective is critical of the separation of personal from economic objectives in education. Instead of separating 'education for personal development' from 'education for employment' (or training), it sees the tension between the intellectual demands of academic subjects and the practical demands from changes in the nature and distribution of work as needing to be at the *centre* of curriculum decision making. In this respect two related questions need to be asked:

1 How does the positive response to work experience by students who have rejected academic subjects become a new possibility for academic subject teachers?
2 How can students make informed vocational choices if this process is part of a rejection of academic subjects and based upon 'common sense'? How can they assess their potential without a systematic understanding of the world of work and economic change?

The personal and the economic cannot be separated because they are deeply intertwined both in reality and in popular imagination in the 1980s. Compared with previous periods there is a far greater density of messages about economic life and work outside of formal schooling. The economic recession of the late 1970s and early 1980s and restructuring of the economy during the second and third Thatcher Governments has sharpened the popular perception of 'life-chances', as students see themselves as market-oriented consumers before having any idea of what it is like to be a producer.

The argument for a relationship between academic subjects and work is based upon two premises. Academic subjects represent both an organised form of knowledge and an existing social order. They cannot simply be replaced by the 'real life' of employer culture (vocationalism) or the 'real life' of working class culture (however mediated it may be by TV and the tabloid press). Curricula based on either set of assumptions, as we will see, become stratified and themselves produce new divisions. Academic disciplines can either go through a process of development or atrophy. Our main argument is that a progressive route for their development can be found in a dialogue with productive life. But there is a second reason, and this is to do with the need for systematic study. Academic disciplines have two major assets – bodies of knowledge (what Gramsci refers to as necessary 'baggage') and methods of enquiry. It is both these components in articulating pupils' real-life experience that must be the basis for a common curriculum for all.

A third implication of the VAAL perspective is the comment it is making about the relationship between specialists and non-specialists. The forging of new relationships between academic subjects and work will mean new forms of specialist knowledge. The VAAL perspective gives a new and crucial, but no longer protected, role to teachers of academic subjects. It no longer sees academic subjects exclusively as routes of access to higher education but as areas of specialisation whose practitioners have responsibilities both to non-specialists (such as parents and pupils) and to other specialists (such as those in other academic subjects and vocational areas), as well as their own professional community, whether in the schools or higher education.

VOCATIONAL, VOCATION AND OCCUPATIONALISM

Any claim to define education in vocational terms has to confront the way this term has been used in educational debates and policy. This means recognising the ways in which demands for 'vocationalisation' of education have reasserted themselves again and again whenever there is a new period of crisis in the economy. This tendency is in no way specific to this country. However, the way in which the concept of vocation, defined as something unique to the 'liberal professions', was separated from the idea of 'vocational education', which prepares people for specific and inevitably low-level occupations, is distinct. 'Vocational' in this sense is usually linked to 'technical' and is familiar in the Technical and *Vocational* Education Initiative, the National Council for *Vocational* Qualifications and the MSC's *Vocational* Education and Training. It is always seen in relation to, and despite claims to the contrary as inferior to, 'academic' education, and as inescapably associated with low-status courses catering for a student population as unrepresentative in social class terms as the intake into Oxford or Cambridge.

In arguing that a concept of the 'vocational' is integral to any democratic model of education, we reject the meanings given to it that we described above, which we would refer to as forms of 'occupationalism'.[6] The term 'occupationalism' can be used in two ways. First, it can refer to the current emphasis on preparing young people for particular jobs rather than adult life in general. In this sense we would wish to draw a distinction between occupationalism and vocational education. But it is also used in another sense, as 'behavioural occupationalism', which serves as an 'ideology of production regulating education rather than an educational ideology servicing production'.[7] This refers to the notions of transferable skills and skill ownership within YTS and other pre-vocational courses.

In arguing that we should go beyond these divisive concepts of 'vocation' and 'vocational' we draw on the Gramscian idea of producers understanding the context of their work and the economic, social and cultural implications of the skills they practise. Instead of the concept of vocation based upon the individualistic and essentially backward-looking notion of a 'calling', we define vocation as the commitment to and understanding of the worthwhileness of work, or what work could represent if changes in its organisation were to take place. Thus to have a vocation, and for education to be vocational, in our terms, requires 'more than mastery of the technical skill and knowledge required to complete an industrial or professional task competently. It also entails an awareness of moral obligation, an appreciation of the political and economic implications of a job of work and often, of the aesthetics of "production"' (Entwhistle, 1979). For school students this can be begun through a study of the economy and working life that makes direct links to a more diverse experience of the workplace as a site of learning. This elaborated view of working life demands a more central role in the curriculum not only for technology but also for a historically based economics and sociology.

Another approach to the idea of vocational education with which we have some sympathy is what Silver and Brennan describe as 'liberal vocationalism' (Silver and Brennan, 1988). This could be described as an attempt to construct an English version of Dewey's belief that all true liberal education was vocational and vice versa. The problem with this approach for us is that it does not face up to the reality that, in the terms set by the division of labour in Western capitalist societies, only a small range of occupations offer vocational opportunities in the sense meant by Dewey. This means that 'vocational' in the sense that we are using it, is also a critical concept; it involves drawing on the academic disciplines to shed light on the social divisions and changes in the current organisation of work. It would build on the schools–industry movement and in particular the important work of Jamieson, Miller and Watts, who examine the diverse ways in which work simulations in schools and school–industry links can enhance the curriculum (Jamieson, Miller and Watts, 1988). In the final part of their most recent work, they recognise the importance of students understanding the causes of economic change and the relationship between these developments and more active forms of pedagogy.

A central aim of going beyond existing definitions of 'vocation' and 'vocational' in developing a broader form of vocational education is to add new dimensions to the new forms of pedagogy which have succeeded in providing new levels of motivation for the most disaffected pupils. In providing a broader perspective, however, it remains important to continue to address the concerns about future employment that many teachers are familiar with among the many 14 and 15 year olds who have failed to find a sense of purpose in 'O' level/CSE (and in many cases also GCSE) programmes.

SOCIAL DIVISIONS AND THE NEW 'VOCATIONALISM'

The VAAL perspective also arises out of a concern that attempts at reform of the 14–19 curriculum are producing new forms of division, even though this was not the intention of those involved in the design or development of the courses. The vocationalisation of the curriculum in the form of separate certification (such as CPVE, RSA Diplomas and Joint Unit Pre-vocational Programmes) is seen by many teachers as meeting the needs of underachieving students, but it is also producing new forms of division. In relation to post 16 initiatives Stewart Ranson has termed this 'tertiary tripartism' (Ranson, 1984). The issue of new forms of division is highlighted by problems of progression between 14–16 and 16+ because of barriers to access to certain vocational courses, particularly for those without 'O' levels (or GCSEs). There are also problems of repetition of learning due to the focus on narrow definitions of social and life skills which are found in all such courses for pupils between 14 and 19.[8]

The separation of academic from pre-vocational courses for pupils as young as 14 means that, for students on the later courses, knowledge content has tended to be replaced by learning process as an educational criterion. In a complex and changing industrial society in which technologies are playing a role in more and more sectors of life, students are not having the opportunity to develop an adequate foundation of knowledge of any kind.

Divisions between the academic and vocational are part of the continuation of the division between mental and manual labour and its role in the reproduction of wider social divisions. Although education cannot in itself bring about social changes, in the absence of broader economic, cultural and political initiatives it can attempt to produce a more open-ended schooling in which the mental and manual divisions are not simply reproduced. The question raised by the 'new vocationalist' initiatives is whether the division between the academic and the vocational which is so widely deplored can be overcome by new forms of active pedagogy and experience-based curricula alone. It is our view that such a change requires not just new pedagogic strategies but more imaginative attempts to create links between academic knowledge and experience; in effect, to create new specialisations within the school curriculum. The VAAL perspective would be that curricular divisions must be challenged by new knowledge, not common sense alone.

ACADEMIC SUBJECTS AND THE 'WORLD OF WORK'

Instead of accepting the division between academic and vocational courses, we are proposing that teachers should draw on academic disciplines to interrogate the world of work. What does this mean for academic subject teachers?

Each academic discipline has a changing set of practices and traditions of its own and in its relations to other ones. For example, physics has changed with the introduction of new topics such as electronics, as well as increasingly becoming part of 'balanced science' rather than a separate subject at GCSE. We could envisage that physics teachers might, together with colleagues who teach economics and history, examine the ways in which particular industrial processes were socially shaped, and what potentials and possibilities were not taken up.

The application of academic subjects to a study and exploration of work involves developments in the nature of those subjects as well as their relations with each other. Despite the priority given to separateness, academic subjects have always had some relationships with each other, though they have been largely restricted to familiar kinds of grouping, such as humanities, natural sciences, languages etc. The VAAL perspective proposes that 'the demands of working life' be treated as a new educational principle. This is not a replacement of one principle with another but the holding of the two in tension. It will involve a number of new and difficult developments for which there is little precedent within existing school subject traditions and often little backing within the school and college timetable. Some examples are:

1 The deliberate creation of new relationships between subjects *across* the academic/vocational divide and not simply between academic subjects.
2 The development rather than the dissolution of disciplines and the creation therefore of new forms of specialisation to reflect new economic, technological and social developments. This points to a less top-down model of the origins of school knowledge than has been typical of most academic subjects. It treats secondary school teachers as specialists in their own right rather than interpreters of knowledge filtered down from the universities.
3 The implications of relating the work experience of pupils to all subject teaching and not simply careers teaching.

TOWARDS A BROADER UNDERSTANDING AND DEFINITION OF WORK

Most resistance on the part of academic subject teachers to making connections to work and the economy reflect the very narrow ways that work has become part of educational policy and practice. There has been a tendency to date to view it almost exclusively in employment or occupational terms. This is not just due to the MSC's desire to see a closer integration of occupational preparation and the school curriculum. Such a focus has its support within the organisation of schools and the close association of work experience with careers education.

We would argue that insofar as work has moved towards the centre of the curriculum, it has remained as occupational preparation largely geared to those pupils who a decade ago would have left school at 15 for vulnerable unskilled jobs. By remaining cut off from the academic curriculum it has sustained divisions in the curriculum without providing any directions of how work experience might have a real educational role. As we said earlier, the concept of work cannot escape being about future employment and preparation for it. However, if it is to realise its educational possibilities it must also be seen to be about developments in the economy, technology and labour processes, and how these structure employment opportunities and the nature of the work. Of equal importance are the relationships between work as employment, work as leisure and work as domestic labour. Making such connections involves a broadening of the concept of work to relate to far more than paid employment; it also indicates the crucial role such subjects as geography, history, economics and social studies can play in a reformed curriculum. It is necessary therefore to explore a new framework for the curriculum which takes *work in all its forms* as the basis for the development of knowledge (historical, sociological, scientific and technological) and skills (intellectual, technical, practical and communicative).

CREATING NEW FORMS OF KNOWLEDGE

In stressing the importance of new relations between academic subjects and between them and the world of work, the VAAL perspective points to new forms of knowledge and the forms that they might take. It aims through its concepts of work and vocation to learn from and go beyond earlier attempts to 'integrate' in both the humanities and sciences. In breaking with existing subject traditions without having any clear principles of their own to define content, such attempts were prone to emphasise only the learning process and all too easily collapse into forms of experientialism.

The challenge is to create new forms of specialisation which all students can feel part of in ways that the old academic subjects did not make possible except for a few. Much work needs to be done on the potential of modularisation as a more flexible means of representing new combinations of knowledge which reflect new social developments (for example, food sciences, media studies, biotechnology, urban studies, political economy etc.) as well as providing a new structure for learner participation. As with any innovation, modularisation is not of itself a solution; it can all too easily be experienced as a kind of self-service cafeteria curriculum with outcomes as divisive as the separated subjects it replaces.

New forms of integration of subject knowledge with work will involve new relationships between groups of teachers who have traditionally kept apart. Overcoming barriers between academic, vocational and pre-vocational courses will involve drawing on each group of teachers' strengths and developing new models of collaboration. Most traditions of specialist expertise have rules of exclusion and ways of defining others as inferior. This has made difficult any collaboration between academic subject teachers, vocational teachers (with their specific conceptions of work-related and technical skills) and teachers on pre-vocational programmes. Each can all too easily see the strengths of the others as weaknesses. The VAAL perspective provides a potential framework for the strength of each to be enhanced in collaboration.

In linking academic subjects to productive life, it offers a more realistic basis for achieving the goals often claimed for the National Curriculum. It will improve the explanatory power of school knowledge, enhance the status of teachers who no longer need to feel subservient to higher education for direction, and expand pupils' participation in their own learning. However, it is still very much a set of principles; the detailed working out in specific cases as well as some of the fundamental questions of organisation and politics remain.

QUESTIONS OF DEVELOPMENT AND IMPLEMENTATION IN THE 14—19 CURRICULUM

Throughout this paper we have stressed the contradictory nature of current curricular developments and the potential space for new approaches that this creates. However, any proposals for ambitious developments in the curriculum are bound to face serious constraints. Most notable are impending National Curriculum guidelines and the approaches of examining and validating bodies. It would also be necessary to take into account school/college organisation, current teacher understanding and morale and, not least, the problem of resources and time. All of these point to the need to evaluate the VAAL perspective, from the point of view not only of its logic but of the forms in which it can be translated from a perspective into a practical strategy.

In this final section we would therefore like to highlight a series of issues and questions with regard to the development and implementation of the proposals.

We hope that these will provide a basis for an ongoing discussion:

1 What are the implications of using 'academic disciplines to interrogate the world of work' for your specialism?

- Are there traditions of curriculum development within your subject upon which we can build, or is the perspective a more radical departure?
- What limitations and constraints do you associate with your subject?
- How can we proceed to establish practical exemplars?

2 The dialogue between academic subjects and work will make new demands of teachers if the relationship between work and education is to be more than a pragmatic response to the needs of the classroom or external certification.

- What do teachers need to know about the world of work in order to develop their disciplines, and how important is a collaborative approach with specialists in technical fields?

3 A critical issue is the *form* in which the dialogue between academic subjects and work takes place.

- What are the specific forms in which the VAAL perspective could be realised within the curriculum?
- How far should identifiable disciplines be retained and how far should forms of integration proceed?
- Does modularisation, as a means for creating new bases for organising knowledge and of giving students a real involvement in planning their own learning, provide a possible route?

4 The relationship between the academic, vocational and pre-vocational approaches and the issue of progression is an increasingly important issue.

- Will our arguments for a broad vocational education in schools (14–16) lay the proper foundation for greater specialisation post-16?
- If so, what are the implications of the proposals for a 14–19 framework of certification and curriculum and in particular the relationship between 14–16 and 16+ certification?

5 What are the wider economic developments required for a perspective to be more fully realised which explicitly challenges divisions between mental and manual labour?

NOTES

1 The first version of this paper was written for *CLIO*, the ILEA history teachers' journal. An amended version was published as a working paper for the Post 16 Education Centre, Institute of Education, University of London.
2 A critique of selective forms of comparison in the HMI report on the FRG is a paper by Lynne Chisholm, 1987.
3 There is a striking resemblance between the subjects of the proposed National Curriculum and those of the 1904 Board of Education regulations. The only difference is that Manual Work/Housewifery has been replaced by Technology and Music. See Aldrich, 1988.
4 By the 'New Vocationalism' we are here referring to the series of government initiatives in the late secondary and college courses – TVEI, CPVE, YTS etc.
5 In the current political climate, there are a range of economic forces which recognise that workers who are more educated and trained may require less supervision, and this is seen as a key to the further reduction of costs. There is also a new tendency in production (just-in-time production) which demands a more creative and responsive worker.
6 The concept of the New Vocationalism as behavioural occupationalism is explored by Rob Moore (1988).
7 Rob Moore, 'Education and Ideology of Production' (draft paper, p. 18).
8 A detailed analysis of the process of division and reform of qualifications can be found in Ken Spours (1988) 'The Politics of Progression', Centre Working Paper No. 2, March.

REFERENCES

Aldrich, R. (1988) 'The National Curriculum: A Historical Perspective', in D. Lawton and C. Chitty, *The National Curriculum*. London: Bedford Way, Paper No. 33.

Chisholm, L. (1987) 'Vorsprung Ex Machina: Aspects of Curriculum Assessment in Cultural Comparison', *Journal of Education Policy*, 2(2).

Entwistle, E. (1979) *Antonio Gramsci: Conservative Schooling for Radical Politics*. London: Routledge & Kegan Paul.

Jamieson, I. M., Miller, A. and Watts, A. G. (1988) *Mirror of Work: Work Simulations in Schools*. Lewes: Falmer Press.

Lynne, R. (1987) *Educational Achievement in Japan: Lessons for the West*. London: Macmillan.

Moore, R. (1988) 'Education and the Ideology of Production', *British Journal of Sociology of Education*, 9,1.

Ranson, S. (1984) 'Towards a New Tertiary Tripartism', in P. Broadfoot (ed.), *Selection, Certification and Control*. Lewes: Falmer Press.

Silver, H. and Brennan, J. (1988) *A Liberal Vocationalism*. London: Methuen.

CORE SUBJECTS AND AUTUMN LEAVES: THE NATIONAL CURRICULUM AND THE LANGUAGES OF PRIMARY EDUCATION

ROBIN ALEXANDER

The contrasts are none the less stark for being so familiar. On the one hand, children's needs and the value of first-hand experience; on the other, society's needs, national norms and the mastery of information. The 'how' of education is opposed to the 'what'; process to product; means to ends; diversity to uniformity; and assessment as diagnosis to assessment as measurement or accounting. From curriculum as a seamless robe, the whole much more than the sum of its parts, to curriculum as a collection of core and foundation subjects. From curriculum negotiated within an agreed framework at school level, to curriculum centrally 'constructed' and 'delivered', postman-style, by the teacher. And many more.

Such polarities (for that, though needlessly, is how they are invariably presented) have been the rhetorical backdrop to the Education Reform Act's inexorable journey from consultation document to the statute book. Government and the primary community all too often have seemed – and seem – to be talking different languages.

Why is this? At the most obvious level, the polarities represent a basic collision of educational values, crystallised in the statement: 'But the primary curriculum isn't core and foundation subjects, it's a walk through autumn leaves.' It's also a matter of political style, as a government with an unassailable parliamentary majority imposes its will. The dumping of much of what progressive primary education has claimed to stand for has been unceremonious but inevitable: the surprise is that people have been surprised.

But, supposing for a moment the protagonists were willing to listen to each other, what of the educators' message? Is the case for primary education being presented as effectively as possible? I suggest that the problem is as much one of *discourse within the primary world* as it is one of communication between the inhabitants of that world and those outside it.

Consider for a moment the languages which are available – and there are many, not just one, since everyone with a particular interest in education has a distinctive way of talking about it: teachers, children, parents, politicians, administrators, researchers, teacher educators, advisors, HMI and so on. Since each of these groups has a legitimate perspective on education, what they say and how they say it

Source: R. Alexander (1989) 'Core Subjects and Autumn Leaves: The National
Curriculum and the Languages of Primary Education', *Education*, 3–13, March, pp. 3–8.

deserve to be attended to. It is too easy for one group to dismiss another's viewpoint and language as 'irrelevant' to the 'real world' of primary education. There are of course many such 'real worlds', and situational myopia is as undesirable among teachers as it is among politicians, parents or academics.

That much is obvious. But *within* the primary profession, too, there is not one language, but several. Elsewhere[1] I've distinguished three 'public' languages of primary education: *everyday, academic* and *ideological*. 'Everyday language' needs no definition. But the directness and validity it gains from being grounded in the unique experiences of one school can also make it less useful for communication between that school and others. One school's common sense can be another school's jargon. In contrast, because of its freedom from the particular school context, academic language can stake a claim for conveying shared ideas across the system as a whole. But of course that very detachment is also its weakness: too often it seems to be about something other than the everyday business of teaching, or about the preoccupations of others than teachers, baffling in a different way.

The dilemma here is that though a vivid account of a particular, live classroom experience is much more arresting to an audience than an abstract analytical framework, to extract general principles from such an account for teachers and children working in very different contexts is a considerably more difficult enterprise.

That leaves ideological language, by far the most familiar form for public utterances on primary education, so much so that we might term it 'Primaryspeak'. Primaryspeak is about assertion rather than argument, rallying the troops rather than reasoning with them. It is peppered with deliberate and carefully nurtured dichotomies like those in the first paragraph above, and with slogans and buzzwords: *flexibility, freedom, spontaneity, start with the child, the seamless robe, integration* and the like; and of course their negative counterparts such as *compartmentalisation, fragmentation, intervention, little boxes* and – possibly the most provocative and hackle-raising word in the Primaryspeak lexicon – *subjects*.

So the choice seems to be between the immediate but not always generalisable language of everyday professional interaction, the sometimes alien or intimidating language of academic analysis and research, and Primaryspeak. In the public area it is the last, more often than not, which tends to prevail. Recently, it has to be said, one factor encouraging this prevalence has been the adversarial style of central government. Faced with an official educational dogma which is uncompromising in content and authoritarian or menacingly populist in tone, and which displays such apparent contempt for professional judgement and expertise, it is hard not to respond in kind. It takes unshakable optimisim (some might say political naivety) to counter ideology with anything other than ideology.

But even before the advent of the present divisive climate we lacked a common language for discussing and analysing primary education across institutional and professional boundaries, which could at the same time encompass both what some call the 'nitty-gritty' of everyday practice and the ideas, values and principles by which such practice is justified.

How does one explain this? In large part, I think, in terms of the particular historical situation of primary schools and those who work in or around them. Here are some hypotheses:

1 Primary schools are historically the poor relation, the Cinderella of the education service, the descendants of those Victorian elementary schools set up to provide a basic education for the working classes. Their teachers were a professional underclass. However much the professional standing of primary teachers may have risen since then, that legacy generated status and resource problems which are still to some extent with us. In this situation, if respect and esteem could not be counted on from outside the profession, then they had to be mustered from within. A language centred on slogans was the inevitable outcome. So too was pressure to convey consensus and a united front against the common enemy of scepticism, exploitation and – perhaps most insidious of all – condescension.

2 Historically too, the primary world has always been strongly hierarchical: employers, advisors, heads and class teachers. One either found oneself in general agreement with the official truths or 'philosophy' and co-operated gladly and constructively, or strategically toed the party line, or came out in open rebellion, or suffered in resentful and increasingly embittered silence. Of course, many LEAs and schools have shifted dramatically in this regard towards a more open and collaborative culture, but not everywhere, or at the same rate. The legacy is a persistent one and the assumption that the class teacher has little to contribute to educational debate is in many places still all too common.

3 A central reality, then, is *power*. Power and powerlessness generate the language of them and us, of bosses and workers, of antagonism to whatever are deemed to be the defining concerns of the other groups; and power denies the validity of the language and perceptions of those at the bottom of the heap. Equally, power breeds *shibboleths*: the 'in' words and phrases by which one proves one's allegiance to current primary orthodoxy. Display, and indeed the strong emphasis on the visual appearance of classrooms, it can be added, are sometimes the visual equivalent of the shibboleth, signalling one's orthodoxy at the point of delivery even more effectively than words. (And more economically too: the instance of the teacher shortlisted for a senior post, merely on the strength of someone looking through his classroom window outside school hours and liking what he saw, bears pondering on in this context.) Moreover, since the power context is also one of patronage, the fact that the attitudes and positions taken up can sometimes be contradictory, or that appearances, words and deeds may not always match, matters less than their strategic value.

Shibboleths change. From 'freedom', 'flexibility', 'spontaneity' and 'discovery' we have moved to the apparent rigour of 'skills', 'concepts', 'match' and 'standards'. We hear now less of 'creativity', 'self-expression', 'making and doing'; more of 'problem-solving' and 'CDT'; less of 'individualisation', more of 'collaborative group work'; less of 'professional autonomy' and more of 'collegiality'. But though shibboleths may change, their function in relation to the power realities of primary education remains the same – being approved, belonging, getting by and getting on. They become mere words, devoid of any precise *meaning*, let alone any sense that they may well connote ideas and issues which are intensely problematic, but serving very precise *functions* nevertheless.

4 Power in primary education may have an added dimension of gender. Primary class teachers have been, historically, mostly female; heads and deputies, except

in infant and first schools, mostly male; advisors and administrators, academics and researchers, union officials and politicians all mostly male. This numerical imbalance may have contributed to a professional culture in which the officially received 'truths' of primary education were man-made and man-defined, while the essential core realities of actually working with children in classrooms, of making learning happen, especially in the early years, were created predominantly by women. (As a male academic I am aware of ironies at this point, but don't see that as cause to remain silent.)

The stage of primary education in which women have always been prominent at senior levels as well as in the classroom – nursery and early years education – tends to support rather than undermine the hypothesis. Here, power may not be complicated by gender in the school itself, but at LEA level and in the wider world consider the still far from finished struggle of early years practitioners to get their job, their expertise and their professional thinking taken seriously by the educational hierarchy.

5 Less controversial is the next point. The more we understand about life in primary schools and classrooms, the more it becomes evident that the latter are arenas of great complexity and subtlety which it is quite difficult to talk analytically about, especially to outsiders, other than conversationally and hesitantly. Certainly the received codes of academic research and analysis seldom approach this complexity, nor do the generalisations of curriculum and policy documents.

Small wonder that the language we may fall back on in such circumstances is Primaryspeak. Few who bother to think about it will argue that 'children not subjects' or 'curriculum is autumn leaves' are exact analytical statements about primary education. But they can serve as a shorthand for a whole mass of assumptions and practices: those working with children every day may not be able to define these exactly, but fundamentally they feel they *know* what it's all about.

Small wonder, too, that since it takes much longer than a fleeting visit to uncover the true nature and extent of children's classroom learning, some outsiders entering classrooms and being required by their position to comment may tend to fixate on the more obvious surface realities: 'Nice display, the children seem to be busy, keep it up . . .' The power differential then upgrades such banalities into 'objective' criteria for judging 'good practice', thus further distorting our sense of what in primary education really matters, and indeed what is real. We then end up with whole checklists of items concerned with something called 'the environment of learning' rather than with learning itself. 'Good primary practice' (now *there*'s a shibboleth) becomes what those with power say it is, outsiders' rather than insiders' realities, surface rather than substance.

6 Primary education is a predominantly oral culture. Schools operate on the basis of a spoken language which is immediate, idiosyncratic and ephemeral, metaphoric and allusive. This doesn't translate well into contexts dominated by the formalism of the written word – whether such writing takes the form of the rhetorical devices of prepared political speeches, the legalism of administrative

memoranda or the rationality (real or bogus) of academic papers. And these latter contexts, to go back to the thread of *power* which runs through all of this analysis, are where the power publicly to define the abiding educational realities so often lies, rather than in the classroom.

7 Being with children and the immediacies of the classroom dominate teacher consciousness. These make for a language in which teacherhood tends to be defined as an extension or consequence of childhood. One of the most familiar outcomes of this is the way the primary curriculum tends to be characterised *in terms of the child's experience rather than the teacher's agenda.* That the first should be a major influence on the second is not in doubt, but they are not synonymous. Hence, then, curriculum defined as 'a seamless robe', 'activity and experience' (or of course 'autumn leaves').

This tendency bears importantly upon the problem of defining and discussing the primary curriculum. The issue of *subjects* crystallises it best of all. 'We mustn't talk about subjects because the child doesn't see the world as subjects, little boxes, compartments and the like . . .' That may well be so, but how does the *teacher* need to see the world, and the curriculum, in order to enrich and extend that childhood vision? What professional agenda does this dictate? Moreover, for the politician or administrator it is this latter agenda, defined as goals, outcomes, means and resources, which matters most; this is the instrumental challenge which has at that level to be met, however much sympathy he or she may have for the child-centred viewpoint.

8 The task of the primary class teacher, in respect of curriculum, is an immense and diverse one and requires considerable breadth of professional knowledge. In terms of our language issue this presents the teacher with a choice: publicly acknowledging that she or he can't know everything; or arguing that it doesn't matter anyway because curriculum is about process, not content, how you teach rather than what you teach, children not subjects.

9 Curriculum codification is incomplete. The areas of the primary curriculum which are discussed with greatest fluency are those like reading and mathematics which are most highly codified – that is to say, defined and structured through generally accepted terminologies and frameworks. Science, the new 'basic', is making rapid progress in this regard. In contrast, much work is still needed in what I have called elsewhere 'Curriculum II' – the curriculum outside the Government's higher status 'core': the arts, the humanities, personal, moral and social development. Without conceptual frameworks there can be no structure, without structure little meaningful long-term planning; without these no real public discourse other than in terms of slogans and shibboleths. 'Whereof we cannot speak' as Wittgenstein said 'thereof we must remain silent.' So, 'What we can define, that can we begin to discuss.'[2]

Yet some may reject this curriculum-defining process on the grounds that it creates subjects. But the issue, surely, is not subjects as such, but what they entail. 'Subject' is a neutral term, indicating merely a labelled component of curriculum. What the labels are, what each label denotes, and how the parts fit together, are all open to debate. So, for example, it is not science as label which ought to be the contentious issue, but the nature and purposes of the particular kinds of early learning that the label 'science', for want of a better, indicates.[3]

These hypotheses about what has created the professional language problem in primary education can probably be added to, and in any case are presented here in simplified and compressed form. But there's another side to the coin. If we now move away from what are essentially the *public* languages of primary education – ideological, academic, administrative, legalistic, political and so on – and ask the question whether, given the problems and limitations of each, there is an alternative, the answer, therefore, is 'Yes'. But it's an alternative which, for all the reasons above, is given little attention or weight and is difficult to gain access to. It's what emerges if you engage in informed and sympathetic conversation with any experienced primary teacher. The vital precondition, too often flouted by those whose conversations take place in a context of unequal power, is that you have to believe, and demonstrate that you believe, that the teacher is a knowledgeable and competent professional from whom you can learn a great deal, rather than someone who is there to learn from you. That sounds so obvious – it is – but consider how often unequal power becomes, anywhere, the inevitable but unadmitted barrier to genuinely open conversation.

The language that emerges, though used by the same people who in *public* contexts may use Primaryspeak, couldn't be more different from it. It is modest and realistic, and avoids the inflated claims which are so prominent a feature of Primaryspeak. It is as strongly affective as it is instrumental: it highlights the classroom as an arena in which feelings – the teacher's as well as the child's – are a powerful influence on events. It emphasises the problematic, and does not claim that all problems in teaching are solved, or even solvable. It acknowledges and worries about the pressure on class teacher expertise created by whole curriculum teaching and the wide ability range to be found in any primary classroom. It is elliptical, qualified and subtle. It deals in shades of grey rather than black and white. It punctures the carefully nurtured front of consensus about 'good primary practice' which has so effectively been conveyed by the primary world to those inside and outside it, and exposes both disagreements about approaches and values and the frustrations of having to act as though these don't exist.

Above all, this more private professional language highlights the daily dilemmas and compromises of classroom decision-making, and reveals a sometimes acute consciousness of the possible mismatch between the reality of what one does in the classroom and what one is obliged to claim, using Primaryspeak, outside it. Thus, though many aspects of teaching of themselves generate dilemmas which need to be (and of course are) resolved, some of the most prominent and intractable can be those about which Primaryspeak delivers its most uncompromising certainties: the holistic, integrated curriculum, activity/enquiry-based learning, group work and so on.

Though many dilemmas are 'in the situation' of teaching as it is, therefore, others are actually created or exacerbated by trying to live up to the sometimes unrealistic versions of 'good practice' which Primaryspeak presents, particularly when delivered by those on whose power and patronage the teacher depends.

The problem here is that the primary world has become the victim of its own rhetoric. The essential realities of teaching may be better expressed in dilemma-language, but Primaryspeak is about unassailable truths and to admit to dilemmas and problems may be taken to signal weakness or even disloyalty. And the worlds of career advancement, of the National Curriculum, and of appraisal and accountability, are about certainties rather than doubts, dogma rather than dilemmas, black and white rather than grey, self-inflation rather than modesty. Who hesitates is lost.

Yet, if I'm right that dilemma-language comes closest to the realities of the classroom and thus to some of the essential and unvarnished truths about primary education, then somehow it has to become part of the accepted language of professional discourse. Doubts, qualifications, dilemmas, consciousness of nuance, alertness to the affective dimension – these are in no sense signs of professional weakness or intellectual flaccidity. On the contrary, they can indicate true insight rather than tunnel vision, inner strength rather than mere professional machismo.

And if dilemmas can be acknowledged as legitimate they can be freely discussed. Freely discussed, they can begin to be resolved. If we are prepared honestly to state and confront the most fundamental challenges of teaching we can begin to deal with them. A problem we are not prepared, or are afraid, to admit to will never be solved.

But the climate is against this. Dilemma-language is driven underground in a context in which the languages of authority veer between the ideological, the legalistic and the adversarial, and in which career advancement is so often about parading certainties, having your 'philosophy' sorted out and sewn up, and saying what 'they' want to hear. In the end we come back to power – and powerlessness – as historical facts in the emergence of today's primary schools.

The language problem in primary education, then, is only partly about language as such: more fundamentally it's about the relationship between language and power. The solutions to the problem, therefore, are structural, and since they pose a challenge to established hierarchies and interests they will inevitably be resisted.

Let me emphasise, however, that this is not a populist bid to give prominence to one voice by shouting down another. The precondition for educational progress is dialogue, and the necessary voices, as I indicated at the beginning of this paper, are many. Insiders' classroom realities are an essential ingredient, but so too are the alternative accounts and perspectives which can be provided by parents, advisors, researchers, politicians and others. Without these, discourse remains as polarised, and as sterile, as ever.[4]

My argument, then, is not that classroom teachers, any more than any other group, know best, but that their consciousness, grounded in the immediacy of classroom experience, is seriously under-represented and undervalued in educational discourse outside the school (and sometimes inside it too), despite the fact that their case for inclusion is so obvious and unassailable. Whatever the reasons for this – and I have suggested several – one result or reaction has been the dominance of a kind of language (Primaryspeak) which does a considerable disservice both to the very consciousness it claims to express and to the educational debate in general. Moreover, though Primaryspeak may induce a much-needed sense of professional solidarity, its persistence seems to have exactly the opposite effect to that intended, keeping the classroom and the class teacher on the periphery of the debate rather than bringing them to the centre.

Hence my argument that both the analysis and the resolution of the problem require attention to professional structures as well as to professional language. Meanwhile we have the immediate challenge of the National Curriculum. Somehow the central classroom realities of primary education, and the perspectives of the teachers who help create them, need to be empowered, articulated and given greater prominence in this critical period of interpreting and implementing the 1988 Act; but somehow, too, we have to find a more fruitful and realistic middle ground between the extremes of Bakerspeak and Primaryspeak, a point of reconciliation between core subjects and autumn leaves.

NOTES

1   The ideas presented here in a necessarily abbreviated form are developed more fully in the following publications: R. J. Alexander (1984) *Primary Teaching*. London: Holt, Rinehart and Winston, revised version Cassell; R. J. Alexander (1988) 'Garden or Jungle? Teacher Development and Informal Primary Education', in W. A. L. Blyth (ed.) *Informal Primary Education Today: Essays and Studies*. Lewes: Falmer Press, pp. 148–88.

2   Whatever else may be said about the National Curriculum subject documents published so far (mathematics and science, at the time of writing), they are undoubtedly useful contributions to this necessary process of becoming more explicit about the content of the primary curriculum and hence replacing Primaryspeak by a language for professional discourse which is at last able to accommodate the complexity of curriculum issues. That being so, the suggestion that some of the non-core areas are to get relatively scant treatment in future National Curriculum proposals, which some have greeted with a sigh of relief, presents a problem. It is true that there is an obvious case to be made for avoiding overly tight or prescriptive statements about, for example, the arts in primary education, but at the same time the continued lack of serious attempts to explicate this area may simply deepen the gulf between the core and the rest, or what I call Curriculum I and Curriculum II, in terms of their relative standing, resourcing, time allocated and quality of provision. For, staying with this example, there is little doubt that primary education has been ill-served to date by the failure properly to engage with the conceptual debate about arts education, and in this respect the assertion that this part of the curriculum is subjective, private, all a matter of personal values and therefore not amenable to definition, let alone assessment, has not helped. Since those who take this line also claim strong advocacy of arts education, this might be counted something of an educational (and political) own goal.

3   By now most people recognise that subjects are on the educational agenda whether we like it or not. The choice for those who are fundamentally opposed to the notion of subjects is continued resistance to their emergence in any form, which will have little impact, or participation in the debate as each set of subject proposals emerges, with a view to exerting maximum influence upon the form that such subjects take in the classroom.

4 Readers may care to note that a new national body, the Association for the Study of Primary Education (ASPE) was launched in September 1988, with the task of bringing together and promoting productive dialogue among the various constituencies and voices in primary education as one of its main aims. Membership of ASPE is open to all: for details and application forms contact Angela Auset, ASPE Membership Secretary, Department of Education, Bristol Polytechnic, Redland Hill, Bristol BS6 6U2 (tel: 0272-741251).

The National Curriculum: A Black Perspective

2.5

Conrad MacNeil

The proposed National Curriculum is not truly national. The culture reflected in it is no more than prevailing white Anglo-Saxon and totally excludes the significant input from the Caribbean, the African and Indian continents and elsewhere. Furthermore, it reflects an imperialist and Eurocentric concept of a static Anglo-Saxon culture which no longer exists. No matter how it is put together, it will inevitably ignore the contributions to knowledge (be it mathematics, science or literature) of Black people that have helped to shape today's society.

Teachers subscribe overall to a Eurocentric perspective, and unless there is guidance for teachers on an appropriate multicultural knowledge base, the Eurocentric approach and subject content is what they will teach. There is no sign that a move to change is projected, nor is it evident in the bulk of in-service training.

There is no evidence that the purveyors of the National Curriculum have in any way taken into account the Black perspective. Indeed there is ample evidence of their indifference, to judge by their disregard of the recommendations of their own government inquiry, the 1985 Swann Report *Education For All*.

The Secretary of State for Education and Science has based his educational policy on the bedrock of parental choice, even though historically those in power have, at best, marginalised by paying lip-service to, and at worst ignored, Black British experience. So Black parents' views are likely to continue to be unheeded. So far there is no structure or system laid down which points to advocacy in the National Curriculum guidelines. There need to be firm and unambiguous statements in the implementation policy to ensure that the implied aims of parental choice and consultation will extend to *all* parents of *all* children in *all* British schools.

If the Secretary of State is sincere in his stated aim that the National Curriculum will, through change, enhance the educational achievement of *all*, then there must be meaningful and *not* token consultation with *all* parents and their representatives on a wide basis, which means that Black parents and their representatives ought to be included on a basis of equality. There has been no indication whatever that such provision will be made.

Source: C. MacNeil (1988) 'The National Curriculum: A Black Perspective', *Multicultural Teaching*, 6(2), pp. 14–16.

LANGUAGE AND THE CURRICULUM

Looking at the content of the National Curriculum, there are further large and worrying omissions.

It is proposed that mathematics, English and science form the core of the curriculum, together with seven other subjects – a modern foreign language, technology, history, geography, art, music and physical education.

As the ILEA's summary of the consultation document points out, although time allocations are set out in the document and would be issued in the form of non-statutory guidelines, the Government does not intend to legislate how *much* time should be allocated to each subject. There is a lack of clarity in the statement that 'where there is good practice, the National Curriculum commonly takes up 80 to 90 per cent of the curriculum'. Questions are immediately raised:

What are the criteria for measuring 'good practice'?
How would the remaining 10–20 per cent of time be utilised?
Would that 10–20 per cent be used for religious education, as statutorily required?

There could then be regional differences in the emphases in the case of the foundation subjects. This certainly will have an impact on the teaching of a modern foreign language because the choice of language to be taught could lead to severe local disagreements, especially where there are many languages spoken in the community. We must bear in mind that there are twelve different languages each spoken by more than 100,000 people in the United Kingdom. Less than half the twelve are European languages, yet there are far more teachers of European languages. This must inevitably lead to discrimination in favour of European language teaching. I suspect that the rationale for choice of language would be not regional needs but national needs because Britain is a member of the EEC. This insular thinking excludes other main trading nations from Africa and the Orient, thus narrowing economic and commercial expansion in the longer term.

My deep mistrust was confirmed by Bob Dunn, the Under-Secretary of State for Education, when he warned that ethnic minority children must not be handicapped by misguided teaching policy. 'Being a citizen', he states, 'means that children must speak English fluently: to read, write, converse, argue and think in English.' He goes on to say patronisingly: 'By all means let families foster and teach the language, customs and religions of their former homeland but it is essential that schools should foster and teach the language of this their adopted homeland.' I agree that command of English is essential, but to suggest that to teach a modern foreign language is misguided and thus a handicap to pupils is not just absurd but insulting.

HISTORY

The inclusion of history as a foundation subject is very interesting in view of the distrust shown by the Conservative Monday Club in its Policy Paper of the Race Relations Policy Committee (No. I.R.4), which I quote: 'History is the subject most marked for re-orientation. Re-orientation of the past is indispensable for ideological dominion in the present. Marxism has always possessed a healthy regard for history as a political weapon and its perspectives have provided much of the basis of anti-racism.' Now read Kenneth Baker on the ILEA's publication *Positive Books on Black People's History*. He accuses the Authority of attempting to censor history texts and rewrite them on party political lines, asserting that the ILEA's approach is 'very close to imposing tight control in London's schools'.

Both make a charge of indoctrination. Both see history as a tool of indoctrination, not of education.

Dawn Gill is clear about the difference: 'To indoctrinate is to present one point of view to the exclusion of others. To educate would involve the examination of alternative and explanatory frameworks.' I suspect that our government would rather have the same old diet of colonial domination which, they claim, benefited the peoples of the territories over which they held dominion for a long time. They might even quarrel with Eric Williams' pronouncement that every age rewrites history. In his preface to *Capitalism and Slavery*, Williams writes 'Every age re-writes history, but particularly ours, which has been forced by events to re-evaluate our conceptions of history and economic and political development.' Constitutions have been revised, economic strategies have been re-examined and re-evaluated, political dogma has been changed – all forced by events. The analogy is self-evident.

GEOGRAPHY

Geography also needs an in-depth approach because of the constant changes brought about either by natural phenomena or by human beings. As a young person, I remember much of the world atlas being coloured red – the British Empire or more precisely British possessions. This is no longer so. Examination of the changes would throw up intriguing issues. For example, we see and read of the poverty in Africa and the Asian subcontinent. Some conclude that the people are feckless and incapable of looking after themselves. Some are more charitable and conclude that mother nature has been unkind. Both are facile conclusions; there is more to it than that. To approach the truth, an examination of the farming and mining policies will inescapably show the indiscriminate extraction of minerals and how the soil was farmed to exhaustion, leaving the land decimated. Like the lack of development, these are issues for discussion. Colonialism must bear some blame. If the Colonists claim that they gave independence to the people, they must also recognise that they left them bereft. Blaming the victim is altogether inappropriate – and in educational terms, quite unsound.

LITERATURE

Literature is a most important subject in the foundation course. It is the most sensitive and at the same time the most powerful medium of thought dissemination and attitude formation; 'the pen is mightier than the sword', still. Gillian Klein observes that 'as writers, editors and publishers select what information to put into their books, they inevitably select also – or censor – what to leave out'. She cites Dorothy Kuya's perception of the process as a vicious circle:

> teachers, parents and others buy books to convey information to children because they conform with their knowledge and understanding ... this information is then regurgitated in the classrooms of Britain. So our children grow up knowing nothing of the diversity of cultures and religions, within which there is a constant dynamic development; they are told nothing of the elements of life which go to make up an individual or a group's existence. Nothing is said about the economic/political/social/religious/ideological framework within which all groups and nations operate. All they encounter are stereotypes, distorting irrelevant information, misleading and ambiguous statements and downright lies – a reflection of the views which were common currency during the period of British Empire: paternalistic, often contemptuous, bigoted and racist.

Black writers have always contributed to the field of literature – James Baldwin, Aime Cezaire, Buchi Emecheta, Derek Walcott, V. S. Naipaul, to name only a few. They offer a broader perspective. Black authorship is not a new phenomenon; what has been happening is that their works have been largely ignored. The works of Black authors are scarcely recommended as textbooks or set books for public examinations. The NCC has a duty to consider this limitation of horizons of pupils.

I have taken examples from history, geography, and literature in order to demonstrate some of the weaknesses and my fear of the one-sided implementation – all on the side of the dominant – of the National Curriculum. There is no in-built assurance that anything other than a Eurocentric and dominant perspective will prevail. The proposals and the implementation seem contradictory.

REPRESENTATION?

It is proposed that the legislation on the National Curriculum will provide for all interested parties to have information on what is being taught and achieved. The interested parties must by definition be the parents and children. But note, they are promised only information – not participation. It is also proposed that the Secretary of State be required to appoint a National Curriculum Council to provide him with external professional advice before he presents legislation to Parliament on the National Curriculum, and that the NCC include people with a range of experience about education. But they will be appointed on a personal rather than representative basis, and with no structural framework for real representation. Representation that is not elected by those being represented is not democratic. Black communities as per the proposal are not allowed to select their representatives. There is no reason to believe that the Secretary of State will necessarily select Black people among his advisors, but even if he does, there is no guarantee that those selected will in fact represent the views of the Black communities. There is an over-riding need for democratic election to ensure fair representation of the views of Black people – let the people choose.

The ILEA draws attention to the Equal Opportunities implications by pointing out that the proposed legislation may inhibit the ability of the Authority to develop curriculum initiatives in response to the needs of particular groups. The Authority also points out that in general there is little recognition of the multi-ethnic nature of the population for which ILEA is responsible. Further, it is significant that among the membership of the two subject working groups so far established there is no one who is Black or from an ethnic minority background. Why not? Black people can hardly feel a sense of belonging if they are not involved in discussion on such a vital issue as education.

If the Secretary of State is serious about equal opportunities in education, he should heed Professor John Rex's statement in the Swann Report: 'To promote equal opportunity without allowing for cultural pluralism is to move towards a policy of false assimilation.' Assimilation (forced or manipulated) will result if the National Curriculum remains statically Eurocentric – an inevitable outcome of the exclusion of Black people from the participation process.

It is crucial now for all doors to be opened for Black people to get on to the higher occupational levels. Through the educational system now in operation and proposed, they are thwarted and will continue to be so, never achieving positions of power.

Professor Rex suggests that 'an open educational system may be the one means through which occupational and status mobility is possible, and the degree of openness may be one of the defining features of a social system, for its participant actors and those who seek to enter it from outside.' Since there is (so far) no intended participation, Black people's means of achieving full and meaningful citizenship are blocked.

A 'MONDAY' CURRICULUM?

Because of the undemocratic ethos of the National Curriculum Council, there is a feeling of unease and suspicion; suspicion that the Conservative Monday Club, if not directly involved, could have had some influence. This is based, for a start, on their statement in their discussion paper of the Immigration and Race Relations Policy Committee (May 1985): 'Curriculum reform is the principal goal of multiculturalism. Changes here will mean success for the multicultural engineers, though not perhaps, the rest of us.' Is this proof of the 'them' and 'us' syndrome which prevails in British society today?

It would appear that paranoia is creeping into their thinking when they conclude that if the aim of multiculturalism should succeed, it would benefit only Black people. The more rational conclusion would be that it would benefit society as a whole.

Their argument that multiculturalism cannot be satisfied by the elimination of prejudice and the growth of understanding 'because these are not the essential aims' does not stand up. Why does the Monday Club believe that the spirit of antiracism is one that itches to punish and remould?' Remould, yes; punish, no – that is futile and unhelpful. Indeed the idea of remoulding is necessary to cope with the metamorphosis which British society has undergone and will continue to undergo.

A splendid opportunity to change society's attitudes through education is being missed. An open education system would inevitably lead to reinterpretation and re-examination of what has been and continues to be excluded from the education agenda. It is the taxpaying consumers' ineluctable right to have their wishes considered about changes and curricular issues. In the case of Black people, their needs, aims, aspirations and ambitions for their children can only be represented by themselves. They must be involved so that the power brokers understand and provide appropriately.

It is useful here to interpret 'education' and to examine whether the National Curriculum is in tandem with the interpretation. At a recent talk in London entitled 'Education Theorising in an Emancipatory Context, A Case for a Caribbean Curriculum', Clement London, an American professor in education, interpreted education as 'culture'. He said that 'Caribbean culture should become an affirmation of the worth, values, and deeds of all Caribbean peoples.' I heartily endorse this statement as appropriate to the diverse ethnic make-up of British society. The last vestiges of monoculturalism are fading fast.

Every avenue, every opportunity must be available to all in order that they might develop and utilise progressive educational practices. Education must be perceived as a liberating investment in a struggle not only to eradicate debilitating economic conditions and thereby social oppression, but also, more importantly, to enlarge the human capacity by allowing the people to share in establishing social systems that foster the sensibilities of citizenship, develop the spirit, and establish attitudes of mind that will redirect thinking away from a siege mentality. Dr London puts forward the premise that education must be used to create, upgrade and harness available potential and expertise. Education content must constitute relevant curricular offerings and address varying assessed and expressed regional needs. This would result in the transformation into viable national systems of shared communities based on local values. Black people view education not only as a social service, an item of consumption, but more pragmatically, as an item of, self-identity and determination.

The format, content and proposed implementation of the National Curriculum will not, I fear, meet Black people's educational aims and aspirations for their children. A radical rethink is urgently required before the unacceptable aspects of the National Curriculum become fixed and irretrievable.

REFERENCES

Education For All, HMSO, Cmnd. 9453 (Swann Report) 1985.
Multicultural Teaching – To Combat Racism in School and Community, Vol. V, No. 3.
Agenda for Multicultural Teaching, Alma Craft and Gillian Klein (SCDC Publications).
Reading into Racism, Gillian Klein. Routledge, 1985.
Capitalism and Slavery, Eric Williams. André Deutsch, 1964.
Race Relations in Sociological Theory, John Rex. Routledge, 1983.
Education for a Multi-Cultural Society, (ed.) Martin Straker-Welds.
Conservative Monday Club Policy Paper, *Immigration and Race Relations Policy*, Committee No. I.R.4, Simon Pearce.
West Indian Children in our Schools, Interim report of the Committee of Inquiry into the Education of Children from Ethnic Minority Groups, Rampton Report, HMSO 1981.

part three
SUBJECT HISTORIES

Competition and Conflict in the Teaching of English: A Socio-Historical Analysis

3.1

STEPHEN J. BALL

[...]

PREHISTORY

One of the most striking features of English as a discipline, for anyone coming for the first time to examine its intellectual and curricular history, is the relative recentness of its emergence as a separately identifiable school subject. This is especially so when one considers the amount of timetabled time devoted to the teaching of English in the contemporary school curriculum. It is probably fair to say that, before the turn of the century, English did not exist as a separately identifiable school subject at either elementary or secondary level. There were certainly very few teachers who could be called or would have called themselves teachers of English. It was not until 1904 that the Board of Education included in its Regulations a directive requiring all state secondary schools to offer courses in English literature and language. Prior to that, English was studied by most children from age 8 upwards in the form of orthography, etymology and syntax. English teaching consisted of subjecting children to systematic instruction in the principles of English grammar. In other words, English took its subject matter and its pedagogy directly from those of the teaching of classics. Indeed many of the teachers were themselves trained in the classics. As a result 'Language lessons were taught ... as expository lessons teaching the rational nature of traditional grammar – or at least traditional school grammar, as proposed by course book writers ... Rote exercises and tests on the facts of grammar were common, and most teachers were convinced of the positive value for the performance of reading and writing of the abstract study of grammatical principles.'[1]

However, these features of pedagogy and content can also be seen to have been shaped in no small part by the constraints imposed by the Revised Code of 1862, which linked 'the prospects and position of the teacher' with pupils' achievements

Source: S. J. Ball (1982) 'Competition and Conflict in the Teaching of English: A Socio-Historical Analysis', *Journal of Curriculum Studies*, 14(1), pp. 1–28.

in examination; that is, payment by results. As Matthew Arnold noted in his *Reports 1852–82*, 'The circle of the children's reading has been narrowed and impoverished all the year for the sake of the result at the end of it, and the result is an illusion.'[2] But even outside of the constraints of the Revised Codes the level of work expected of children, in both elementary and secondary schools, was modest to say the least. According to Joyce, writing in 1864 in his book *School Management*, composition 'in the highest sense of the term' could 'only be mastered by a mature intellect, but the ability to write a common letter, or any simple statement in plain intelligible language with correct spelling, fairly punctuated and free from ... obvious or gross grammatical errors' was thought to be all that it was possible to achieve in the ordinary national schools.[3] Thus most of the work done in 'English' during this period, or in what were in fact normally separate composition[4] and grammar lessons, was based on imitation for composition work and parsing for grammar work. And, in this, composition remained 'a poor relation ... merely a testing device, the proof of the grammar pudding'.[5] A typical example of grammar work, which Shayer describes as 'frankly, nasty', would be Mushet's *Exercises in English*.

> '*I had rather go* home this way, please.'
> had: – Verb. defect. intrans. – act, subj. past indef. sing.
> 1st – agreeing with I
> rather: – Advb. of degree. old comp. from – mod. 'had'
> go: – Verb, strong, intrans. – act. infin. pres. – dep. on 'had'
> please: – Verb, weak, intrans. impers. – act. subj. pres. sing.
> 3rd – agreeing with it.[6]

As for literature, in 1872, 71,507 children (3·6 per cent of all those in elementary schools) were examined in 'specific subjects', and grammar was the second most popular of these specific subjects, with 18,426 being examined. English literature was the fourth most popular with 11,085. By 1875, when the percentage of children examined in 'specific subjects' had risen to 3·7 per cent, English literature was the second most popular, with 39,211 examinees. By 1882, the number of examinees in English literature was up to 140,772. However, the Board of Education pointed out in Circular 753 of 1910 that 'These figures might, however, easily give rise to quite erroneous impressions unless the scope and meaning of the term "English literature", as explained in the list of "specific subjects", be clearly defined.'[7] The syllabus for the examination of English literature as a 'specific subject' in 1876 was as follows

> 1st year ... One hundred lines of poetry, got by heart, with knowledge of meanings and allusions. Writing a letter on a simple subject.
> 2nd year ... Two hundred lines of poetry, not before brought up, repeated; with the knowledge of meaning and allusions. Writing a paraphrase of easy prose.
> 3rd year ... Three hundred lines of poetry, not before brought up; repeated; with knowledge of meanings and allusions. Writing a letter or statement, the head of the topics to be given by the Inspector.

For the period 1882–90 the Board notes 'the continuance of the emphasis in English which had prevailed in the previous period'.[8] But for the period 1902–10 it goes on 'Grammar instead of being taught as an isolated subject was taught in relation to composition.'[9] Indeed in the first ten years of this century there was a marked degree of opposition to the teaching of grammar as a separate and predominant aspect of English. However, several *Journal of Education* reports published during this period attest to the continuing influence of classics as a model for the teaching of English (for example, Barnett and Zimmern).[10]

Three matters of issue emerge from this brief examination of the teaching of English during the earliest period of state education. One is the occurrence of territorial disputes involved in the claims made for English to be a specific, separate and coherent subject entity included in the curriculum of all elementary and secondary schools. Another is the emergence of competition and conflict within the boundaries of English between rival claimants to the definition of the corpus of knowledge and associated pedagogy which should constitute the subject. The third is a process of curriculum change marked by a considerable complexity of influences and slowness of pace. It is with those main themes that I shall be concerned in the remainder of this paper.

THE FIRST STRUGGLES

The Struthers 1907 primary school memorandum recommends that 'Only so much grammar need be taught as can thus be applied; the phenomena treated should be such as can arise naturally in reading and writing.' During this period a campaign was begun to disassociate English from the overbearing domination and competition of classics teaching, to establish English once and for all as a separate subject in its own right, with its own content and at secondary level its own specialist teachers. But this was not a campaign that was easily or quickly won. While English was established fairly quickly, if not over-confidently, as a separately timetabled subject, the role of the teaching of grammar continues to be one basis of disputation within the subject until the present time, as we shall see later.

An important part of the strategy of establishing English as a separate subject with its own content was the inauguration of the English Association in 1906. The Association was set up with the explicit aims of promoting English as a subject in its own right, with its own place in the curriculum, and to counter the stultifying and conservative influences of the classical tradition. In the original articles of the Association, article (c) states that the Association is 'to promote the due recognition of English as an essential element of national education'.

It is clear that the Association came into being very much as a source of support for the establishment of an autonomous epistemic community for English teachers and a response to the pressures from and opposition of the classicists. 'As Classics, Modern Languages and other subjects had supporting associations, one was needed to uphold the claims in education and otherwise of the mother tongue.'[11]

Rudduck notes that 'Participants at this first Annual Meeting of the Association thought fit to urge that the general overall purpose of the new Association was to secure "a prominent if not a foremost place" for English in the curriculum of every school and college in the Empire.'[12]

In 1907 the Association had 300 members. By 1927 the number had grown to over 7000. And over a period of thirty years from its inception, members of the Association were to have considerable influence upon the thinking about the teaching of English in schools.

By 1906 the lines of battle were drawn for a conflict which in effect continues to the present day, although we must recognise that, during the 1910s and 1920s at least, this battle was to be fought on two fronts; on the one hand, it is a territorial dispute between English as a subject and classics – as Smetherham notes, 'Each subject speciality perceives itself as having a unique contribution to the purpose-at-hand that it alone was able to make'[13] – on the other hand, here we have the origins of the internecine dispute within English about the definition of the subject. This latter is a dispute between a view of the subject as 'grammar' and a view of the subject which gives a central position to the role of 'literature' and pupil expression. The former view has embedded firmly within it a conception of English teaching as being concerned with the 'correct' use of English, based on the belief, reiterated in the 1929 General Report on the Teaching of English in London Elementary Schools, that 'the use of English . . . is a fine art, and must be taught as a fine art'. However, additionally, Shayer argues that 'the linguistic emphasis came to represent a further attempt to make English a respectable discipline'.[14]

The early phase of the development of 'English' in competition with the teaching of the classics parallels closely Bucher and Strauss's account of the problems ensuing from the emergence of new specialisms in the medical profession:

> the emergence of new segments takes on a new significance when viewed from the perspective of social movements within a profession. Pockets of resistance and embattled minorities may turn out to be the heirs of former generations, digging in along new battle lines. They may spearhead new movements which sweep back into power. What looks like backwash or just plain deviancy, may be the beginnings of a new segment which will acquire an institutional place and considerable prestige and power.[15]

This conflict is evident in pamphlets published by the English Association right through into the 1930s. So too is what Bucher and Strauss refer to as 'the sense of mission':

> It is characteristic of the growth of specialities that early in their development they carve out for themselves and proclaim for themselves unique missions. They issue a statement of the contribution that the speciality, and it alone, can make in a total scheme of values and, frequently, with an argument to show why it is peculiarly fitted for this task.[16]

Interestingly and significantly, the intellectual battle to establish English as a discipline in schools was closely related to and allied with the very similar battle to establish English as a contemporary discipline in the universities. English was accepted as part of a Bachelor of Arts degree at London University in 1859 and was subsequently adopted by several other provincial universities, but in every case it remained an essentially linguistic rather than a literary area of study and held an uneasy and subordinate intellectual position, somewhere between history and grammar. Oxford and Cambridge were less ready to recognise English as a subject worthy of their attention, and such courses as were introduced were based on philology and the study of Old English. Cambridge did not appoint its first professor of English, Arthur Quiller-Couch, until 1912, at which time it is reported that he had just one student.

Initially in both the grammar schools and in the universities, English came to be seen as more appropriate and acceptable as a subject for girls and women. This tended to reflect and reinforce its low intellectual status and continuing subordinate position to the classics – which were considered to be over-taxing for the female mind.[17]

This also contributed to the considerable unevenness in the development of English as a subject at secondary level. This is evident in the 1922 Board of Education *Report of the Consultative Committee on the Differentiation of the Curriculum for Boys and Girls Respectively in Secondary Schools*:

> English language and literature – The general conclusion expressed by our witnesses and on the whole corroborated by the evidence furnished by examining bodies was that in this subject the average achievement of girls was distinctly superior to that of boys. This result is largely due to the more assured position given to the subject in girls' schools, and to the larger proportion of well-qualified women teachers and the better teaching which is consequently given.[18]

It is also apparent from the evidence submitted to the Committee that the teaching of English that was done in boys' schools was oriented and defined differently from the teaching in girls' schools. In the boys' schools, English continued to be taught very much in the classical mould. Thus the Committee recommended: 'That more care and attention should be given (a) in boys' schools to the use and comprehension of English and to the study of English literature as a means to this end, and (b) in girls' schools to the analysis and understanding of the logical content of works of literature.'[19]

[...]

THE 1920s, 1930s AND 1940s

It would be a mistake to portray the growth and penetration of the 'new English', as I have dubbed it, as a contested but inevitable process or indeed as a very rapid process. While the revised conceptions of English as a literary and expressive discipline continued to make steady headway in the elementary schools from 1904 onwards, change in the secondary schools was significantly slower and in certain respects more conflictual. What needs to be considered is why the grammarian paradigm in English teaching continued to be so resilient against the challenge of alternative 'assertive' paradigms up until the 1950s, and why it continues to be represented in the teaching of English even today. In examining these concerns we must face an immediate problem; that is, whether these competing paradigms of English teaching are to be considered simply in terms of their rhetorical development in the writings of respective advocates, or in 'official' pronouncements of the reports, recommendations and suggestions issued by the Board of Education, or in terms of the realities of classroom teaching. Obviously, all three are important, and they cannot be treated as mutually exclusive fields of activity, but it would be naive to take them to be synonymous. However, there is a further difficulty, in that any attempt to portray the classroom teaching of English during this period must rely upon the indirect accounts of commentators, rather than firsthand accounts of researchers or practitioners. What emerges from these former sources is a fairly standard picture, at least at secondary level, of the continuing pre-eminence of a grammarian, classicist approach to the teaching of English. The dominant image of the period is of the pervasive and conservative influence of the public school curriculum:

> In the majority of secondary school syllabuses up to and including the 1950s the language element predominated. Drill in the mechanisms of writing: spelling, punctuation, paragraphing and so on, practice in identifying and explaining the various parts of speech – this has been 'the stuff of' English since the turn of the century.[20]

> As recently as 1960 English as a school subject was in a state of suspended animation that had hardly changed over 40 years.[21]

> It seems clear that there was a widespread adherence to traditional ideas especially in the public schools and grammar schools, and in its essence English teaching was not substantially different in the thirties from the methods of the preceding fifty years.[22]

> If the term reader has a 1900 sound, its persistence as a school textbook (indeed as a school *course*) must not be underestimated. The reader could be said to take care of the literature side of many schools, with no necessity to look further.[23]

> For over fifty years this Latin-based norm of 'correct' English was firmly entrenched in schools. It was enshrined in the School Certificate and in the Ordinary Language syllabus and once established there it was difficult to dislodge.[24]

One of the reasons for the persistence of the grammarian tradition during the 1920s, 1930s and 1940s, a 'pale substitute for Classics', as Shayer puts it, is undoubtedly the continued importance of the classics at university level and in the public schools. But there are a number of social and situational factors that also had their part to play; that is, features of the schools themselves and the social structure within which they operated. One factor of relevance is the relationship between English and other school subjects apart from classics, for it was not only from this direction that competition emerged. The ownership of areas of the corpus of knowledge claimed by English was contested also by history. Shayer notes 'Literature was particularly vulnerable to the inroads of History and the distinction between the two was not completely established until the 1920s.'[25] Furthermore, as noted already, English literature in particular had become accepted much more readily as a subject for girls. The preponderance of single-sex schools in the secondary sector thus tended to isolate boys' schools from many of the developments in English teaching. Importantly, despite the founding of the English Association and the steady stream of reports, suggestions and recommendations from the Board of Education and elsewhere, English continued to be regarded as a subject that all teachers were capable of teaching. This fact was noted in the 1910 Circular 753 issued by the Board of Education. 'The teaching of English in a school is not only being treated as a water-tight unit, but is being taught by any member of staff who can be induced to "take a few periods" to fill in time.'[26] The Circular also noted that in many schools English was not taken 'seriously'. (The problem of unqualified staff teaching English has been highlighted once more by the recent HMI Survey: *Aspects of the Secondary Curriculum*.)[27] The idea, which has recently returned to the forefront of debate following the publication of the Bullock Report, that 'every teacher is a teacher of English', tended to operate against the claims made for English to be considered as a subject in its own right. While the widespread practice of using non-specialists for English teaching continued, both the credibility and the progress of English was inhibited. Meanwhile the universities continued to produce 'English' graduates imbued with philology and language studies. Additionally, the structural stability of the schools themselves did not encourage a rapid dissemination of new educational ideas. The structure of teacher employment during the inter-war years provided for stable staffs and little geographical mobility. And the teaching profession did not escape the effects of the world depression of the 1930s, and this brought its own stultifying influence to bear upon the teaching of English:

> There were, of course, progressive measures at work in the thirties in education but the depressed state of the profession, with problems of unemployment of teachers and stagnation of promotion, led to a climate in which most teachers were more prepared to perpetuate tradition as it was found in the prescribed books of a given department, than to experiment and introduce new directions of study.[28]

However, the state of affairs in the secondary schools during this period is not indicative of a total lack of development in the state of thinking about English as a discipline and in the teaching of English in schools and universities. Rather, the opposite is the case, for an examination of the work of the English Association and the members of what came to be called the Cambridge School of English reveals the emergence and establishment of two separate but related paradigms of English teaching that were to come to have a major impact upon classroom practice during the 1950s and 1960s. Abbs distinguishes these as the 'Cambridge School of English' and the 'Progressive Movement', the latter advocating and promoting the importance of self-expression and individuality and the role of play in learning English. 'The progressives asserted the need for a freer and more spontaneous approach allowing the child to generate much of the curriculum according to his basic needs.'[29] The key figures in the progressive movement in its early stages were: Percy Nunn, Greening Lamborn, Edmund Holmes, W. S. Tomkinson and Caldwell Cook. Later came Marjorie Hourd and Herbert Read. In discussing Read and Hourd, Abbs notes that they 'emphasize the power of creativity in education, to recognize the place of feeling and of imagination, to perceive the value of psychic wholeness'.[30] This approach to English teaching had its impact most directly upon the elementary schools and later more broadly contributed to the underlying philosophy of practice of the progressive primary schools of the 1960s. [. . .]

At the point of the outbreak of the Second World War the three paradigms of English teaching so far introduced in this account were clearly articulated, both in theory and practice, and contending with one another for predominance – with, in practical terms, the progressive movement making headway against grammar in the elementary schools and the Cambridge school making inroads in the secondary schools.

It is possible to begin to conceptualise the reasons for the emergence of these competing paradigms in two ways: (1) in terms of the inexorable adjustment of the school curriculum to the needs or forces of the social structure; or (2) as the outcome of the strategies, pressures and influences of particular groups or individuals with investments in the teaching of English. In practice, I intend to go some way towards conflating these approaches by discussing both the *conditions of change* – the changes in the economic and social conditions of schooling which allowed, inhibited or provided for changes in the process and content of school knowledge – and the *relations of change* – those activities and strategies which actually initiated change. [. . .]

The mid-1960s were marked universally by a change in the climate of opinion about education, from Freire's work in Brazil and Illich's in Mexico to the Cultural Revolution in China, to compensatory education in the USA and the Plowden Report. In Britain, there was a marked rethinking of the role, content, structure and process of educational provision. Also in Britain there was a massive concatenation of contextual variables, *conditions of change*, stimulating and reflecting educational change. Several of these should be mentioned here:

1 The growth in the number of comprehensive schools and the spread in the commitment to comprehensive reorganisation among teachers, politicians and educationalists, with the concomitant questioning of and weakening of the grammar school tradition.

2 The changing structure of the teaching profession (the introduction of scale posts, posts of responsibility etc.).

3 The changing patterns of career and promotion in teaching with the shortage of

teachers in many subjects and a massive school building programme.

4 The changing pattern of teacher training (the increasing numbers of graduate teachers entering postgraduate training courses and more recently the requirement for them to train).

5 The opening of teachers' centres, the founding of the Schools' Council and the subsequent funding of large-scale curriculum development projects in many subject areas.

6 The introduction of the CSE ('O' level) examination and in particular the mode III form which involved teachers for the first time in designing their own courses for examination (although, as Allen notes, 'The new CSE examination was the focus for the critical reform but we felt trammelled also by aspects of the O-level GCE [both language and literature] and A-level literature').[31]

7 The problems faced by teachers involved in comprehensive reorganisation and ROSLA [Raising of the School Leaving Age] with 'pupils who appear to neither know how to "learn" the "academic" knowledge, nor appear to want to'.[32]

8 The rediscovery of poverty and the discovery of cultural deprivation with the resulting concern with schools as agencies of compensation for social problems accompanied by greater awareness of children's learning problems.

9 The political and social radicalism of the 1960s, particularly that which addressed itself to the form of and control over the process of education.

Specifically in English, the emergence of the *socio-linguistic* paradigm reflecting and responding to the points listed above was supported by the funding of a number of curriculum projects by NFER and the Schools Council:

The Written Language of 11–18 Year Olds (1966–71). James Britton and Nancy Martin.
Language Development in the Primary School (1969–71). Connie Rosen.
Oracy (1967–72). Andrew Wilkinson.
Linguistics and English Teaching (1964–70). M. A. K. Halliday.
English 16–19 (1975–9). John Dixon. [. . .]

A contemporary picture of English in schools emerges which is not starkly dissimilar in many respects from the situation that existed when English was first established as a separate curriculum subject. There is: (1) disputation within the subject involving a very real struggle for intellectual sovereignty, with competing paradigms seeking to control the definition of analytic problems and methods and the pedagogic form for the realisation of the subject; and (2) threats to the continuing independence of English as a school subject from the inroads of adjacent curriculum areas. However, the contemporary situation differs in the degree of complexity involved in the competition with the subject community. As noted previously, the opposition between paradigms involves both issues of content and issues of method (pedagogy). Implicit in the former is the polarisation of *elite* and *mass* concepts of culture, and in the latter is a concomitant separation of child-centred and subject-centred orientations. [. . .]

Clearly, the politico-economic climate of the later 1970s has brought about conditions of change which have led to a reassertion of the utilitarian functions of English teaching in schools. To quote Cashdan, 'The school needs to be seen, by both pupils and parents, as a facility (for which they have paid) provided for their use.'[33] The dominant concern is once again for 'correctness' and the improvement of standards of language used by children.

In many ways, in attempting to explain these changes the *conditions of change* can be identified and specified more straightforwardly than the *relations of change*. As Allen notes 'Of course, any attempt to make sense of recent history is beset by obvious problems of clarity, selection and perspective. When the "historian" is attempting to account for changes which had both personal and public dimensions, the problems are compounded.'[34] At any point in time, there is a whole set of influences at work in shaping and changing a particular school subject. While it is possible to accept at an abstract level that school knowledge 'is a selection from the available knowledge within the culture' and that, 'those in positions of power will attempt to define what is to be considered as knowledge',[35] it is much more difficult to identify those in 'positions of power', the extent to which their attempt is successful, and the extent to which alternative definitions compete for ascendancy within any subject. Nor is it very clear whether the process of definition concerns simply states of knowledge or must also be taken to include ways of knowing and matters of pedagogy. [...]

What emerges from this analysis of curriculum change is a model of curriculum innovation which is perhaps at the same time both humanistic and reactionary. Curriculum change is seen to be a long-term and interpersonal process, based upon the establishment of subject paradigms via networks of communication and apprenticeship (with many of the teachers who are not exposed directly to experience of these paradigms being influenced marginally or not at all by them). Thus it is important to reiterate that there is no direct equivalence at any one point in time between the establishment of these paradigms at universities or colleges and the work of most teachers of English. The variation of generational, regional and apprenticeship effects tends to ensure that at the school level all possible paradigm positions are represented in the allegiances of teachers, and this often provides the basis for disputation and conflict within a single school subject department.[36] [...]

NOTES

1 W. B. Currie (1973) *New Directions in Teaching English Language.* London: Longman, p. 19.

2 M. Arnold (1908) *Reports on Elementary Schools 1852–82.* London: HMSO, p. 126.

3 P. W. Joyce (1864) *School Management.*

4 'Composition' does not refer to any sort of creative writing on the part of pupils, but was used to refer to the skills of correct expression or manner of presentation.

5 D. Shayer (1970) *The Teaching of English in Schools.* London: Routledge & Kegan Paul, p. 22.

6 J. Mushet (1912) *Exercises in English*. Edinburgh.

7 GB Board of Education (1910) *The Teaching of English in Secondary Schools: Circular 753*. London: HMSO, p. 4.

8 Ibid., p. 14.

9 Ibid., pp. 24–5.

10 P. A. Barnett (1902) 'English Literature and English Schools', *Journal of Education*; and A. Zimmern (1900) 'Literature as a Central Subject', *Journal of Education*.

11 F. S. Boas (1979) Undated paper, quoted in J. Rudduck 'A Study of Traditions in the Development of Short In-Service Curriculum Courses for Teachers'. Unpublished PhD Thesis, University of East Anglia.

12 J. Rudduck 'Notes on the English Association and National Association for the Teaching of English'. Unpublished.

13 D. Smetherham (1978) 'Identifying Strategies'. Paper given at the SSRC-funded Conference: Teacher and Pupil Strategies, held at St Hilda's College, Oxford, 15–17 September, p. 22.

14 Shayer (1970), p. 9.

15 R. Bucher and A. L. Strauss (1976) 'Professions in Process', in M. Hammersley and P. E. Woods (eds), *The Process of Schooling*. London: Routledge & Kegan Paul, pp. 24–5.

16 Ibid., p. 20.

17 See: C. Dyhouse (1976) 'Social-Darwinistic Ideas and the Development of Women's Education in England 1880–1920', *History of Education*, 5(1), pp. 41–58.

18 GB Board of Education (1922) *Report of the Consultative Committee on the Differentiation of the Curriculum for Boys and Girls Respectively in Secondary Schools*. London: HMSO, p. 102.

20 M. Saunders (1976) *Developments in English Teaching*. London: Open Books, p. 19.

21 G. Allen (1973) 'English: Past, Present and Future', in N. Bagnell (ed.), *New Movements in the Study and Teaching of English*. London: Temple Smith, p. 30.

22 W. B. Currie (1973) *New Directions in Teaching English Language*. London: Longman, p. 25.

23 Shayer (1970), p. 33.

24 L. E. W. Smith (1973) *Towards a New English Curriculum*. London: Dent, p. 3.

25 Shayer (1970), p. 19.

26 Ibid., p. 33.

27 DES (1979) *HMI's Secondary Survey: Aspects of the Secondary Curriculum*. London: HMSO.

28 Currie (1973), p. 25.

29 P. Abbs (1980) 'The Reconstitution of English as Art', *Tract*, 81, pp. 4–31.

30 Ibid., p. 9.

31 D. Allen (1980) *English Teaching since 1965: How Much Growth?*. London: Heinemann, p. 2.

32 M. F. D. Young (1971) 'An Approach to the Study of Curriculum as Socially Organized Knowledge', in M. F. D. Young (ed.), *Knowledge and Control*. London: Collier–Macmillan.

33 A. Cashdan (1979) *Language, Reading and Learning*. Oxford: Basil Blackwell, p. 18.

34 D. Allen (1980), p. 3.

35 Young (1971), p. 32.

36 S. J. Ball and C. Lacey (1980) 'Subject Disciplines as the Opportunity for Group Action: A Measured Critique of Subject Sub-Cultures', in P. E. Woods (ed.), *Teacher Strategies*. London: Croom Helm.

Training the Mind: Continuity and Change in the Rhetoric of School Science

3.2

Robin Millar

[...]

Two paradigms of science education

Since the earliest days of science instruction in schools, the relative importance of scientific *content* and scientific *method* have been almost continually under discussion. Few, if any, educational writers have portrayed the value of science as a school subject as residing wholly in its content or in its method. Instead, we might regard their views as lying at some point on a continuum with these end-points. Advocates of a content-biased approach usually stress the idea of science as 'useful knowledge', whilst a method-biased approach will characteristically state (or imply) that pupils can benefit from exposure to the 'scientific method' or to 'scientific' modes of thought.

In his book *Science for the People*, Layton[1] portrays the development of science as a subject in elementary education during the period from 1820 until the 1860s in terms of a continuing dialectic between these two paradigms: the idea of science as 'useful knowledge'; and the view of science as a vehicle for training mental 'faculties' like observation and classification. It seems clear that a concept of the mind as made up (in some sense) of a series of faculties which were capable of development (in much the same way as muscles could be developed by suitable exercise) had become a part of the tacitly accepted 'knowledge' of the day. These ideas are closely associated with those put forward by the nineteenth-century phrenologists, of whom the best known is, perhaps, George Combe.[2] Although their use of the notions of mental faculties led them into conflict with the scientific establishment of the day, it seems clear that a conception of the mind as being composed of discrete faculties had become accessible to a wide range of educated opinion. The unselfconscious way in which nineteenth-century educators make use of such ideas indicates the extent to which the ideas were consensually held.

Source: R. Millar (1985) 'Training the Mind: Continuity and Change in the Rhetoric of School Science', *Journal of Curriculum Studies*, 17(4), pp. 369–82.

The theory of 'faculties of mind' provides a physical basis for the belief in what is generally referred to as 'transfer of training'. It is, of course, clear that writers may use the idea of 'transfer' without of necessity espousing the full 'faculty' model of mental functioning. Indeed, as the 'transfer' idea has evolved, the associated picture of the structure of the mind appears to have steadily become less concrete.

The 'faculty' paradigm is associated by Layton with the work of John Stevens Henslow, who emphasised the training which science (and particularly the natural history sciences) could provide for improving the faculties of observation, classification and rational thought; the idea of science as a form of 'useful knowledge' whose possession could help to shape an individual's future life and work, and whose study could provide a forum within which rational thought might be exercised, is related to the work of Richard Dawes on 'teaching the science of common things', and the work of the HMI, Henry Moseley.

During the 1840s, the conjunction of Dawes's and Moseley's views ensured that the 'useful knowledge' paradigm of science education became more widely disseminated than did Henslow's ideas. However, a combination of circumstances led to the emergence from comparative obscurity of a programme promoting the educational value of the natural history sciences based on a fully articulated faculty-training rationale.

THE EMERGENCE OF A SCIENTISTS' LOBBY

The Great Exhibition of 1851 showed Britain to be pre-eminent in industrial development, but simultaneously revealed how little of this supremacy had been achieved as a direct result of a satisfactory infrastructure of scientific education. The technological advances of the industrial revolution were the work of applied scientists and gifted (and largely self-educated) artisans – men with direct experience of the industrial situations in which their innovations were applied. The major verdict of the commissioners of the 1851 Exhibition was that a need existed for a system of scientific instruction suitable for an industrial population.[3] In response, it was decided to mark the centenary of the Society of Arts in 1854 by holding an international Educational Exhibition, whose aim was to promote educational goals in the way that the 1851 Exhibition had furthered industrial ends.[4]

Part of the Exhibition took the form of a series of public lectures on education. With more than sixty contributions, this was the most comprehensive attempt to this date to air educational matters in England.[5] In the event, the lecture series was to indicate a developing polarisation within the science lobby between the movement for 'teaching the science of common things' and the advocates of 'pure' science.

These lectures, and a similar series at the Royal Institution in the summer of 1854 gave some prominence and cohesion to a scientists' lobby, concerned both with education and with the advancement of science itself, some of whose members were in positions of considerable influence.[6] They tended to espouse a faculty psychology view of the benefits to be had from science education, not pressing the claims of science in competition with those of the established curriculum subjects, but instead arguing for a role for science in the training of mental faculties entirely distinct from those developed by other subjects like classical languages and literature. In following this line of argument, their choice of this particular comparison is revealing, for it shows how the Royal Institution lecturers were primarily concerned with issues relating to the teaching of science in the public schools and the maintained grammar schools – classics not being part of the elementary school curriculum. Thus the scientists' lobby appears increasingly to have focused its concern on the curriculum of schools for the children of the upper and middle classes, whilst the supporters of 'teaching the science of common things', though often men of impeccable education and scientific training, were invariably outside the mainstream of scientific advance, and were concerned exclusively with education, and predominantly, indeed, with the education of the working classes.

THE FACULTY PARADIGM ASCENDANT

The movement for 'teaching the science of common things' received a severe setback in 1857, when Moseley's successor, Frederick Temple, abandoned the policy of attempting to generate a supply of teachers trained to teach science in elementary schools. The introduction of Robert Lowe's Revised Code in 1862 prevented any revival.[7] The Code applied to state-supported elementary schools. Its central principle was 'payment by results' – the results being pupils' achievements in reading, writing and arithmetic. Not unnaturally this had the effect of constraining instruction in these schools to the three Rs and little else.

The position of science in the public schools and endowed grammar schools was not, however, affected directly by the 1862 Code, and the 1860s and early 1870s saw many developments in this sector, notably the activities and subsequent reports of the Clarendon Commission,[8] the Taunton Commission,[9] the British Association for the Advancement of Science committee of 1866–7,[10] and the Devonshire Commission.[11] The findings of all these groups indicated that science education in the public schools and the grammar schools was, with a few exceptions, in a very underdeveloped state. Yet the activities of the Commissioners helped to create an atmosphere in which changes might occur. As the Commissions assembled their evidence, they provided the advocates of science and of the classics with an opportunity to state their cases clearly and openly. It is, I think, in noticing that the case for teaching science in the public and grammar schools had to be advanced against the claim of the classics that we can begin to understand how the advocacy of science came to take the form it did. For the classics were traditionally defended in terms of mental training, rather than content, and the scientists fought their battle by contending this ground – not by arguing against the mental training view itself, but by promoting science as a device for such training. As Thompson has observed:

> Wilson's [J. M. Wilson of Rugby] plea for science did not rest on a criticism of the classical curriculum but on the positive advantages to be gained through a study of science. He argued: 'There is another and even stronger ground for advocating the introduction of science as an element in all liberal education and that is its peculiar merit as a means of educating the mind . . . it encourages the habit of mind which will rest on nothing but what is true.'[12]

I do not imply that the science lobby in any sense took a calculated decision to use a 'mental training' argument to combat that of the classics lobby. It has been observed above that the 'training' ideas appear to have been widely accepted at the time. The argument advanced here is rather that external circumstances resulted in the dominance of these ideas (and the form of science education to which they led) within the science lobby as a whole. The effective rebuff to the teaching of science in elementary schools which followed Lowe's Code meant that those arguing for the advancement of science education were obliged to concentrate their attention during the 1860s and early 1870s on the public and endowed schools – on the education of the upper and middle classes. In doing so, they were led to use the 'faculty training' argument to counter similar arguments used to defend the existing curriculum of classical languages and mathematics.

FROM ARMSTRONG TO NUFFIELD[13]

The dominant figure in science education in the later part of the nineteenth century was H. E. Armstrong. As an enthusiastic advocate of the heuristic (discovery-learning) approach, Armstrong fully endorsed a faculty-training rationale for science education:

> It is . . . mainly on other and far higher grounds that we should advocate universal practical teaching of the elements of natural, and more particularly of so-called physical science; viz. that it tends to develop a side of the human intellect which, I believe, I am justified in saying is left uncultivated even after the most careful mathematical and literary training: the faculty of observing and of reasoning from observation and experiment.[14]

There seems little doubt that the term 'faculties' is being used here in a rather different sense from that of earlier writers. Certainly the phrenologists' ideas of physical 'organs' within the brain are not necessarily involved. The emphasis is, nonetheless, on the educational value of the *forms* and *methods* of science, rather than on its *content*. In placing his emphasis on the training of faculties, Armstrong was adapting his earlier arguments on behalf of the natural history sciences to his needs in the promotion of chemistry in schools.

Enthusiasm for heurism began to wane during the early years of the twentieth century, influenced in part by an apparently widespread perception of the need for broader, more balanced science provision, perhaps more relevant to everyday concerns.[15] In the wake of the extension of educational provision following the 1902 Education Act, the movement found expression both in increasing pressure for the expansion of biology teaching[16] and in recurrent criticisms of the inefficiency of the heuristic method. The experiences of war, seen by many as evidence of longstanding 'neglect of science'[17] in British education ended (at least for the time being) the sway of heurism. In striking parallel with current concerns (though the possible reasons for such parallels are not further explored here), the ideas of 'science for all'[18] and 'general science'[19] (for which, read 'integrated' or 'balanced' science) became dominant in public writings about the science curriculum, and a greater emphasis on science 'content' held sway for almost four decades.

The 1960 Ministry of Education *Pamphlet No. 38: Science in Secondary Schools*,[20] the work of a group of HMIs, forms a bridge between the general science era and the Nuffield era which was soon to follow. Its long first chapter is a historical review, unusually detailed for a curriculum pamphlet of this kind, which indicates the extent to which the authors perceived their work as falling within an established tradition. With a retrospective view extending as far as H. E. Armstrong, they write: 'Concentration upon "method", almost to the point of obsession and to the exclusion of all else, which at one time flourished, is rarely found today.'[21] In elaborating this theme, the Inspectors draw attention to the accumulating evidence from psychological research which casts severe doubt on the efficacy of 'transfer of training'. However, the developing argument in *Pamphlet No. 38* demonstrates very clearly how a shift of emphasis from the 'transfer of training' rhetoric to that of 'the work of the scientist' enables very similar motives to find more acceptable expression:

> It is necessary to balance the twin aims of acquiring knowledge which is valuable in itself and of training in the methods of investigation and logical thinking in a practical context ... The qualities, both moral and intellectual, which go to make up the devoted scientist carry with them much of great value for a liberal education.[22]

THE NUFFIELD 'O' LEVEL PROJECTS

The work of the Nuffield 'O' Level Projects, begun in 1962 and published in 1966,[23] inherited the same rather unpromising climate of opinion as regards transfer of training. The Nuffield Physics writers spelt out the position as they saw it:

Fortunately there is some transfer ... but *only in certain favourable circumstances* ...

1 Transfer is ... likely to occur when there is common ground between the field of training and the field to which you wish it to transfer ...
2 Far-reaching transfer does occur sometimes when ... the pupil develops ... feelings of enjoyment, interest, inspiration with his studies ...
3 Transfer is more likely if the pupil knows of its possibility and seeks it.[24]

The cautious approach to transfer which this quotation from the *Nuffield Physics Teachers' Guide* demonstrates may owe much to the influence of E. M. Rogers, the Director of the Physics Project, who was all too aware that psychology had not dealt kindly with educators' aspirations *vis-à-vis* mental training. In his textbook *Physics for the Enquiring Mind* (written before Nuffield),[25] he admits that transfer is likely only in the somewhat limited circumstances listed above. Yet he appears to feel intuitively that a practical approach, designed to promote 'understanding', will produce benefits which go beyond the mere acquisition of factual knowledge: 'laboratory [work] can provide much more important gains if it can teach you scientific ways and give you a more general understanding of science ... If you work as a scientist yourself, you are on common ground with scientists, gaining an understanding of science.'[26]

'Understanding' is, perhaps, the cornerstone of the Nuffield Projects' response to this situation. Rogers's comments, and those of many others associated with the Nuffield Physics, Chemistry and Biology Projects, indicate that the Projects hoped to promote such understanding by enabling pupils to participate in a simulation of 'the work of a scientist' in the school laboratory. From work of this kind, an enjoyment of science would follow. Understanding will not only generate enjoyment, it is argued, but will also promote a wider awareness in society of the cultural influence of science. Such influence is seen to stem from the scientist's approach: 'We say we want to teach for understanding, but what does that mean for the general pupil? ... Scientists have a characteristic way of thinking and planning and working, which we call scientific attitude or scientific method or science itself, that offers intellectual resources and guidance to all.'[27] Although the Nuffield Projects are now almost twenty years old, there seems little doubt that they have had a profound influence on almost all subsequent science curriculum development in Britain. Whether this debt is specifically acknowledged or not, the Nuffield Projects were major landmarks of the environment within which subsequent curriculum projects were developed. [...]

COMPREHENSIVE INFLUENCES

As the 1960s progressed, the concerns of educators turned inwards, and the focus of attention became the secondary school itself, and in particular, the reorganisation of secondary schools which was proceeding at this time. I would suggest that it is in implicit response to these internal pressures that most of the projects which follow the Nuffield 'O' Level Projects return to a greater emphasis on the possibilities of 'transfer of training'.

As comprehensivisation gets under way, the emphases perceptibly shift from the liberal education stance of Nuffield 'O' level rhetoric towards a more overt emphasis on the ethical aims associated with the 'transfer' view. Some of this change of emphasis is no doubt because the comprehensive intake poses the basic question of the relevance of any science teaching whatsoever, in a more acute form. There also appears to be an increasingly perceived 'need' to achieve non-cognitive objectives with this 'new' group of pupils.

The concerns of teachers are reflected in the numbers of articles in *School Science Review* and *Education in Science* on such topics as the suitability of Nuffield 'O' levels for less able pupils, and the problems of mixed-ability organisation, and strategies to deal with them.[28] *Nuffield Secondary Science*[29] is a product of this period. It is a collection of resource material from all the sciences, available for use with 13–16 year old pupils not taking science 'O' levels. The *Teachers' Guide* makes the following observations:

> All pupils can be given opportunities and encouragement to observe phenomena accurately.[30]
> The spirit of the work should be one of investigation in which first-hand observation and experiment provide essential opportunities for acting and thinking scientifically.[31]
> We all acquire knowledge from films, photographs and books but it is important that the pupils should be as critical of indirect evidence as they are in examining their own first-hand evidence.[32]

This last comment is followed by some elaboration on the need to be critical of advertisers' claims. Transfer of attitudes learned in the science laboratory to outside life is thus explicitly sought. This is a theme which is elaborated in the following longer extract: 'Everyday life brings the need to solve problems, to predict the consequence of actions, and to evaluate the assertions of politicians, advertisers, or scientists ... The attitudes of mind and habits of thought needed can be encouraged within the science lesson.'[33]

Similar concerns are evident in Scottish science curriculum writings of the same period. The Scottish Education Department's *Curriculum Paper 7: Science for General Education*[34] deals with a course for all pupils in first and second years of the Scottish secondary school, and for lower-achieving pupils in years 3 and 4. In the *Curriculum Paper*, general and specific objectives are explicitly stated following the terminology of Bloom.[35] They propose, as general aims, that pupils should acquire:

(i) Some knowledge of the empirical world around;
(ii) A little of the vocabulary and grammar of science;
(iii) An ability to observe objectively;

(iv) An ability to solve problems and think scientifically;
(v) An awareness of the culture which is science.[36]

In a subsequent paragraph, the meaning of 'thinking scientifically' is expanded. It involves the following 'kinds of thinking':

In Comprehending Knowledge	In Application of Knowledge	In Analysis, Synthesis and Evaluation of Knowledge
observing	re-arranging	justifying
comparing	relating	assuming
classifying	explaining	inferring
summarising	predicting	imagining
interpreting	estimating	inventing
discriminating		discovering
illustrating		generalising
extrapolating		hypothesising
		testing and re-evaluating hypotheses
		judging.[37]

Many of the old 'faculties' are here in a new guise. There is, of course, no inference that these 'kinds of thinking' are located in specific areas of the brain. Yet it seems clear that the authors see these as 'kinds of thinking' which are of use outside the laboratory, as well as inside.

As the 1970s progress, publications of the Scottish Central Committee on Science (a subcommittee of the Scottish Consultative Committee on the Curriculum) make increasing use of the idea of 'processes of science'. Within the framework of this article, the 'process' rhetoric is clearly seen to be the latest variant of an established line of argument. In *Memorandum No. 28: Science in S1 and S2*,[38] from the Scottish Central Committee on Science, the 'process' approach is seen as an alternative to the 'objectives' model of the curriculum: 'While it is common to think of a syllabus in terms of objectives and content, a complementary viewpoint which is particularly appropriate to science, is to reckon in terms of the concepts and processes which it is hoped to develop.'[39] *Concepts* which pupils might grasp are such things as temperature, pressure, vertebrates, acids, matter as particles, etc. The idea is that through the science instruction, pupils will come to appreciate for themselves the meaning of these concepts. *Processes*, on the other hand, are seen as 'the skills in which pupils become practised in the doing of science as they learn about science'.[40] These are listed as: 'observing, classifying, measuring, laboratory techniques, communicating, inferring, predicting, defining operationally, formulating hypotheses, interpreting data, controlling variables, experimenting.'[41] 'Transfer' of these processes outside the science laboratory is not explicitly discussed in this particular document. Yet, although the terminology is different, there can be, at best, a very narrow distinction between teaching the 'processes' of observing and classifying, and the old claims that science developed the mental faculties of observation and classification. In both cases, we are surely to infer that the learning will be of use outside the context in which it was acquired.

There is no indication in more recent science curriculum writings, whether of English or Scottish origin, that enthusiasm for the rhetoric of science 'method' or science 'process' is on the decline.

[...]

NOTES

1 D. Layton (1973) *Science for the People*. London: George Allen and Unwin.
2 For a short account of Combe's contribution to education, see W. A. C. Stewart and W. P. McCann (1967) *The Educational Innovators*. London: Macmillan, pp. 280–6.
3 Layton (1973), p. 100.
4 D. Layton (1972) 'The Educational Exhibition of 1854', *Journal of the Royal Society of Arts*, 120 (5188), pp. 253–6.
5 The important contributions to this lecture series were published in *Lectures in Connection with the Educational Exhibition of the Society of Arts, Manufactures, and Commerce* (1855). London: Routledge & Kegan Paul.
6 The texts of the Royal Institution lectures are reprinted in Sir E. R. Lankester (ed.) (1917) *Science and Education*. London: Heinemann.
7 An account of these shifts of policy can be found in Layton (1973), Chapter 7. For a brief statement of the terms of Lowe's Code, see J. S. Maclure (1965) *Educational Documents: England and Wales: 1816 to the Present Day*. London: Methuen, pp. 79–80; a short account of its effects can be found in W. H. G. Armytage (1964) *Four Hundred Years of English Education*. Cambridge: Cambridge University Press, pp. 124–6.
8 *Report of Her Majesty's Commissioners Appointed to Inquire into the Revenues and Management of Certain Colleges and Schools, and the Studies Pursued and Instruction Given Therein* (Clarendon Commission) (1864). London: HMSO. A more accessible précis is found in Maclure (1965), pp. 83–8.
9 Schools Enquiry Commission (Taunton Commission) (1868) *Report of the Commissioners*. London: HMSO.
10 British Association for the Advancement of Science (1868) *Report of the 37th Meeting, 1867; Report of Farrar's Committee*. London: John Murray, pp. xxxiv–xliv.
11 Royal Commission on Scientific Instruction and the Advancement of Science (Devonshire Commission) (1871–5) Eight Reports, Minutes of Evidence, Appendices, Index. London: HMSO.
12 D. Thompson (1956) 'Science Teaching in Schools During the Second Half of the 19th Century', *School Science Review*, 133, p. 300; the quotation is from Wilson's contribution to F. W. Farrar (ed.) (1867) *Essays on a Liberal Education*. London: Macmillan.
13 This subtitle is a reference to E. W. Jenkins *From Armstrong to Nuffield* (1979). London: John Murray, where a much fuller account of this period may be found.
14 H. E. Armstrong (1884) 'On the Teaching of Natural Science as Part of the Ordinary School Course and on the Method of Teaching Chemistry in the Introductory Courses

in Science Classes, Schools and Colleges', reprinted in W. H. Brock *H. E. Armstrong and the Teaching of Science, 1880–1930*. Cambridge: Cambridge University Press, p. 75.

15 D. Thompson (1958) 'General Science – Its Origin and Growth', *School Science Review*, 140, pp. 109–22.

16 (1912) 'Educational Conferences Considered in Relation to Science in Public Schools', *Nature*, 88, pp. 393–4.

17 This term relates to a letter signed by thirty-six eminent scientists which was published in *The Times* (1916), on 2 February, and to a committee subsequently formed by some of the signatories.

18 (1920) 'Science for All', *School Science Review*, 6, pp. 197–212.

19 Jenkins (1979), Chapter 3, pp. 70–106.

20 Ministry of Education (1960) *Pamphlet No. 38: Science in Secondary Schools*. London: HMSO.

21 Ibid., p. 25.

22 Ibid., p. 157.

23 *Nuffield Biology* (1967). London: Longman/Penguin; *Nuffield Chemistry* (1966). London: Longman/Penguin; and *Nuffield Physics* (1966) London: Longman/Penguin.

24 *Nuffield Physics, Teachers' Guide I* (1966), pp. 70–1.

25 E. M. Rogers (1960) *Physics for the Enquiring Mind*. Oxford: Oxford University Press.

26 Ibid., p. 63.

27 *Nuffield Physics, Teachers' Guide I* (1966), p. 65.

28 A few examples of the many such articles are: M. Shayer (1972) 'Conceptual Demands in the Nuffield O-level Physics Course', *School Science Review*, 186, pp. 26–34; P. J. Kelly and G. Monger (1974) 'An Evaluation of the Nuffield O-level Biology', *School Science Review*, 192, pp. 470–82; J. A. Hunt (1969) 'Nuffield Chemistry in a Comprehensive School', *School Science Review*, 173, pp. 915–19; L. M. Sturges (1973) 'Problems in Teaching Science to Non-streamed Classes', *School Science Review*, 191, pp. 224–32.

29 *Nuffield Secondary Science* (1971 onwards). London: Longman.

30 *Nuffield Secondary Science, Teachers' Guide* (1971). London: Longman, p. 15.

31 Ibid., p. 19.

32 Ibid., p. 20.

33 Ibid., p. 15.

34 Scottish Education Department (1969).

35 B. S. Bloom (ed.) (1965) *Taxonomy of Educational Objectives: The Classification of Educational Goals. Handbook I: Cognitive Domain*. London: Longman; and D. R. Krathwohl, B. S. Bloom and B. B. Masia (1965) *Taxonomy of Educational Objectives: The Classification of Educational Goals. Handbook II: Affective Domain*. London: Longman.

36 Scottish Education Department (1969), p. 11.

37 Ibid., p. 12.

38 Scottish Curriculum Development Service (Dundee Centre) (1977) *Memorandum No. 28: Science in S1 and S2*. Dundee: Dundee College of Education.

39 Ibid., p. 30.

40 Ibid., p. 31.

41 Ibid., p. 35.

CURRICULUM REFORM IN MATHEMATICS: BEYOND THE IMPOSSIBLE
3.3 REVOLUTION?

AGNIESZKA WOJCIECHOWSKA

TWENTIETH-CENTURY REFORM ACTIVITIES IN MATHEMATICS EDUCATION

This paper focuses on two major changes that took place in the mathematics curriculum patterns of secondary schools in this century. One of those occurred in the early 1900s, the other one in the 1960s. As the reforming attempts of those periods have many features in common, they may be analysed jointly, thus enabling a more adequate answer to be given to the question of what made them collapse and what should be done to find a way out of the present critical situation.

Up to the turn of the nineteenth century, mathematics education involved a traditional canon consisting of the subjects of arithmetic and elementary algebra, as well as Euclidean geometry and trigonometry. This does not mean that all reforming activity was abandoned; in fact, some changes did take place within those subjects, but – since the beginning of the eighteenth century – they were introduced smoothly, without disturbing the adopted canon. In the academy, however, these subjects had been out of favour for a very long time. The same applied to the associated teaching methods: mathematics educators, and particularly geometry teachers, persisted in holding on to longstanding practices. On the other hand, there was an increasingly active concern for change in the overall curriculum pattern in many European countries at the beginning of the twentieth century. One of the greatest mathematicians of the turn of the century, Felix Klein (1849–1925), professor in Göttingen, was a pioneer and a leading advocate of syllabus change at this time. Writing in 1907, he and his co-worker, R. Schimmack, came to the following conclusions:

> The normal development of science shows the more difficult and complicated areas becoming elementary by the incremental explanation of basic concepts and by their simplification ... The task of the school is then to see if the inclusion of the simplified subject would enhance general education. In our time, this necessary process has been obstructed, especially in mathematics. The high science given to a teacher-candidate at the university has no

Source: A. Wojciechowska (1989) 'Curriculum Reform in Mathematics: Beyond the Impossible Revolution?', *Journal of Curriculum Studies*, 21(2), pp. 151–9.

importance for him in his later profession. The school curriculum isolated itself from the university science and stagnated, leading to the idea that there is an invariable canon of school mathematics.[1]

In 1904, the German Society of Natural Historians and Physicians called into being a commission to project curriculum reform in mathematics and science. The project had been accepted at the Society's meeting in September 1905 in Merano and it became known as the Meran Programme. This programme focused on the scientific approach to the subjects taught in secondary schools; on the pupils' understanding of the problems taught; on their ability to use their knowledge; on practice in describing natural phenomena in terms of mathematical symbols; on the relations between mathematical subjects; and on the relationship between mathematicians and other scientific disciplines. Following Klein's philosophy and his belief that the principal goal of mathematics teaching was to develop the pupil's geometrical imagination and functional thinking, the authors of the Meran Programme focused on these goals.

The movement initiated by the Meran Programme began to spread throughout Europe,[2] and these ideas were more or less successfully implemented. The reforming process, however, was stopped by the outbreak of the First World War.

Both world wars, to say nothing of the economic depression of the inter-war period, had an inhibiting effect on the implementation and dissemination of reforming ideas. In the 1950s, quiescence in curriculum reform seemed to be interrupted. Opinions that mathematics education involved obsolete methods – based on traditional canons which were no longer able to meet modern requirements – began to spread. It is interesting to note that similar arguments had been put forward fifty years earlier.

J. G. Kemeny was amongst those who had a particularly critical approach to the problem in question. In 1965, he wrote:

> Most parents would not believe it if they were told their son could study a certain subject in our school for 14 years without finding out what the subject was actually about, or what has been happening in this subject in the last 150 years. Yet, this is precisely what the present mathematics programme is designed to do. Students can take eight years of primary school, four years of secondary school and two years of college mathematics, without hearing a single development less than 150 years old, and without acquiring any real insight into the subject.[3]

It appears that the impulse which gave rise to the second reforming wave was similar to the one that gave rise to the former wave. Again, emphasis was laid on bridging the gap between the mathematics taught in schools and mathematics as science, on the pupil's understanding of basic mathematical notions, and on the significant role of mathematics in technology. Postulates put forward concerning the methods of mathematics education called for the recognition of the psychological laws governing mental development. The differences in implementing this postulate may have resulted from the rapid advances in psychology and pedagogy in the past decades.

As in the early 1900s, the active concern for change in the curriculum pattern was, again, supported by outstanding authorities in mathematics. In the 1960s it was the 'collective mathematician' – the group of French mathematicians publishing since 1939 under the pseudonym Nicolas Bourbaki – who took over the leadership from Klein. It seems worthwhile to quote a statement of an eminent member of this group, Jean Dieudonné, which resembles that of Klein.

In the last 50 years, mathematicians had been led to introduce not only new concepts, but also a new language which had won universal approval. But until now the introduction of this new terminology has been steadfastly resisted by secondary schools, which desperately cling to an obsolete and inadequate language. And so when a student enters the university, he will most probably never have heard such common mathematical words as set, mapping, group, vector space, etc. No wonder he is baffled and discouraged by his contact with higher mathematics. Some elements of the calculus, vector algebra and a little analytic geometry have recently been introduced at the last two or three years of secondary school. But such topics have always been relegated to a subordinate position, the centre of interest remaining as before 'pure geometry taught more or less according to Euclid with a little algebra and number theory'. I think the day of such patchwork is over and we are now committed to a much deeper reform – unless we are willing to let the situation deteriorate to the point where it will seriously impede further scientific progress.[4]

The Bourbaki philosophy of mathematics, which became the basis of the novel mathematics education, was quite different from Klein's ideas. Following this philosophy, explained in the paper 'L'Architecture des Mathématiques',[5] a central role in mathematics is played by the abstract notion of structure, based on set theory. The acceptance of the Bourbakist ideology as a basis of mathematics education should be attributed also to the psychological theories developed by Piaget and Bruner. On the other hand, it should be emphasised that the radical criticism which originated in the early 1960s involved more than just the Bourbakist approach. Furthermore, the changes that had taken place were highly differentiated. Thus, Howson *et al.* distinguished five basic trends, while another classification was given by Krygowska.[6]

A comparative analysis of the two reforming activities enables the following generalisations to be made. The earlier reforming attempts were inhibited by the outbreak of the war, when they were still in the phase of discussion on both national and international levels,[7] and were far from being implemented in teaching practice. The more recent attempts found acceptance and application, but the range of dissemination was much smaller than had been expected.[8] The two reforms of mathematics curricula in schools owe their origin to similar inspirations. They also put forward similar goals. And that is why they will be considered here as two phases of one phenomenon, as two stages of a single process which – despite its long duration – displays a revolutionary nature. This revolutionary nature manifests itself in the radical criticism of the state of the art in mathematics education and in the radical break with longstanding tradition.

To these preliminaries one explanation should be added. We will deal mainly with syllabus – the mathematical content of curriculum. Methods and the whole context of teaching will play only a secondary role. The reason for this lies partly in the structure of the educational systems in which the modernising movements started, both Germany at the turn of the century and France in recent times having centralised arrangements.[9] More importantly, such centralisation is characteristic of the educational systems of the majority of UNESCO members,[10] including the Polish one, from which the personal experience of the author is derived. For such a system, the detailed syllabus is the most important part of the curriculum, since it can be administratively ordered and its realisation can be controlled *ex post facto* by school authorities.[11]

CRITICAL JUDGEMENT BY MATHEMATICIANS

Although both phases of the revolutionary reforming process owe their origin to the interest and contribution of outstanding scientists, a number of mathematicians refused to approve the principal ideas of the intended changes, even in the period of enthusiasm and reforming zeal. Thus A. N. Whitehead, in 1916, rejected the postulate of eliminating 'drill exercises' and substituting for them the pupil's 'thinking and understanding':

> It is a profoundly erroneous truism, repeated by all copy-books and by eminent people when they are making speeches, that we should cultivate the habit of thinking of what we are doing. The precise opposite is the case. Civilization advances by extending the number of important operations which we can perform without thinking of them.[12]

The number of adversaries increased markedly in the second phase of the reforming process. Among them were Morris Kline, Hans Freudenthal, Jean Leray and René Thom.[13] What they primarily disapproved of was the Bourbakist concept of the 'architecture of mathematics' which influenced the overall vision of the 'new maths'. But there were also objections to the method of implementing modified syllabuses and to the functioning of these curricula in school practice.[14] As Semadeni indicated, there is one more important factor that might have contributed to the failure of the reform: some of the main ideas found wide acceptance among mathematics educators just as the mathematical world began to approach them with scepticism; for example, axiomatic method and set theory as a basis for the whole of mathematics.[15]

Another idea, also based on Bourbakist philosophy, which assumed that 'poor' mathematical structures were more natural and more easily perceived by the child's mind than 'rich' structures, for example real numbers, was refuted by Freudenthal.[16]

Let us recollect some of the ideas that were the guiding principles of the two phases in the reforming process:

1 Strengthening the relationship between mathematics as it appears in schools and its counterpart in university education and scientific research.
2 Constructing the curricula so as to give the student real insight into the subject and nature of contemporary mathematics, or what is regarded as the most important part of mathematics.
3 Making use of such methods and means as meet the requirements of up-to-date psychology and didactics.

It should be noted that the approach to these principles in the first phase of the reforming process differed significantly from the one practised in the second phase. The difference is to be attributed to the time that had elapsed, during which a new generation of mathematicians had grown up and many substantial changes had taken place, not only in mathematics and socio-cultural life, but in almost every domain – owing to the tremendous developments in science and technology. There is, however, one more factor that should be emphasised here. Of the three postulates mentioned above, the first one puts forward objections to the canon of school mathematics, whereas the remaining two make it impossible to create a new canon. Mathematics develops constantly and it often happens that changes take place rapidly, so that it is difficult for the experts to come to a unanimous opinion on what is the most important part of contemporary mathematics, and what part of it should be introduced to common education. Educators are doomed to some second-hand opinions following mathematicians, especially well-known figures in mathematics. And, usually, a working mathematician is open to the conviction that the centre of this science lies somewhere near his own specialism.

Thus, amongst mathematicians there are many different opinions and there is little hope of agreement on that question (see, for instance, recent writings by Ulam and Zeeman).[17] This lack of agreement is equally true as far as selection of psychological, pedagogical and didactic principles is concerned. A pluralism of ideas is current in those areas as well.

One could now claim that the revolution in the content of mathematics education failed to be successful or, at least, was refuted by mathematicians because of the invalidity of the Bourbakist vision of mathematics which served as a base for it. But the problem is more sophisticated. It is not the problem of the inadequacy of Bourbaki's architecture of mathematics and its rejection by the mathematical world. What seems to be of importance is the fact that it was accepted by the leaders of the reform as the unique, valid vision and ideology of mathematics. In fact, Bourbaki's vision might well have been the last monolithic ideology of mathematics for a long time. Since the moment it was refuted, no agreement has been achieved so far, and many different trends have begun to appear. Each of them may influence educational practices in its own manner.

It is clear that creative mathematicians can work without making use of a philosophy or vision of mathematics as a whole, but this does not hold for mathematics educators. That is why they were prone to accept 'Bourbakism' as their sole ideology, and why they found themselves in a critical situation when the Bourbakist concept collapsed. These days, mathematics educators have a two-part 'metaproblem' to solve, namely (1) how to formulate the complete set of reasonable postulates concerning general mathematical education, and (2) how to practise them in actual school life. We should avoid the situation where the objectives are attractive and desirable but impracticable.[18] [. . .]

REQUIREMENTS FOR A SUCCESSFUL REFORM

The postulate of allowing a variety of approaches is also valid for mathematics taught in school. It is worth remembering that ever since the 'Bourbakist ideology' was rejected, no dominant conceptualisation has been available. Instead of one total vision of mathematics serving as an ideology of mathematics education, there are a number of different trends and ideas which coexist, and exert an influence on mathematics curricula. This variegated influence has produced a wide spectrum of curricular offerings which range from 'engineering mathematics' through 'algorithmic mathematics' to 'logicised mathematics' and, also, from the 'back to basics' approach to an educational maximalism in which a thorough mathematics education of the entire population of pupils is intended. Consideration should also be given to the variety of the teaching methods suggested. These have varied from 'teaching through playing' to the behaviourist 'drill and practice', and from teaching many subjects separately to the integration of them and to the creation of pupil teams with the aim of investigating and solving scientific interdisciplinary problems.

Thus the following generalisation can be made: it is advisable to abandon the non-effective and non-successful revolutionary trends and replace them by an evolutionary approach allowing a pluralism of concepts, as well as their verification in everyday practice and the comparison of results achieved by different methods.

A similar conclusion may be drawn when the problem of interest is considered, by making use of a sociological approach. The education system and its environment in general, and mathematics education in particular, constitute a specific society. This society consists of mathematicians, the school administration, supervisors, teacher-training organisations, teachers, pupils and their parents, and other related populations. The society as a whole is hierarchical in nature and shows a strong tendency to conservatism. It is interesting to note that even academic educators proposing an immediate modernisation of mathematics curricula in schools are obdurate conservatives as far as the method of educating their own students and, specifically, prospective teachers is concerned. The conservatism and the hierarchical nature of this society enable comparison of the school system to the organisation of the Church. The revolution in school mathematics discussed in the first part of this paper may be thought of as being an analogue of what is known as the Reformation in Church history. In both instances, the existing canon was questioned, but nothing equally firm and attractive was proposed instead. Every radical postulate raised radical objections and gave rise to a wide spectrum of trends and concepts.

As far as the crisis in mathematics education is concerned, the most reasonable way of overcoming the existing difficulty is tolerance. And 'tolerance' means acceptance of many different trends which owe their origin to the inspiration of various sources, but act in coexistence.

Based on this postulate, many practical recommendations can be formulated. Yet, taking into account the fundamental role of mathematics in contemporary education, it is necessary to eschew 'exaggerated' tolerance and hold oneself back from running into extremes – a tendency that is easily imaginable for non-centralised education systems. In the highly centralised ones there is no danger of exaggerated tolerance. On the contrary, it is necessary to throw open the door to coexistence of different curricula. The first step in that direction could be made by admitting alternative, essentially different textbooks with the same underlying syllabus,[19] by describing the 'minimal syllabus' with various possible extensions,[20] or by giving a general description of the range and skill to be acquired by pupils. In the last case, prescribed knowledge and skills may be reached in different ways and by using various methods, a wide spectrum of which should be offered to teachers.

All of this should be subject to further investigation, especially by mathematics educators in countries with centralised education systems, but knowledge and experience of others will be invaluable as well.

NOTES

1 F. Klein and R. Schimmack (1907) quoted in H. G. Steiner (ed.) (1980) *Comparative Studies of Mathematics Curricula: Change and Stability 1960–1980*. Bielefeldt: Institut für Didaktik der Mathematik, p. 12.

2 For instance, in Poland in the period between the two wars the teaching programme involved elements of differential calculus and analytical geometry; attempts were made to include probability theory. None of these subjects existed twenty-five years later. See K. Wuczynska (1982) 'Selected Problems of Mathematics Teaching in Secondary Schools in Poland in the 1920s' (in Polish), *Dydaktyka Matematyki*, 2, p. 83.

3 J. G. Kemeny (1965), quoted in W. W. Joyce, R. G. Oana and W. R. Houston (eds.) (1970) *Elementary Education in the Seventies: Implications for Theory and Practice*. New York: Holt, Rinehart and Winston, p. 1.

4 J. Dieudonné (1959), quoted in A. G. Howson, J. Kilpatrick and C. Keitel (1981) *Curriculum Development in Mathematics*. Cambridge: Cambridge University Press, p. 102.

5 N. Bourbaki (1948) 'L'Architecture des Mathématiques' (*Les grands courants de la pensée mathématique*), *Cahiers du Sud*, pp. 35–47.

6 Howson *et al.* (1981); A. Z. Krygowska (1981) *The Common Mathematical Education in Curricular Reforms 1960–1980* (in Polish). Cracow: WSP.

7 See A. G. Howson (1984) '75 years of ICMI', *Educational Studies in Mathematics*, 15, pp. 75–93.

8 New maths established in less than 15 per cent of American schools according to P. J.

Hilton (1981) 'Avoiding Math Avoidance' in L. A. Steen (ed.) *Mathematics Tomorrow*. New York, Heidelberg, Berlin: Springer, pp. 73–82.

9 The high positive correlation between revolutionary consciousness and centralistic subconsciousness is well documented in H. Arendt (1963) *On Revolution*. New York: Viking, or even in A. de Tocqueville (1952) *L'Ancien Régime et la Révolution*. Paris: Mayer.

10 As an illustration we quote here the discussion in the educational section of the International Congress of Mathematicians (Warsaw, 1983), where representatives of developing countries complained that textbooks used in their schools were translated from European languages without being adapted to local conditions. (On the other hand, one textbook author replied by pointing out the cheapness of such large-scale publication initiatives.) See R. C. O'Brien (1980) 'Mass Media, Education and the Transmission of Values', *Prospects* (UNESCO), 1.

11 Polish official programmes explain the goals and methods relating to particular syllabuses, items etc. We have observed that teachers do not read these comments, regarding them as unimportant ornaments.

12 A. N. Whitehead (1916) 'The Aims of Education: A Plea for Reform', *Mathematical Gazette*, 8 January, p. 191.

13 See, for example, M. Kline (1974) *Why Johnny Can't Add*. New York: Vintage Books; J. Leray (1971) 'Les mathématiques "Modernes"', *Gazette des mathématiciens* (Nice), G4 (October), pp. 13–19; R. Thom (1971) 'Les Mathématiques Modernes: Une Erreur Pédagogique et Philosophique', *L'Age de la science*, 3(3), pp. 225–45 (English translation in the *American Scientist* (1971), 59, pp. 695–9); and H. Freudenthal (1963) 'Enseignement des Mathématiques Modernes ou Enseignement Moderne des Mathématiques', *Enseignement mathématique*, 9(2), pp. 28–44.

14 For a critical account of the 1960s reforms, see A. Z. Krygowska (1979) 'Mathematics Education at the First Level in Post-Elementary and Secondary Schools', in *New Trends in Mathematics Teaching IV* (UNESCO: Paris), pp. 31–45.

15 Z. Semadeni (1974) 'Remarks to the Papers by Leray and Thom' (in Polish), *Wiadomości Mathematyczne*, 18, pp. 142–4.

16 That was the objective of Freudenthal's lecture presented at the Symposium in Honour of A. Z. Krygowska, Cracow, 1984.

17 S. M. Ulam (1976) *Adventures of a Mathematician*. New York: Charles Scribner's Sons, pp. 273–303; E. C. Zeeman (1979) 'Research, Ancient and Modern', in E. C. Zeeman *Catastrophe Theory, Selected Papers, 1971–1977*. Reading, Mass.: Addison-Wesley, pp. 605–14.

18 The utopian character of the reform was pointed out by Whitehead in 1916 (see note 12).

19 For example, in Poland in 1979 three different textbooks for grade 4 were introduced, and in the next year two for grade 5. Unfortunately, the 'experiment' was cut off before one could appreciate its significance. The causes had nothing to do with textbooks themselves, but with the conservatism of teachers, the disfavour of the administration and indolence on the part of the institutions involved (including the publisher and printing house). For some details, see J. Waszkiewicz and A. Wojciechowska (1982) 'On introducing the Alternative Mathematics Textbooks at Grade 4' (in Polish), *Wiadomości Matematyczne*, 24, pp. 203–18.

20 It is interesting to look from this point of view at the discussion of 'mathematics for all', such as the one at the ICMI session at the ICMI in Warsaw (see note 10). See the comments of P. Damerow, Z. Krygowska. J. de Lange, B. Cornu, D. Wheeler, W. Walsch, G. Howson, A. Ralston, S. Turnau and H. G. Steiner in Polish in *Dydaktyka Matematyki*, 6 (1986).

part four

INTERNATIONAL PERSPECTIVES

PATTERNS OF CONTROL: SCHOOL REFORM IN WESTERN EUROPE

4.1

BOB MOON

THE CONTEXT OF REFORM

In an earlier study (Moon, 1986) I looked at the ways in which national systems of education controlled the form and structure of the school curriculum. The advent of new or modern mathematics in the 1960s and 1970s was examined in a variety of Western European countries. Analysis showed that the assumptions taken for granted about the formal systems for control (centralised or decentralised, for example) were challenged by the evidence from a series of case studies. New maths appeared in thousands of French primary classrooms long before the '1945' regulations were changed in 1970. Conversely, in the decentralist Dutch context, highly centralist, government-funded initiatives inspired a significant degree of reform. A number of factors were seen as significant in providing the means to bypass the formal system. Influential university mathematicians, for example, provided the status and legitimacy to override inspectorial controls in France. Textbook publishers in countries such as France and the Netherlands, where official approval for texts does not need to be sought, were also important in promoting new approaches. The evidence began to draw into question some of the theoretical work that tended to confirm the importance of formal structures (see, for example, Archer, 1979). This paper picks up this earlier work and carries the analysis forward to the events of the 1980s experienced in England and Wales, France and the Netherlands. In that period, mathematics reform in each of the countries became embroiled in a wider ranging debate about the quality and standards of schooling across the whole curriculum. Towards the middle and end of the 1970s each country began to move towards legislative responses to the pressure for reform of a very different character. The form that this took, which will be considered in an integrated way across all three countries, provides further evidence against which the assumptions about the writings of educational systems can be analysed. It also provides a further indication of the influence of cross-national movements in the European educational context of the 1980s.

Source: Extract from Bob Moon (1990), 'Patterns of Control: School Reform in Western Europe', *British Journal of Sociology*, 41: 3.

THE CENTRALIST AND LEGISLATIVE MOVEMENT TOWARDS CURRICULUM REFORM IN THE 1980s

In each of the national studies a growing political disillusion with reform was noted. Textbook sales of new mathematics series dropped markedly throughout the 1970s. Media reporting became almost wholly hostile. Political intervention is recorded through parliamentary debates in all three countries. In France *Le Figaro* (21 October 1980) heralded the new 1980 primary mathematics regulations, the first full changes since 1945, with the headline *'Maths: retour à la raison'*; alongside was a cartoon showing a harassed schoolteacher pointing to the blackboard sum '2 – 1 =' and exclaiming to dispirited looking pupils, *'Soyons encore plus clair: je vous donne deux bonbons, vous en mangez un. Il reste?'* The build-up to the new proposals was marked by the resurgence of inspectorial intervention. In 1980, ministerial and inspectorial control over the new regulations was more evident, with a number of interest groups relegated to the more token advisory groups appointed by the Minister.

In England and Wales, mounting pressure on educational standards was symbolised in the historic intervention by Prime Minister James Callaghan in a speech at Ruskin College, Oxford, where he talked of 'concern about the standards of numeracy of school leavers' and went on to say that he was 'inclined to think' that there should be a basic curriculum with universal standards. It was a theme that was pursued by the Conservative Government elected in 1979 through a series of curriculum papers published in the early 1980s. In mathematics, a committee of enquiry, the Cockcroft Committee, established by the Labour Government to defuse cross-party concern, reported in 1979 and proposed an 'inner core' of essential mathematics that should be taught in all schools. In France the new 1980 regulations were introduced with an extensive, centrally organised, programme of regional meetings and seminars. In England and Wales the Cockcroft recommendations were supported by designated funding for the updating of both primary and secondary teachers in the new approaches advocated.

The apparent excesses of the new maths programmes attracted political and media attention in the Netherlands during the latter part of the 1970s. *De Volkskrant*, originally a Catholic newspaper but now a widely read left-of-centre publication sometimes referred to as 'the social workers' daily', gave extensive and critical coverage to the reforms – for example, on 6 February 1974 the headline read 'Chaotic situation facing schools, maths becomes stumbling block'.

In each of the three countries such concerns helped provide the backcloth against which centralist and highly interventionist policies began to be formulated. Again, the parallel process of development, what Ambler (1987) has called 'common experiences' across countries, began to shape policy options.

Pressure groups played a significant part in promoting the case for interventionist policies across the whole of the school curriculum. Mathematics was frequently cited to illustrate the excesses of the 1960s. In France, whilst the Minister of Education in the new socialist government, Alain Savary, battled with the issue of private Catholic schooling that ultimately led to his downfall, others within the socialist party were planning a new and radical initiative. Through the latter part of 1983 and early months of 1984 Jean-Pierre Chevènement, working with a small group of advisors within the context of *République moderne*, his *club de réflexion*, developed a range of policies to foster 'republican elitism' with a reaffirmation of the value of rigorous, orthodox study in the basics throughout primary and secondary schooling. It is now clear that well before Savary's final demise the decision had been taken that Chevènement would succeed. His political advisors, led by two former Maoists, Philippe Barret and Jean-Claude Milner, comprehensively established a reform programme with a populist appeal. Milner's book *De l'école*, published in 1984, provided a key text for the overall design, and Chevènement taking the educational world by storm was seen by one of the more conservative teacher union leaders, Guy Bayet, as providing *'le plus beau virage depuis 1968'* (*Nouvel Observateur*, 4 January 1985). Other teacher union leaders were less impressed, but Chevènement appealed, through widespread media exposure, over their heads to the public generally. Opinion polls (*Le Point*, September 1985) showed substantive support.

In adopting this tactic Chevènement was working outside the normal consultative structure of interest groups, what Milner in his book had called the triple alliance of the corporation (teacher unions, the educational bureaucracy and progressive Christians) – a grouping that in his view had rendered educational change slow and cumbersome. In England, a remarkably similar process characterised the slightly later period 1986–8. There is an intriguing parallel in the way the Chevènement socialist kitchen cabinet on one side of the channel formulated proposals similar (albeit with different purposes) to those of Mrs Thatcher's advisors in Downing Street. A more shadowy professor, Brian Griffiths, fulfilled the same role as Barret in France, orchestrating the inflow of advice and ideas from the range of right-of-centre pressure groups (Hillgate, Centre for Policy Studies, Institute for Economic Affairs) that had published numerous pamphlets and tracts in the early part of the 1980s, advocating a return to traditionalist values in curriculum and the dismantling of the local authority monopoly control in state education. (The Hillgate Group's 1986 publication *Whose Schools?* provided a blueprint for the 1988 legislation that was to follow.)

John Quicke (1988) has analysed the processes leading up to the quickly taken government decision to introduce a centralist and statutory National Curriculum in the period shortly before the 1987 General Election (see also Chitty, 1988; Johnson, 1989). He describes the tensions within the Conservative party, and among its advisors, between the neo-liberal and neo-conservative elements; between those who saw market principles extending across the full spectrum of educational agents, and those who saw defence of traditional and nationalist standards within a managed system as the direction in which policy should be pursued. Despite these internal tensions, the style that evolved for curriculum was interventionist and regulatory.

As in France, the reforms represented a sharp break from the corporate policies that had been distinctive of post-war educational politics, including the first phases of the Thatcher administration. The change is starkly illustrated by these short quotations, the first from *Better Schools* (DES, 1985), the much-publicised document that marked the high spot of Sir Keith Joseph's ministerial career at the Department of Education and Science (DES), and the second, published after the 1987 election, from the consultative document on the curriculum (DES, 1987).

> The Secretary of State's policies for the range and pattern of the 5 to 16 curriculum will not lead to national syllabuses. Diversity at local education authority and school level is healthy, accords well with the English and Welsh tradition of school education, and makes for liveliness and innovation. (p. 4)
> The Government has announced its intention to legislate for a national foundation curriculum for pupils of compulsory school age in England and Wales ... Within the secular national curriculum, the Government intends to establish essential foundation subjects – maths, English, science, foreign language, history, geography, technology in its various aspects, music, art and physical education ... the government wishes to establish programmes of study for the subjects, describing the essential content which needs to be covered to enable pupils to reach or surpass the attainment targets. (p. 35)

In France Chevènement pursued his policies vigorously. *Le Monde de l'Education* of March 1985 (pp. 8–9) reports his new instructions to inspectors to oversee teacher quality in the teaching of the basic subjects rather than make general observations about the system as a whole. Instructions were also issued to the presidents of curriculum commissions set up by his predecessors to make sure that the emphasis would be on the acquisition of knowledge rather than explorations of any idealistic teaching approaches (*Nouvel Observateur*, 4 January 1965). In England the proposals for curriculum, despite all the objections from educationalists (Haviland, 1988), passed unaltered onto the statute books through the 1988 Education Reform Act. Implementation was immediately vigorously pursued through DES working parties and the establishment of new national bodies directly appointed by the Minister and responsible for curriculum and for examinations and assessment.

In centralist France, therefore, the political, as opposed to bureaucratic, centre reasserted influence. In decentralist England a very similar process, characterised by similar strategies for outmanoeuvring the normal range of interest groups, was put in place. The rhetoric was on whole curriculum reform, raising standards (in England), democratising excellence (in France) and modernisation (in the Netherlands), all objectives necessitating governmental intervention.

Overall, the theme of quality reverberates through political advocacy for new directions and new approaches. It was in many ways a more manageable aim for government policy. The terms in which it was defined could be adapted to resource constraint. For socialist administrations it also achieved what Wise (1979) has termed goal reduction. Governments could appear, within the terms they defined, to be making progress, whereas progress in terms of previous commitments to ideas of equity, access and opportunity had proved singularly disappointing.

In the Netherlands similar forces were at work. The formation of a right-wing coalition government comprising the *Christen Democratisch Appél* (a grouping of three Christian Democrat parties) and the Conservative *Volksparty voor Vryheid en Democratie* opened up education policy to influence from business interests, which had been campaigning for educational reforms and increased governmental intervention. In 1979 a working paper on 'determining, measuring and improving quality' was produced (van Bruggen, 1987) which led in 1982 to a national testing programme, firstly in Dutch and then extending over the next few years to a range of other subjects including mathematics. In 1985 there was a Primary Education Act with a number of curriculum regulations, followed by the more prescriptive Education Bill of 1987 proposing a national core curriculum of fourteen subjects and an assessment programme linked to attainment targets; a development that paralleled similar proposals in England.

Proposals such as these were not unique to European countries. Across most of the industrialised countries of the world the 1980s saw national reappraisal and the development of national policies to combat what was variously termed educational decline or crisis. The publication in the USA of the 1983 'open letter to the American people' from the US National Commission on Excellence in Education, 'A Nation at Risk', attracted worldwide attention for its indictment of the 'mediocre educational performance' (p. 5) of the American school system. In Japan, Prime Minister Nakasone's Extraordinary Council on Education has been seen by some commentators (Horio, 1988, p. 376) as an attempt by business interests to impose an even more directive and unaccountable policy meeting structure than the highly centralist if rather more paternalist Central Council of Education controlled by the Ministry of Education. A right-wing think tank, the Kyoto Round Table, is widely reported as inspiring a number of the reform proposals.

Again, these developments show how educational systems very different in structure and historical lineage can be worked similarly where orchestrated reform is vigorously pursued. The increasingly centralist intervention of government in France, England and the Netherlands shows a striking homogeneity, given the very different traditions from which each emanated. Numerous observers (such as Westbury, 1984; Apple, 1986; Altbach, 1986) have explored the underlying social and economic forces that have, in the last decade, motivated the new style of legislative and centralist intervention. These observations of the way in which different educational systems responded to these pressures point to the difficulty of sustaining the characteristic of systems in terms such as 'centralised' or 'decentralised'. Over significant periods of time changes have occurred, working through different institutional arrangements, without reformers necessarily feeling the constraints or controls of the systems in which they moved.

Autonomy and Control – the Evolution of Educational Systems

The difficulties of accommodating specific accounts of change processes within prevailing assumptions about the structure of formal systems is reflected in a number of studies in other areas of social and public policy. As in this paper, the juxtaposition of apparently centralised and decentralised systems occupies much attention. Interest in the centralised structure of French government and administration has attracted considerable attention. The fate of reform programmes initiated by socialist governments between 1981 and 1986 have stimulated particular concern over a number of years and across a range of administrative contexts.

Ashford (1982) has pursued a central concern of this paper, the reliability of the concepts of centralisation and decentralisation for understanding change. His analysis points to the dangers of allowing traditional and formal procedures to obscure the way systems work in practice. In a comparative study of French and English bureaucracies he concludes

> that central–local relations, viewed through the multidimensional components of the subnational system, are paradoxically more formal and rigid in Britain, a country often admired for its pragmatic politics. In France [however,] the subnational system is more important to the political system and the formalities of administrative and political behaviour can easily cloak the more flexible and diverse ways that political action has devised to influence each other. (p. 367)

Ashford has been accused of pushing his conceptual model too far, a criticism similar in kind to the criticisms made of Archer's overarching theoretical structure. Sharpe (1983), for example, suggests that the 'incredible fragmentation' of French local government set alongside the closely intertwined structure of local, regional and national office holders (a consequence of the *cumul des mandats*, or holding of multiple offices) creates a symbiotic relationship of mutual dependency that Ashford's categorisation ignores. Overall, however, he sees Ashford's study as 'an important corrective to many of the standard assumptions on the nature of French central–local relations' (p. 32). Duclaud-Williams (1981, 1983, 1988) has also questioned many of the general assumptions about French educational administration. He sees the system as having its own pattern of inter-bureaucratic and politico-administrative relations, and questions, therefore, the validity of applying general French models to this very specific policy area.

Duclaud-Williams is also critical of the concept of change within the French administration advanced by Michel Crozier (1964) in *The Bureaucratic Phenomenon*. In this work Crozier described organisational or bureaucratic change as a process in which long periods of routine, during which nothing alters, are interspersed with crises, and it is these crises which have to bear the entire burden of adaptation. Although Crozier's name does not appear in her index, Margaret

Archer has incorporated this perspective into her model of change within centralised systems. For Archer,

> changes are evidenced and documented at the centre by laws, decrees and regulations ... education can change very little in the centralized system between such bouts of legislative intervention. Patterns of change, therefore, follow a jerky sequence in which long periods of stability (i.e. changelessness) are intermittently interrupted by polity directed measures. This has been termed the *Stop–Go* pattern. (p. 617)

Massey (1986), looking at governmental policy development in France, is critical of attempts to premise analysis on formal, legalistic descriptions of the French state, and she points to the rich variety of sources of local power and autonomy that stand in opposition to the centralist model of the authoritarian Gaullist Fifth Republic. In her terms, 'given the importance for public policy making of external pressures, conflicting interests, local and regional factors, the variation in the state–groups relations, financial conditions and changes in all these variables over time, and between policy sectors, any attempt to discover a single French policy style is doomed to fail' (p. 425; see also Wilson, 1983). Finally Ambler (1985) shows how effectively one interest group, in this instance the teachers' union *Fédération de l'Education Nationale* (FEN), could obstruct Savary's reform proposals. He points in a later paper (Ambler, 1987) to the parallels that could be drawn with Sir Keith Joseph's difficulties in circumnavigating the interests of teacher union and local authority influence over the same period of time.

These examples illustrate the difficulties of existing overarching theories of change, of the sort advanced by Archer. Within the political sociology of education, Smith (1989) has argued that, rather than trying to understand change through any particular theory, 'better understanding may be gained through the more modest development of models that are wide in scope, are flexible and whose usefulness depends on how well they contribute to understanding complex relationships over limited periods of time' (p. 176).

In the concluding part of this paper, therefore, drawing on the evidence from the curriculum reforms described, some indication of the points from which such models could be established are explored. Two areas merit particular attention: the evidence of local influence and control, and the activities of interest groups in initiating and sustaining reform movements.

Firstly, there is clear evidence of local autonomy, even control, within systems that would fall within the centralised model policy formulation and decision making. In the French mathematics reforms the local, school-based authority to purchase new textbooks provided an important means of bypassing central directives, and parallel evidence for this exists in other areas of curriculum. Hörner (1981), for example, describes how, despite the dissolution by ministerial dictat of a reform commission for science, the members reconstituted themselves and set about publishing textbooks to 'salvage as much as possible' of the original proposals. Broadfoot *et al.* (1988), following a comparative study of the roles of

French and English teachers, has shown how 'the actual constraints to which French teachers are subject, and the controls which are exercised over them, are relatively limited' (p. 282). In looking at the working of the French system it is possible to see how, contrary to popular perceptions, significant decisions about curriculum can be made at the level of the schools or the commune. The *Maire*, for example, with the *conseil municipal*, can decide whether to fund the teaching of languages other than German or English in the local *collèges*.

In the early part of the 1990s countries such as England and the Netherlands have embraced more centralised models for administering the curriculum. It will be important to monitor the extent to which these inhibit local autonomy. Overall, however, the linear model of the centralised system is inadequate for understanding the system in action and the way these processes enhance or impede reform.

Secondly, and more significantly, therefore, it is necessary to look at the activities of interest groups. In the examples of subject-based reform in the 1960s and legislative intervention in the 1980s the activities of interest groups are prominent. University mathematicians were instrumental in promoting change in each of the three countries. Key individuals as well as the groups they led played a leading role in working the system to their ends. The tactics adopted, however, varied from country to country and were always strategically distanced from *traditional structures* of control and decision-making.

In the first subject-based phase of reform, university mathematicians wielded significant influence. To achieve this influence required acknowledgement of and accommodation to other groups. Alliances had to be created, sometimes involving the central administration or the inspectorate, but not always so. Publishing interests were significant in all three countries. These groupings, however, were temporary reflections of a particular configuration of circumstances. As conditions changed so new alliances were established. Publishers in France, for example, were only willing to back reformers working outside government guidelines for a relatively short period of time.

A volatility of interaction between interest groups and between groups and government is characteristic of developments in each of the countries. Freudenthal, the recipient of major Dutch government finance in 1970, had all funding withdrawn within a decade as business interests rather than professional educators gained influence. The inspectorate in France, bypassed by the reforming zeal of university mathematicians in the 1960s, painstakingly reasserted influence throughout the 1970s. The reforming zeal of Margaret Thatcher's third administration led to the exclusion of all the significant educational interest groups that had played a significant role under previous Labour and Conservative administrations.

Regan and Wilson (1986) have described the way 'groups constantly seek new avenues of approach, new structures and new tactics to sway decision makers'. Like Smith (1989) they question the suitability of existing models, such as pluralist and neo-corporatist, for understanding the significance of interest group strategies. Within the context of educational systems, attempts by Archer and others to pattern the interaction of interest groups according to system traditions appear equally problematic. Abrupt changes in political and economic conditions, for example, can upset the transitory balances of power. Numerous commentators (such as Papadopolous, 1980; Shipman, 1981; Fowler, 1981) have pointed to the impact of the 1973 oil crisis on subsequent policies for educational change. Anweiler (1988) has talked of the tremendous pressure on government to achieve and assure the modernisation of the state (in this case France) through educational reform: 'The advances of neighbours and competitors like West Germany and Japan, the expectations of its own industrial and commercial élites, a diffuse but real sense of national pride – these all created a context in which the state was under increasing pressure to help the society move forward, to pave the way towards new economic and technological frontiers' (p. 264).

This process of transformation, responding to changes in economic and demographic conditions, has strengthened the hand of government, creating patterns of interest group politics very different from the proliferation of strategies more characteristic of the 1960s. In the 1970s and early 1980s, as resources became restricted and economic and political success became tightly intertwined, government acquired significantly greater authority. Centrality, therefore, is synonymous in the 1980s with government across each of the educational systems described here. In earlier circumstances the centre was often, to use Lattimore's phrase, more nomadic, with professional educators, in certain contexts, wielding significantly greater authority than government.

The strategies and evolution of interest groups offer a more significant opportunity to understand the processes through which educational change occurs. While the conditions of change may alter, characteristic patterns in the relations of change, however complex, appear to remain constant. Hence the plea by more than one observer for the development of middle range theories within which developments can be conceptualised.

The evidence from each of the countries in both phases of curriculum reform points to the importance of interest group strategies for determining the way in which reforms were instituted. Where circumstances are appropriate (for instance, in a period of constrained resources within a centralised structure) the traditional structure could be embraced. Chevènement's reforms in France provide an example. In the same system, however, twenty years earlier, it was more expedient to bypass the formal structures, to such an extent that the study of the formal decrees would give a wholly inaccurate picture of reform. Strategic decisions about how to proceed became crucial to the success of interest group activity.

The process therefore of *orchestrating* (see Fullan, 1982) key parts of the formal and informal network of interests within educational systems merits the closest attention. Where reform initiatives developed, one group appears to have played a leading role in orchestrating support. University mathematicians were significant in the Dutch and French context in the 1960s. In England, civil servants and the central inspectorate were equally influential, although working through the Nuffield Foundation network to establish a centrally directed curriculum project. In the 1980s political think tank groups, closely allied to ministerial or prime ministerial interests, have played a similar role.

Groups working in this way are required to develop a variety of strategies. The dimension of *inclusiveness or exclusivity*, for example, is the first to face any group attempting to gain influence. Different contexts throw up different approaches. The mathematics reformer in France in the 1960s and the New Right think tanks in Britain in the 1980s adopted the policy of *exclusion*, bypassing many of the adjacent interests, which would normally expect to be brought into reform initiatives on a national scale. The way in which the exclusion strategy is implemented then becomes significant. The cultivation and exploitation of the media, appealing over the heads of those who may attempt to inhibit reform, is now a familiar tactic. The availability of television as well as press coverage provided the reformers of the 1960s with a particularly powerful means of seeking support outside the normal political and bureaucratic structures. The revolution in communications, continuing apace in the present day, presents a further challenge to the structure of traditional systems. *Communication strategies* therefore represent an important part of the orchestration process.

Resource targeting is a further strategic area criticial both for sustaining the group and for presenting reform. Again, this is realised in different ways and is often shrouded in secrecy, particularly where groups operate very closely alongside politicians. International as well as national sources of funding can be sought, and the significance of the former for providing a source of legitimacy beyond national concerns is in itself a strategic decision. The *internationalisation* of issues is an important and underestimated way of advancing reform, and looks like becoming even more significant in the coming decade.

A final example of the strategic planning required in the process of orchestration relates to *pace*. Is the process of mobilising support to be developed over an extended period of time or will a rapid development of policy be more likely to succeed? In both mathematics reform and nationally interventionist curriculum policy the latter appears to have been, in the short term, more effective. Interest group activities, however, continue unabated within and around education systems, providing a more accurate understanding of the way systems work in practice than does the formal bureaucratic structure. The pace of reform can be accelerated or retarded as new alliances are formed and power redistributed. Interest groups, for example, can be transformed as a consequence of the successes or failures of the causes pursued. Mathematicians who, in the 1960s, were primarily mathematicians with an interest in education had, by the end of the following decade, become professional mathematics educators spawning new journals, new institutes and an agenda very different from that associated with school reform. Strategic planning by interest groups, however intuitive, involves decisions that integrate each of these dimensions. The pace of development, for example, is inextricably linked with the extent to which other groups are included or excluded. Planning also evolves over time as the context or setting is changed and as the consequences of actions provide new information for subsequent policy formulation.

Closer examination, therefore, of these processes is important in developing a richer appreciation of the way educational systems promote or respond to change. New parameters will need to be established and some constructs, however firmly embedded in current understandings, will require substantial modification. Most significantly, given the focus of this paper, the idea that the way in which events unfold within educational systems is predicated on the formal structural properties of the system has assumed mythical status. Attempts at school reform in Britain can be seen as markedly similar to developments in other European countries. Explanations therefore must extend beyond national boundaries. As Kogan (1983) has eloquently pleaded, we should guard against taking 'centre–local relationships as processes and structures in themselves. They are all transitive concepts requiring objects, namely the work and life of prime institutions, if they are to become meaningful' (p. 83).

REFERENCES

Altbach, P. G. (1986) '"A Nation at Risk": The Educational Reform Debate in the United States', *Prospects*, XVI(3), pp. 337–47.

Ambler, J. S. (1985) 'Neocorporatism and the Politics of French Education', *West European Politics*, 8(3), pp. 23–42.

Ambler, J. S. (1987) 'Constraints on Policy Innovation in Education: Thatcher's Britain and Mitterand's France', *Comparative Politics*, October, pp. 85–105.

Anweiler, O. (1988) 'The Politics of Reform and Non-Reform in French Education', *Comparative Education Review*, 32(3), pp. 251–6.

Apple, M. (1986) 'National Reports and the Construction of Inequality', *British Journal of Sociology of Education*, 7(2), pp. 171–90.

Archer, M. S. (1979) *Social Origins of Educational Systems*. London and Berkeley, California: Sage Publications.

Ashford, D. E. (1982) *British Dogmatism and French Pragmatism*. London: George Allan & Unwin.

Broadfoot, P., Osborn, M., Golby, M. and Paillet, A. (1988) 'What Professional Responsibility Means to Teachers: National Contexts and Classroom Constants', *British Journal of Sociology of Education*, 9(30), pp. 265–87.

Chitty, C. (1988) 'Central Control of the School Curriculum 1944–87', *History of Education*, 17(4), pp. 321–34.

Crozier, M. (1964) *The Bureaucratic Phenomenon*. London: Tavistock.

DES (1985) *Better Schools*. London: HMSO.

DES (1987) *The National Curriculum 5–16: A Consultation Document*. London: HMSO.

Duclaud-Williams, R. (1981) 'Change in French Society: A Critical Analysis of Crozier's Bureaucratic Model', *West European Politics*, 4(3), pp. 235–51.

Duclaud-Williams, R. (1983) 'Change and Authority in France: A Reply to Warwick', *West European Politics*, 6(2), pp. 163–4.

Duclaud-Williams, R. (1988) 'Policy Implementation in the French Public Bureaucracy: The Case of Education', *West European Politics*, 11(1), pp. 80–101.

Fowler, G. (1981) 'The Changing Nature of Educational Politics in the 1970s', in P. Broadfoot *et al.* (eds), *Politics and Educational Change*. London: Croom Helm.

Fullan, M. (1982) *The Meaning of Educational Change*. New York and London: Teachers College Press.

Haviland, J. (1988) *Take Care Mr Baker*. London: Fourth Estate.

Hillgate Group (1986) *Whose Schools?* London.

Horio, T. (1988) *Educational Thought and Ideology in Modern Japan*. Tokyo: University of Tokyo Press.

Hörner, W. (1981) 'The Relationship between Educational Policy and Educational Research: The Case of French Curriculum Reform', *European Journal of Science Education*, 3(2), pp. 217–21.

Johnson, R. (1989) 'Thatcherism and English Education: Breaking the Mould or Confirming the Pattern', *History of Education*, 18(2), pp. 91–122.

Kogan, M. (1983) 'The Central–Local Government Relationship – A Comparison Between the Education and Health Services', *Local Government Studies*, 9(1), pp. 65–85.

Massey, S. (1986) 'Public Policy-Making in France: The Art of the Possible', *West European Politics*, 9(3), pp. 412–28.

Milner, J. C. (1984) *De L'École*. Paris: Seuil.

Moon, B. (1986) *The New Maths Curriculum Controversy: An International Story*. Lewes: Falmer Press.

Papadopolous, G. S. (1980) 'Educational Reform Trends in the Western World: The Current Debate', *Prospects*, 10(2), pp. 159–68.

Quicke, J. (1988) 'The New Right and Education', *British Journal of Educational Studies*, 26(1), pp. 5–20.

Regan, M. C. and Wilson, F. L. (1986) 'Interest Group Politics in France and Ireland: Comparative Perspectives on Neo-Corporatism', *West European Politics*, 9(3), pp. 393–411.

Sharpe, L. J. (1983) 'Review Article: Dogmatism and Pragmatism in France and Britain', *West European Politics*, 6(1), pp. 129–33.

Shipman, M. (1981) 'The School Curriculum in England 1970–1980', *Compare*, 11(1), pp. 21–32.

Smith, D. M. (1989) 'Unintended Transformations of Control over Education: A Process of Structuring', *British Journal of Sociology of Education*, 10(2), pp. 175–93.

Van Bruggen, J. C. (1987) 'Survey of Trends in Curriculum Reform in the Netherlands'. Unpublished Mimeograph. Enschede: National Institute for Curriculum Development (SLO).

Westbury, I. (1984) 'A Nation at Risk', *Journal of Curriculum Studies*, 16(4), pp. 431–45.

Wilson, F. L. (1983) 'French Interest Group Politics: Pluralist or Neo-Corporatist?', *American Political Science Review*, 77(4), pp. 895–910.

Wise, A. E. (1979) *Legislated Learning: The Bureaucratisation of the American Classroom*. Berkeley, CA: University of California Press.

4.2 FRENCH CURRICULUM REFORM

ANNE CORBETT

INTRODUCTION

No country is an island, least of all France, so conscious of its place at one of the great crossroads of European geography and history. Yet in moments of national boastfulness the French like to suggest that their way of life is unique: 'The school is in France, as in no other country, a living part of our heritage, a source of common pride, the crucible in which the national identity has been forged', said the minister of education, Lionel Jospin, in June 1989, introducing a major new law on education.

In looking at French curriculum developments over the last decade this paper explores the dynamic of the relationship between general trends and the culture of the French, finding an inspiration in the work of the historian Fernand Braudel. It was he who formulated for the French the not always welcome idea (so powerful is the nation state's legacy) that when we study national history we need to keep in mind what is shared with other nations as well as what is distinctive. We are shaped by much the same climate and geography. We are caught up in the same social and economic trends. The history that individuals bring with them has to be squeezed into the general frame. Braudel talked about 'a house with three storeys'.

In that spirit this paper picks on some similarities of the educational scene in the industrialised countries of Western Europe on the eve of 1992 to show how the French are responding to external change, and what this is doing to the traditional structures for the creation and control of programmes. The French, too, appear poised on the brink of major change, but it is not in the same vein as in Britain.

SIMILARITIES . . .

Over the last thirty or forty years the education system in France, as elsewhere, has become nominally more democratic with the vast extension of secondary and higher education. Selective entry for secondary school has lost its legitimacy.

Source: commissioned for this volume.

Reforms designed to ensure greater equality of access and a fairer share-out of knowledge have been set in train. Familiar perverse effects have been noticed: selection still operates but in less visible ways than in the past. Today it is seen in such practices as choice between high-prestige and low-prestige subjects. A classic example is the foreign language chosen on entering secondary school: German, a minority choice, has high prestige; English has low prestige. Similarly with the choice of *Baccalauréat*: the maths-dominated *Bac* ranks higher than the arts-based *Bac*, the 'general' *Bacs* rank higher than the commercial and technical ones. As elsewhere, the extension of educational opportunity seems to have had little effect on closing the gap between the most and the least privileged.

The period has also been marked by violent argument and intense academic debate. If, as in Britain and the USA, the period 1945–65 was one of great hope raised by education, accompanied by the reconstruction and expansion after the Second World War, so the period 1965–75 saw a similar disillusion, since which a government has launched a major reform, recently culminating in the most important legislation for decades.

. . . AND DIFFERENCES

But there has been a tone to the debate in France distinctively different from that in Britain, in which, rather than crisis, the French talk about 'creating a dynamic for renovation' and 'making education the national priority'.[1] All the governments of the 1980s have supported the aim of getting 80 per cent of the age group to *Baccalauréat* level.

This basic optimism about education can be explained by two strands in French history. One is the attachment to a highly centralised education system as a tool for underpinning French identity, its hallmarks the national curricular programmes, national diplomas, a national recruitment of teachers. The *académies* in the provinces are administrative outposts of the ministry, not education authorities in their own right.

Until very recently France has lived with the *ancien régime* idea that its national unity is fragile. The Jacobins of the first Republic and then Napoleon were in complete accord with the view developed by Louis XIV that only a strong nation would provide a bulwark against internal opponents and external enemies. To quote Vincent Wright's authoritative introduction to modern France:

> France is a country of great geographical and cultural diversity and was created by bringing together (with the persuasion of the axe and the sword) peoples as distinct as the Basques and the Bretons, the Béarnais and the Burgundians, the Alsatians and the Auvergnats, the Normans and the Provençals. Parts of France such as Nice and the Savoy are recent acquisitions, and Alsace has twice this century been taken back from the Germans.[2]

National boundaries have been violated four times in the last 170 years.

In an interview in 1987 Georges Laforest, then the chief inspector in philosophy and responsible for co-ordinating the new programmes under Jean-Pierre Chevènement, put the case for the centralised education system in these terms:

> The unity of the French nation is not something abstract. It is a unity which lies in knowledge and culture. It is thus vital that from the primary school to the *lycée* young people can have access to the same knowledge and in particular those aspects which are concerned with France's past: literature, history, civic education. It is a matter of principle that national programmes should provide an identical culture – with naturally the variations that personal enrichment can bring – so that there are the common references which provide the basis of a society. That is the fundamental principle.

> The second strand lies in France's revolutionary history. The concept of national programmes grew alongside the development of constitutional thought and the creation of a public education system in which merit would be rewarded and privilege would not be bought. Argued over during the period of the French Revolution, programmes became institutionalised under Napoleon for the select few who aimed to go from *lycées* to the scientific and technical *grandes écoles*. When the functions of state education were given a broader definition in the 1880s, compulsory primary education too was characterised by a standard common curriculum; there were similarly common programmes in secondary schools. Accompanied by the notion that a common programme was integral to the concept of equality of educational opportunity, they have been a keystone of a system in which public education has been the norm and a means by which its essential functions could be identified.[3]

But what the French elliptically call 'changes in science and society' have been forcing rethinking about programmes for the last twenty years. The 1960s were marked by abrupt changes in content and a lack of change in teaching methods and organisation; some of the problems which ensued have been described in the English press.

The 1980s have brought new concerns. Not only are there the same technical problems – that is to say, content needs to be updated in a number of subjects, and many schools still need help in coming to terms with the diverse abilities of their pupils. A significant number leave school without any qualification, making the aim of getting 80 per cent to the *Bac* look wildly out. Almost a quarter of the under-25s are jobless; one of the highest percentages in any developed country. Calls to break the 'encyclopedic nature of programmes' and other uniformities in the system, 'to multiply the paths to success', have become commonplace.[4]

There has also been a change in the political climate. As a highly centralised system has become both democratically inappropriate and impossible to manage, 'decentralisation' and 'deconcentration' and the 'opening up of schools to their community' have become keywords. As yet the impact on curriculum is negligible. Under the law of 1982, completed by 300 decrees, a number of the powers held centrally by the state have been distributed between the three tiers of territorial authority: *communes*, *départements* and *régions*; it is only the maintenance of schools which is at issue. But a question mark is raised for the future. Local pride is being invoked, a key idea being to release resources which would be difficult to raise via taxation. Does this not inevitably herald a time when there will be a local stake not only in what schools look like, but in what they teach?

TRADITIONAL STRUCTURES FOR THE CURRICULUM

THE USE OF LAW

The myth dies hard outside France that a French minister of education can look at his watch at 3 p.m. on a Monday and tell you what is happening in every school. But the formal structures of creation, diffusion and control still look highly centralised and programmes have the force of law. They must be respected by the publishers who devise the textbooks and the teachers concerned.

The *sine qua non* of curriculum reform in France is that it should be approved at the highest level of the state. To make major changes in programmes, a minister of education needs the approval of the council of ministers, which the President of the Republic chairs. The general lines of a reform are enunciated in decrees following such councils. Draft ministerial orders specifying the details of the programmes and hours bring them into effect, following approval by a national consultative committee on which teachers' unions and parents' organisations sit. When ready for implementation they are published in the *Bulletin Officiel*, the official guide for the public service.

These revisions take place cyclically. René Haby, a minister of education during Valéry Giscard d'Estaing's presidency, launched a major reform in 1975, covering the range of compulsory schooling. Ten years later the socialist Jean-Pierre Chevènement put through a similarly large-scale revision, forming the basis of the programmes now in use. Innovative in emphasising that a wide public has a legitimate interest in the programmes, he published them in accessible paperback form.

Programmes consist of four elements: a notice of the hours to be accorded to a subject, a statement of objectives, instructions to teachers and a broad syllabus outline. To take an example from the 1985 civic education programmes for secondary schools, which are designed to stimulate critical reflection, not simply tell pupils how to behave:

> [Objectives] Civic education presupposes an understanding of the rules of democratic life, how they were brought into being, an understanding of institutions with their historic background and a reflection on the conditions and the means by which respect of the human being and his rights is exercised: by tolerance and solidarity, by refusal of racist behaviour, in a wish to live

together under democratic rules. It should enable pupils to respond to questions about rights . . .

[Instructions] Civic education is a subject to be taught and a practice to be exemplified . . . the role of the teacher is not to impose a pattern of acceptable behaviour but to help pupils acquire the tools of independent thought.

The four-year programme works up to a study of the key texts including habeas corpus, the Declaration of the Rights of Man and the Citizen 1789, and the conventions of the European Declaration of Human Rights, as well as a consideration of how these work in practice. The last of the four years also looks to the institutions of the USA and USSR and international organisations, and asks teachers to set these, too, against what happens in practice.

INSPECTORS IN THE 'BATH'

Inevitably the process of curriculum reform has started long before a minister puts his signature to the relevant documents. Curiously, however, in a society in which so many of the rules are written, the responsibility for curriculum change was not defined until the education law of 1989.

Subject associations and university research groups play a role. But the final responsibility has been clearly seen as lying with the corps of the *inspecteurs généraux*, the 140 or so people mostly recruited from the very special group who teach the *classes préparatoires* for the comparative entry to *grandes écoles*, and who are almost exclusively subject specialists. They are vastly superior in prestige to the other inspectorial corps, like those with territorial responsibilities.

Back in 1977 the then doyen of the inspectorate, Lucien Géminard, drew a diagram to explain to the *TES* that the system by which the programmes were devised was not operating in a vacuum.[5] Though there was a hierarchy of control, there were also channels of information which enabled the inspectorate to decide what needed changing. 'Most of my colleagues are in and out of their establishments for much of their time. One learns a very great deal that way'; whereas, he added, firmly, 'those in the bath [as the French call the chalkface] see nothing'.

He reacted sharply to the accusation that, by definition, such programmes would be out of touch with what most pupils could achieve. 'We are always sandwiched between the demands of the universities and the subject experts on one hand and teachers on the other . . . It is our duty to advise the minister on how his pedagogic policy can be conveniently and practically executed. There is no point in recommending a programme which half the teachers cannot teach.'

Ten years later a maths teacher, who was part-author of a textbook, confirmed that in essentials nothing had changed.[6] She was there as a *classe préparatoire* teacher, working with inspectors, who are much in demand by publishers to give the textbooks an extra cachet. The direction for innovation was still *de haut en bas*. An *inspecteur général* for English and the deputy chief inspector, M. Max Délaquis, suggested that nothing *could* change, at least not easily. 'We have been trying to get more flexibility into the system for ten years but no one will let us. Everyone believes that you must have the same programmes, the same numbers of hours devoted to subjects, the same kinds of textbooks, the same training for teachers.'

IN THE NAME OF JUSTICE AND MOBILITY

De facto doubts about the degree of centralisation have been raised by a number of English specialists.[7] But as noted by Pascale Gruson, a CNRS (*Conseil National de la Recherche Scientifique*) research fellow in the sociology of education, there is a double phenomenon at work which means that programmes are, basically, respected: 'The teacher is given a certain freedom of approach but is not really able to enjoy it: teachers' working conditions are not compatible with a collaborative approach to introducing change' (*Times Educational Supplement*, 6 March 1987). At the same time, 'although secondary school teachers often have reservations about the programmes, most would be reluctant to give up the principle. This is not because they are afraid of leaping into the unknown, but because they understand what is at stake: sharing a culture, acquiring the means of communication, which can help a community to become acquainted with its own democracy (ibid.).'

A teacher of English in her 20s, working in a *lycée professionel* in a largely immigrant Paris suburb, speaks for many:

I know that among my terminale class of 36 there are about six who follow the programme effectively, the others struggle. And when they have come out of five hours of infernally noisy workshops and there's English for the last hour of the day and I'm supposed to be teaching them about Reagan or the women's liberation movement in the States ... I just say 'My God ... maybe Monory[8] is almost right in his attempt to reduce the programmes: these ambitious ones are irrelevant.'

I always calm down eventually and realise it would be a grave error not to give these students the chance the national system offers them. One pushes on. But how individual teachers react depends ultimately on their professional ethics and their stamina (ibid.).

DEVELOPMENTS OF THE 1980s

THE EDUCATION ORIENTATION LAW 1989

France goes into the 1990s, like Britain, with a new law on education. The Education Orientation Law of 10 July 1989 has a number of provisions of crucial importance to the curriculum.

First, it establishes a national programmes committee of 'qualified persons'. That is to say, it breaks the monopoly of the general inspectorate, while reaffirming the role of programmes as defining for each cycle of education, in terms of a national framework, what it is essential that pupils should be taught and the methods they need to assimilate. From the moment the council is named and the decrees applied, it will have the responsibility of advising the minister on the general conception, the main objectives and the adequacy of existing programmes.

Secondly, it redefines the role of the general inspectorate as being to evaluate the system in general, by department, by academy, by region or at national level as appropriate, and in conjunction with the administrative service inspectorate, and to make known innovative practice. The inspectorate is required to report to parliament and to make an annual report.

Thirdly, a national evaluation committee with responsibility for public cultural and scientific institutions is established as an entity independent of the inspectorate.

Behind the clauses is a conviction which is original for France. It is that 'equality and diversity must go hand in hand', as it was put by Jospin, minister in the Rocard government, in his presentation of the bill to the National Assembly. 'The principle of equality of opportunity has been the force of our schools. But has our system too often imposed a single model of excellence? We know the problems: repeating a year, programmes which are beyond the capacity of pupils to assimilate, absence of support . . . and a rate of failure which is hard in human and economic terms.'

How have these major changes come about? We can pick on two factors.

THE END OF CULTURAL ABSOLUTISM? CURRICULUM COMMISSIONS 1981–1984 AND 1988–1989

Before the 1981 election, which was to bring the Left to power for the first time for twenty-three years, there was a huge movement in favour of social change. Grassroots initiatives could be counted by the score. There were also manifesto promises from Mitterand, designed to restore history, geography and philosophy to the place they had enjoyed before Giscard and his minster Haby reduced them as incompatible with mass secondary education.

The first months were propitious for change and the first education minister, Alain Savary, was the sort of person to encourage dialogue. He commissioned a number of reports on various stages of the education system: on teacher training (A. de Peretti), on the *collège* (L. Legrand) and on *lycée* education (A. Prost). He also established four curriculum commissions.

The chairman of one of them, Professor Jean-Claude Chevalier, the eminent specialist of the French language, has described how he got involved. His own interest in pedagogy had some years before created a close working relationship with Legrand, at that time director of the national institute of educational research, the INRP. It involved him chairing a group of *collège* teachers anxious to change the teaching of French. 'This was post-1968. Teachers weren't satisfied with taking ideas out of books or from university specialists. It was our job to help and get their ideas published.'

'The importance of Savary was that he wanted ideas from outside the usual channels of the inspectorate.' The commission that Chevalier chaired included librarians, sociologists and language teachers as well as teachers of French. 'We wanted to draw on a wide range of views in order to situate French in the context of other subjects and within the social system.' In terms of content the commission's greatest innovation was to insist on a recognition of the three languages of the mother tongue: 'the written language, the oral language and the language of images are a trilogy.'

A second innovation was to insist that programmes should be in the most general terms and force better trained teachers to make a choice.

> Those of us with INRP experience knew how difficult that would be. The climate in schools was rarely conducive. But under Savary teachers' centres were established. And intellectually it was essential to make teachers responsible. We no longer live in an age in which culture can be defined by what a bourgeois elite knows. There are no longer cultural absolutes. The philosopher Michel de Certeau talked about culture as an archipelago. We may cross over to each other's cultural islands. Or we may not.

When Chevènement, a much more authoritarian figure, became minister, the influence of the inspectorate was re-established and he set in motion the revision of programmes by the inspectorate (see below) leaving the commissions in abeyance. 'It wasn't until Monory's time that we were finished off. And that without a word of thanks ... and no official ministry publication.'

But the commission's work was not lost. 'I've been an activist for a long time', said Chevalier. 'I know from experience that when direct routes do not work you can often succeed by indirect ones.' The report was eventually published by the departmental educational publishing centre at Angers in the Loire valley, thanks to some complicated financing through the INRP.[9] 'We expected that the report would in any event be taken up by the *inspecteurs généraux* once the absurd quarrel was over and we thought the French teachers' subject association would fight for it. And indeed, its message was taken up in the revised programme. A good example of grassroots activity, don't you agree?'

Nor was that the end of the story. In December 1988, Jospin called for the formation of ten working parties on the content of the curriculum under the chairmanship of two professors from the prestigious Collège de France: the sociologist Pierre Bourdieu and the biologist François Gros. Chevalier chaired the working party covering modern and classical languages and French. An agreed set of principles was published in March 1989.[10] The reports of the working parties followed three or so months later.

The main report put the seal on the still controversial idea that there is no cultural absolutism. It forms the basis of the philosophy of the new act. For the commission the programmes form a whole, and a national programme council should ensure that elements of them can be modified 'as science or society' suggest: 'It is not possible to say at any moment and for any area what is valid and what is out of date. But the relationship between the necessary perpetuation of the past and the equally necessary adaptation to the future should be a matter of permanent reflection.' A second key idea is that the needs of pupils should be taken into account overtly, and teaching methods adapted. Teaching ways of thinking is crucial: 'The programmes should be a frame not a shackle.' It is essential nevertheless that there should not be inadmissible gaps in what is learned: 'Teachers' own concern that teaching should be coherent should lead them to think about interdisciplinary co-operation.'

As for the programmes: 'It was not the commission's responsibility to intervene either directly or in the short term on the construction of programmes', but rather to point 'to what should be the progressive transformation of curriculum content in line with actual or likely evolutions in society.' And also to help teachers.

French teaching, for example, to take again Chevalier's report, had not recovered from 'its brutal transformation' in the 1960s from something 'deliciously anachronistic' into a battleground for the social sciences, with a heterogeneity among newly recruited teachers and pupils hitherto unknown on the French scene. What they were talking about now was 'a profound modification of a training and exam system with professionals capable of mastering modern culture and keeping up with a form of teaching which is in perpetual motion'.

Moon has drawn attention to the circumventing of the inspectorate in times of crisis, such as that surrounding the reform of mathematics in the 1960s. What is striking about the 1980s is that those with official positions never used the word crisis.

ASSESSMENT AND PLANNING

The idea that the output of the education system should be evaluated has been a second major element to mark thinking about the curriculum in France this last decade. It is a phenomenon common to the developed world. But it is evident too that the word means different things in different systems.

The OECD commentary on its project on the development of educational indicators underlines the different concerns. 'Leaders ... want this information for many purposes: for national reporting, to guide school improvement, to help in priority setting, and to discharge increased demands for accountability.'[11] The French have approached the question of evaluation in ways which are distinctively different from, for example, the British.

The service of the French ministry of education concerned with evaluation and planning was formally set up in February 1987, when René Monory was education minister. It had grown out of the ministry's statistical services and in response to two needs. As described by its director Jean-Pierre Boisivon, on the one hand the ministry needed better planning mechanisms than it was obtaining with budget exercises. Medium-term planning (for five years) had become vital (for example, for teacher recruitment). At the same time there was growing pressure for better information about the output of the system. For Boisivon this development is linked 'with a revolution in the ministry and of which public opinion is still scarcely aware'; that is to say, deconcentration and decentralisation. Policy makers can no longer assure the coherence of the system by the resources they feed in. They also need to know the results.

Since its creation the planning and assessment service has, says Boisivon in a characteristically French way, been concerned with 'three main objectives and four fields of study'. Its customers are policy makers, 'partners' and teachers. The policy makers are obvious. The partners 'are those on whom we count to play a more active role . . . parents, employers and local councillors, for example through schools projects which will be a bit like those pioneered at firm level'. It is also working for teachers. 'Teachers want us to develop the evaluation tools which will enable them to work more effectively.'

And the evaluation of individual children's attainments? 'To produce league tables? That does not interest us', says Boisivon categorically. The performance of pupils and students is indeed included as one of the four fields of study with which the evaluation service is concerned. The others concern teaching and non-teaching staff, educational policy and teacher training. Boisivon stresses that in each case the concern is to use the information gathered not to make 'simplistic judgements' but to plan. For example, in searching for ways to improve the quality of the system, the evaluation and planning unit will be following samples of pupils and teachers throughout their careers, and samples of families and firms, and taking note of their attitudes as well as results.

The first major national exercise, which took place in 1989, consisted of testing the reading and maths skills of all pupils in the second year of primary school (8 year olds) and the first year of secondary school (12 year olds). It did not teach the evaluation service much that was new. The service had done work on pilot samples. But it did bring home in a spectacular way to the public that a significant number of pupils do not achieve what programmes take as the norm. It also brought home the programmes' ambitions. For example, 80 per cent of the second year primary school children can make sense of a text, even though 30 per cent confuse Cs and Ss and plurals. However, by secondary school, when it was expected that pupils would be able to do quite sophisticated comprehension exercises and, for example, transform an affirmative phrase into the negative or interrogative form, there was no noticeable improvement. That is to say, the vast majority (90 per cent) could recognise alphabetical order, but less than a third could manipulate the phrases as asked.

And the consequences? Such national testing is designed to give a boost to campaigns for improved teaching ('a differentiated pedagogy which takes into account the diversity of pupils' and 'the amelioration of programmes and teaching methods') and to have an information role useful over time and hopefully within an international framework. But 'individual evaluation is best carried out by other means. That is the inspectors' role.'

This work seems another marker for the future.

THE INSPECTORATE RENASCENT?

What of the inspectorate in all this? So widely seen as a privileged caste, are the *inspecteurs généraux* living a moment of 'rupture' or of 'continuity', to use a favourite French phrase? The answer is usually both at the same time, and that seems to be the case here.

It is interesting in this respect to look back at a report entitled *Investing in Intelligence*, written in 1987 by Georges Laforest,[12] now the doyen of the *inspecteurs généraux*. In it he defines a future in which there will be greater diversity, greater openness to the environment, more contact with parents, 'for the state cannot do everything' and 'in the world of tomorrow in which demands for education and training will certainly increase, new sources of finance will have to be found. Within a general framework, contractual policies will be the model.'

Interviewed in 1990 he stressed the continuity in the fundamentals of the general inspectorate's role, though under the new act some of the form will change as the inspectorate drops its assessment of individuals and moves over to a triple mission: the evaluation of innovations, such as modern languages in the primary school and the teaching of general culture on technical courses, the evaluation of teacher training, initially with particular emphasis on the technical area; and the evaluation of the way the system functions. Here, for example, there will be studies of the effectiveness of the apprenticeship cycles in primary and secondary schools and the controversial cycles of observation and orientation at the end of the second and the fourth year of secondary school, 'with conclusions to be drawn on the more pupil-oriented learning'.

But at the base of their work the inspectors will still be directly involved in defining *'la culture pour l'Homme moderne'*, even if the inspectorate is no longer the only body to be involved. Laforest, an outgoing man, maintains that the national commission on programmes is a bonus: 'I don't believe that a corps should have a monopoly.' And it is after all this body, of which the inspectorate will be part, which will be defining the general framework and proposing areas for change: 'In the past change has been a matter of development in knowledge, but also of political will.' He quotes the changes in the 1985 programme as stemming from these diverse sources: the emphasis on technology and images, the introduction of civic education. And the issue is still how to 'arm the pupil to face society: to be part of it *and* to be critical'.

CRITIQUES

Counteracting official optimism, critics have not minced their words. Among the titles dealing with the fall in standards are *Vos Enfants M'Intéressent Plus* by Maurice Maschinno,[13] and *L'Enseignement en Détresse*[14] by Jacqueline de Romilly, the famous professor of classical Greek, the first woman given a Collège de France chair, and now a member of the Académie Française. They are the latest in a long line which can be traced back over a century.[15] Flaubert's remark in 1872 still stands out by its style: 'The dream of every democracy is to raise the member of the proletariat to the level of stupidity of the bourgeoisie.'

The case that there is decline is however challenged. In one of the best known of the recent replies, 'Le niveau monte', Christian Baudelot and Roger Establet point out that at the end of the nineteenth century 60 per cent of the population left school without a diploma. Today the figure is 20 per cent. The educational skills of army conscripts have improved measurably. And so on.

However, more interesting for our purposes are the critiques which debate the relationship of the education system and the individual, centred on what children ought to learn and can learn. Shaped by trends in sociological and psychological thought, they are part of the intellectual climate of our times.

The pendulum has now swung against the appeals for diversity and the breaking of the elite mould pioneered in the 1960s and 1970s. Pierre Bourdieu with *Les Heritiers*, published in 1966, and *La Réproduction* (1970) and Alain Touraine with *Lettre à une étudiante* (1974), and regular newspaper articles during the 1970s (collected in *Mort d'une gauche* (1979)) produced classics.

But such a view has come under attack as it has become more obviously rooted in the education system. In France, trends which are seen as detrimental to learning have been denounced quite as strongly by the Left as by the Right.

Thus the highly polemical book *De L'École* is said to have been much appreciated by Jean-Pierre Chevènement when he was minister of education. By Jean-Claude Milner, professor of linguistics at the University of Paris VII, it was published in 1984. Milner's object was to denounce the mechanisms which, in the name of pedagogy and efficiency and even devotion to teaching, were in reality destroying education and with it a concept of active democracy: 'To speak of the school is to speak of four things: (i) knowledge, (ii) transmissible knowledge, (iii) the specialists charged to transmit that knowledge and (iv) the institutions with the function of bringing together the specialists who are to transmit and those who are being transmitted to.' But, argued Milner, all were devalued by a 'three-pronged machine'. The elements have not always been in harmony but, taken together, they have been powerfully destructive. These are (and what an un-English analysis!) the administration, the majority in the teaching profession and the Christian lobby.

Why are they so destructive of education? The interest of the administration is to reduce costs, says Milner. The interest of the majority of the teaching profession is to fight the privileges accorded to teachers teaching an elite (a reference to the opposition of primary and lower secondary school teachers to *agrégés*, who are better paid and teach shorter hours), and thereby secure themselves a monopoly. Christians for Milner are a menace because it is they who have articulated ideas which are subversive of education. Charity replaces thought. Their 'phrasing', their 'desires', produce a situation in which the 'loyalty' invoked is 'disloyal' (p. 31). The community takes precedence over the institution; devotion takes precedence over knowledge; education meaning upbringing takes precedence over instruction, the emotional takes precedence over the cognitive.

And why is this so serious? Because France is 'the only country in which democratic concepts and knowledge are so intimately linked . . . Britain has habeas corpus, the Netherlands have a special concept of tolerance, the Americans have their constitution'. But in France the decisive limits on power 'cannot be resumed by a single symbol . . . they are rooted in a multiplicity of historic events, dates, names, concepts to which one only has access by knowledge'. Freedom, as the revolutionaries put it so aptly in 1793, must be the power for the individual to use all his faculties as he wishes. In consequence, says Milner, the aim of education must be to guarantee as far as possible to each citizen the right and the means to accomplish that. And much of that lies in access to a common content: 'Gaps cannot be tolerated.'

La Défaite de la Pensée, by the philosopher Alain Finkielkraut, is another example of an attack on the notion that the content of education should be differentiated according to needs and capacities: 'European society has all but given up the struggle to inculcate elements of universalist culture based on reason – one of its hallmarks. The social scientists have a lot to answer for' (indeed, he takes on Bourdieu by name). In favouring a pluralistic approach, on the grounds that the values which underpin social systems are arbitrary, they risk strengthening ethnicity, nationalism and other collective values. And that, says Finkielkraut, is the 'undoing of thought'.

CONCLUSION

In the past the curricular programmes of French schools have had their philosophical roots in general convictions about the role of the education system in creating equality and democracy, with the idea that such principles are best guaranteed by a nationally uniform system. Now that a measure of decentralisation is on the way, with quite possibly a better educational environment for many pupils, France is a particularly interesting test case. At issue is whether it will be possible to define a clear national framework of common objectives in terms which are compatible with the new encouragement for diversity. In the common European house there will be some attentive eyes on Braudel's 'third storey'.

NOTES

1 François Mitterand has made education the priority of his second term of office.
2 Vincent Wright (1989) *The Government and Politics of Modern France* (third edition).
   Unwin Hyman.
3 See Corbett and Gruson (1987) 'Pascale', *Times Educational Supplement (TES)*, 6 March.
4 See for example Jean-Claude Barbarent (1989) Secretary General of the SNI,
   Les Enfants du Condorcet. Editions Laffont.

5 *TES* (1977), 4 February.

6 *TES* (1987), 6 March.

7 Moon (1986) 'The New Maths Curriculum Controversy: An International Story'. Lewes: Falmer Press.

8 Minister 1986–8 in a Right-wing government.

9 *Réflexions sur l'Enseignement de Français* (1986). Texte collectif. Angers: CDDP.

10 *Principes pour une Réflexion sur les Contenus de l'Enseignement* (1989). Commission présidée par Pierre Bourdieu et Françoise Gros. Available from Ministère de l'Education Nationale.

11 OECD/CERI (1989) *Project on International Educational Indicators*.

12 Georges Laforest (1987) *Investir dans l'Intelligence, Rapport sur l'Education et la Formation*. République Moderne, Journées de Réflexion des 24–5 janvier.

13 Maurice Maschinno (1983), *Vos Enfants M'Intéressent Plus*. Paris: Hachette.

14 Jacqueline de Romilly (1984), *L'Enseignement en Détresse*. Paris: Julliard.

15 This and the following examples are taken from Christian Baudelot and Roger Establet (1989), 'Le Niveau Monte', quoted in *Le Monde*, 7 January.

4.3 A SCOTTISH TRADITION OF CURRICULUM REFORM

JIM RAND

INTRODUCTION

There is a tendency for those who write about curriculum to imply that there is a unitary system operating within the United Kingdom. Many write, and lecture, about curriculum development in 'Britain' when, to be accurate, they should refer to curriculum development in England (and sometimes in England and Wales). There is one part of Britain where the General Certificate of Secondary Education (GCSE), the National Curriculum, key stage testing and records of achievement are of academic interest only, having no practical significance. For example, not one of these features in contemporary curriculum developments in Scotland.

It is striking that many comparative studies of curriculum seek to compare activities in the UK (usually England) with countries on the other side of the world. There have been very few serious attempts to explore and analyse the various systems for curriculum design and development which exist *within* the United Kingdom. There is, however, a rich seam to be drawn on in such comparative reviews. For example, the way in which the Scottish and English 'systems' have responded to the last two decades of unprecedented interest in curriculum provides a pointed illustration of the complexity of forces which shape and change the curriculum.

PERSONAL EXPERIENCE

A brief item of anecdotal evidence might be helpful. In 1975, after working as a lecturer in curriculum studies in a college of education in England, I moved to what appeared to be a similar job in Scotland. In England I had worked with pre-service and in-service students on a wide range of projects which had emerged from the confident and heady early years of the Schools Council; for example, the Humanities Curriculum Project, Nuffield Science, Integrated Studies, Geography

Source: commissioned for this volume.

for the Young School Leaver, and others such as MAN: A Course of Study (MACOS) and Resources for Learning. It is clear that my experience may not have been typical of all working in England, but by any measure these were exciting initiatives, and there seemed to be an optimistic assumption that 'curriculum innovation' would change schooling.

I found my move to Scotland a professional culture shock. Curriculum development north of the border was centrally controlled and managed: I thought it staid, conservative and unresponsive. Fifteen years later, however, when I meet former colleagues from England, instead of expressing optimism for the challenge of innovation they talk of political intervention, the erosion of professional autonomy and the imposition of a 'testing driven' model for curriculum. Many claim to look with envy on those of us who work within the 'Scottish system' where, they believe, the worst excesses of political intervention have been fought off and the major developments of the 1980s have been accommodated within a much more 'reasonable' framework.

Thus my justifications for claiming that there are important insights to be gained by comparing curriculum design and innovation north and south of the border are both professional and personal. This paper is a preliminary attempt to identify some of the key issues. Since the structure and operation of curriculum development in England is relatively well documented, the paper will concentrate on a description and analysis from a Scottish perspective.

The paper highlights a paradox. Since the 1960s, curriculum design and development in England and Wales have tended to operate through a devolved structure where considerable emphasis has been placed on the professional autonomy of teachers. By contrast, in Scotland the curriculum has been tightly controlled and managed from the centre. However, in 1990 teachers working south of the border find that a National Curriculum and key stage testing have dramatically reduced their own autonomy, whilst their colleagues in Scotland find that they are operating within less restrictive guidelines. The more liberal professional framework appears also to have been more vulnerable to political intervention.

THE SCOTTISH SYSTEM: PARTNERSHIP AND CONSULTATION?

The curriculum experienced by pupils in their classrooms is the product of a complex network of influences. Each learner's experience of the curriculum is unique, and the 'real' curriculum is what the learner takes away from the classroom, not what the teacher intends or brings to it. Nevertheless the curriculum, intended and experienced, emerges as a result of decisions and actions taken at national, education authority, school and classroom levels. The ways in which these decisions and actions occur at each level differ in the Scottish and English systems.

In 1985 Sir James Munn, who was at that time Chairman of both the Consultative Committee on Curriculum (CCC) and the Manpower Services Commission (Scotland), summarised what he saw as the framework for curriculum policy making and development in Scotland:

> Neither the Secretary of State for Scotland nor the Scottish Education Department (SED) has any direct responsibility for the school curriculum. It is, however, accepted and indeed expected that the Secretary of State will issue guidance on the curriculum to education authorities and schools. While the Secretary of State may on occasions take the initiative, he will normally issue curricular guidance only after taking advice as appropriate from HM Inspectorate, the Consultative Committee on Curriculum and, on assessment issues, the Scottish Examination Board. (Munn, 1985)

Although some details have changed since 1985, the system remains essentially the same. The statement makes it clear that central direction of curriculum design is the basic premise. The statement also highlights the prominence in the process of agencies such as HM Inspectorate (HMI), the CCC and the Scottish Examination Board (SEB).

In Munn's view, further distinctive features of the system are the notion of 'partnership' and the close and 'harmonious' relationships between the various elements. A small system should ensure that key decision-makers are well known to each other, that they meet regularly and that consultation becomes a less formal and more responsive process than would be possible in a larger system. For example, many major developments in Scotland have been devised, promoted and managed by a small committee or working party of less than a dozen people (Gatherer, 1989).

Munn claims that:

> The partnership principle extends well beyond the bodies with national responsibility. Formal responsibility for the school curriculum lies with Education Authorities. By and large they are willing to accept central guidance, provided they have some say in its formulation and guidance is couched in fairly general terms, leaving reasonable scope to take account of local needs and preferences.

Such an optimistic interpretation is not held universally. Not everyone is prepared to take such a benign view of the central tendencies of the Scottish system; some critics find the principle of partnership less convincing in reality than is suggested by Munn; and there is mounting evidence that curricular guidance couched in 'fairly general terms' may introduce structural or apparent change, but is not the most effective way to promote and sustain innovation which has real impact on the curriculum experienced by pupils at the classroom level.

Before examining critically the view that the Scottish system is characterised by partnership and consultation, it is necessary to consider the main structural elements of the system. The Scottish Education Department (SED), in particular

HMI, the CCC (now the Scottish Consultative Council on the Curriculum – SCCC) and the SEB are key aspects of the structure. Contextual factors such as the entry requirements and expectations of Scottish universities, the training and career structures for Scottish teachers and the traditional roles of education authorities and churches also have a very significant influence on the design and development of the curriculum in Scotland.

SED/HMI

A recurring theme of the recent debates in England has been the struggle for control over the curriculum and in particular the more assertive role adopted in recent years by the Department of Education and Science (DES) and HMI. There has been no such public struggle north of the border. As should be clear from the extracts above, a feature of Scottish education for many years has been the dominant influence on curriculum matters of the SED and HMI.

Unlike their counterparts in England, members of HMI in Scotland have traditionally played a key role in the design, implementation and evaluation of all recent major curriculum initiatives (with the exception of the Technical and Vocational Education Initiative – TVEI). In the mid-1960s, with the establishment of the Scottish Certificate of Education Examination Board and the CCC, some members of the Inspectorate assumed overt leadership roles in the management of curriculum development. Since that time the SED, through HMI, has played a dominant role on all the major committees and working parties responsible for curriculum design and development in Scotland.

The Munn and Dunning development programme re-emphasised the central and decisive role of the Inspectorate. Whilst in England confusion and uncertainty appeared to characterise attempts to revise certification procedures, in Scotland, according to one well-informed source:

> There was no question about the methodology to be adopted for the design, piloting and promulgation of the new S3–4 (14–16) curriculum during the 1980s. A Development Unit was set up in the SED, and the administrators and inspectors who manned it rigorously controlled the management of funds, staffing and the dissemination of materials. (Gatherer, 1989)

Such a system may be decisive and able to respond quickly to the need for structural change, but critics have pointed to the high price which is paid for conceding so much power to a small 'policy community'. In addition to the criticisms levelled at the Scottish Inspectorate for the narrow base of experience, qualifications and outlook from which it recruits, growing levels of political intervention in curriculum matters have raised other concerns. Can Inspectors who are expected to be the 'eyes and ears of the Minister' also accommodate, let alone promote, divergent or alternative views and priorities arising from the profession or other parts of the service? A crucial feature of any account of the Scottish system would be the distinctive and powerful position assumed by the SED and HMI.

CCC

The CCC, which is sometimes described erroneously as the Scottish Schools Council, was established in 1965 to advise the Secretary of State for Scotland on the curriculum in primary and secondary schools. It was remodelled twice before it became the SCCC, a company limited by guarantee, in 1988.

Unlike the establishment of the Schools Council, which was surrounded by professional and political controversies, the establishment of the CCC was regarded as little more than an administrative reshuffle. It was clear that it had been carefully designed to have a limited advisory role. It was to be wholly controlled by the SED. It was chaired by the Secretary of the Department, and dominated by SED members, administrators and inspectors. The non-SED members were handpicked and appointed by the Secretary of State 'as individuals for their knowledge and expertise rather than as representatives of particular organisations'. These procedures lend a different interpretation to the notion of 'partnership':

> the idea of partnership fudges the issue of power. Are the partners equal? If not, how do the dominant and subordinate partners limit and influence each other? The problem concerns values. It only makes linguistic sense to describe a relationship as a partnership if the partners share the same goals and pull in the same direction. (McPherson, 1985)

South of the border, in marked contrast, attempts by the Minister in the early 1960s to create a centralised curriculum body were defeated, and the establishment of the Schools Council in 1964 was regarded as a compromise. It was a way of reconciling the competing interests of central government, local authorities and the professional autonomy of teachers. An accurate grasp of the differences between curriculum policy and innovation north and south of the border depends on an understanding of the operation and effects of the different forces responsible for the establishment of the CCC in Scotland and the Schools Council in England, within a year of each other, in the mid-1960s.

In 1976 John Nisbet summarised a decade of operation for both systems:

> The Scottish structure has the advantage that the proposals which emerge are more likely to be in line with national policy. They will generally be practicable; they arise from consensus of informed opinion within the system; they are seen as carrying the approval of authority; . . .
> The critic alleges that only what is feasible within existing assumptions is

suggested; the defence argues that the present need is for practicable, realistic suggestions for gradual reform. In contrast, the Schools Council, by farming out projects, can take risks and tolerate eccentricities more readily and can float ideas tentatively, but it is in constant danger of becoming a fringe activity, lacking effective leverage on policy. (Nisbet, 1976)

Nisbet spotted clearly the feature of the Schools Council which would ultimately make it vulnerable to its critics and to closure by Sir Keith Joseph. He also identified as the distinctive feature of each system the relative level of centralisation or devolution.

Unlike the Schools Council, the CCC was dominated from the outset by central influence. Until regional reorganisation in the 1970s, education authorities in Scotland were not only few in number but also relatively small in size. Only three or four of the larger authorities could afford a full and professionally serviced, authority-wide support structure. Typically, Scottish education authorities employed fewer subject or specialist advisors than was the case in England and Wales, and the growth of teachers' centres, as a local focus for school-based curriculum development, was an English phenomenon which had no direct parallel in Scotland.

According to Gatherer, 'Scottish education authorities traditionally have shown little interest in curriculum development as one of their prime functions. They have not substantially influenced the structure or content of the curricula in their schools' (Gatherer, 1989). It is important to note that more recently (1990) there have been radical changes in the organisation of administrative and professional support in several Scottish education authorities. This, together with an anticipated change in resourcing arrangements for in-service support, which will shift funding from colleges of education to authorities, will alter the pattern described by Gatherer.

A further point of comparison is the level of involvement of teachers' professional associations in curriculum policy and development. The elaborate structure of the Schools Council gave the teacher unions a place, by right, on the policy making bodies. In Scotland, teacher unions had no such entitlement; although union members may serve on committees as individuals, they do not represent the union. However, during the 1980s teachers demonstrated their real power to influence curriculum development. The perception grew that excessive demands were being made on the teaching profession by a high-handed and insensitive government and central administration, and this was a major factor leading to a protracted and bitter period of industrial action. A central feature of the action was a boycott of staff and curriculum development activities. The ultimate threat to a centre–periphery model for development is that of classroom teachers refusing to respond to centrally devised plans or directives. Scottish teachers, unlike their English colleagues, have a formal contract of employment, which in the mid-1980s did not specify curriculum or staff development. It is not surprising that central and local government made it a condition of the settlement in 1987 that teachers accept these as part of their normal duties.

This development is in itself a valuable insight into the extent and limitations of a centrally managed development framework. Theoretically, teachers have limited influence on curriculum policy making, but actually they have very real power with regard to implementation. A characteristic of the period since the industrial action has been that local authorities and HMI in particular have been at pains to demonstrate their sensitivity to the demands made on teachers by programmes of curriculum development. A consequence of this is, of course, that curricular innovation is frequently designed in the light of pragmatic considerations of what teachers will accept.

SEB

The SEB (formally SCEEB) has a statutory function of advising the Secretary of State on matters relating to examinations and certification for secondary pupils. It is also the body responsible for the organisation of the Scottish Certificate of Education (SCE) examinations (Standard Grade and Revised Higher, formerly Ordinary Grade and Higher Grade). The major influence on the curriculum in the secondary sector in Scotland has been the existence of a single examining body. Certification has been available only through the SEB, and a form of national curriculum and assessment has existed as a consequence of the common examination.

Although Standard Grade developments have introduced reforms to certification and assessment in Scottish secondary schools, critics increasingly complain that, as in many aspects of GCSE, the innovation has been more apparent than real. The changes implemented through Standard Grade certainly fall some way short of the intended outcome described in the Dunning Report. It remains true, in 1990, that most Scottish 14–16 year olds follow a curriculum dominated by two-year courses, leading to certification through assessment procedures which are mainly external and terminal and where awards still depend on normative assumptions regarding levels of performance – Credit, General and Foundation. The SEB has, throughout the development programme, opposed attempts to promote more fundamental change in certification procedures (MacIntyre in Brown and Munn, 1985).

The Scottish Universities Council on Entrance (SUCE) has had a major influence on the position adopted by the SEB. SUCE is represented on all of the major committees and panels of the Board. Scottish universities have demonstrated an inherently conservative view of the purpose of schooling and they have exerted their considerable influence to resist attempts to change. Kirk (1982) quotes the evidence from SUCE to the Munn and Dunning Committees:

> The evidence from the Scottish Universities Council on Entrance disputed the necessity for able pupils to undertake the broadening activities associated with minority time. The general educational development of such pupils it was maintained could safely be entrusted to their own private reading or to the liberating effects of life at university . . .

The Scottish Universities Council on Entrance made it clear that it would not recognise awards based on internal assessment.

SCOTVEC AND NATIONAL CERTIFICATE MODULES

The most fundamental and rapid development programme in Scotland was that associated with the 16–18 Action Plan. It was designed to reform the provision for non-advanced further education, and it introduced to Scotland a completely new modular system for curriculum delivery, assessment and certification. Scottish Vocational and Educational Certificate (SCOTVEC) and National Certificate modules have already had a dramatic impact within schools, as well as in further education. By 1990 over 1,000,000 National Certificate modules had been awarded, and 40 per cent of presentations were by that time coming from secondary schools. Although there is some evidence that teachers have experienced difficulties in coming to terms with internal certification procedures, the fact that modular courses are now a feature of secondary schools is a substantial achievement.

APPROACHES TO CHANGE

Any attempt to describe and explain the differences between the English and Scottish systems, with regard to curriculum design and innovation, would need to consider both structural characteristics and operational experience. The structural elements have been considered above and three particular features of development experience are discussed below, as a means of illuminating distinctive characteristics of the two systems. The three features are: the use of evaluation and its link to teacher-centred approaches; the development of records of achievement; and TVEI.

EVALUATION AND CRITICAL REVIEW OF PRACTICE

In England, external evaluation became a requirement of the first generation of Schools Council projects. A model of development emerged where typically the Council devolved responsibility to a project team, frequently external funding was involved, and there was a need to provide the sponsors with an 'account' of the project, in terms of both activities and outcomes.

The requirement for public evaluation which was built into the early Schools Council/Nuffield projects prompted a fierce but productive conflict about theory and practice. Out of this conflict, alternative models of evaluation were developed and tested, which actually came to challenge the basic assumptions of the systems-led and RDD (research, development and dissemination) models for innovation which were then favoured.

The Humanities Curriculum Project (HCP) and the work of Lawrence Stenhouse and his colleagues were especially significant because their work laid the foundations for the establishment of a very influential network of practitioners and researchers. This network has sustained a range of innovative and influential developments. Stenhouse and others began a series of projects which placed teachers at the centre of the process of innovation. Fundamentally important projects (such as the Ford Teaching Project, SAFARI, MACOS, TIQL, and GRIDS), together with key developmental concepts, such as classroom action research, self-evaluation and the teacher as researcher, were all, to a greater or lesser degree, influenced by the experience of those involved in HCP. Each initiative subscribed to the view that real and effective innovation at the classroom level depended on individual teachers becoming committed to 'critical and systematic reflection on practice'. This provided curriculum development, in parts of England at least, with greater access to a view of curriculum as 'learner experience'. In Scotland, however, the structural view of curriculum as grand plan, or teacher intention, remained the principal perspective.

In Scotland, external or public evaluation of the kind which characterised Schools Council projects played a much less significant role. The Scottish Education Department, or one of the central agencies, was usually both sponsor and developer for the major curriculum initiatives, and so evaluation never assumed the same public importance. Where it did occur, evaluation was usually a restricted and internal affair. Although there was an extensive programme of research linked to the first phase of development work arising from the Munn and Dunning reports, in effect the whole of the Standard Grade development programme has been designed and managed, over more than a decade, by HMI without a single commissioned, external evaluation. The introduction of the TVEI Pilot in the mid-1980s was the first major initiative in Scotland to incorporate a commitment to external and public evaluation. In examining the two systems, north and south of the border, this differential experience of public and professional evaluation is significant. Both the system and teachers north of the border lacked experience of the value, as a basis for development, of critical and systematic reflection on practice. This arose in England through evolving approaches to evaluation and later self-evaluation.

The developments in England were possible only because of the devolved model for innovation which was used in the late 1960s and early 1970s. In Scotland, curriculum development was a more closely managed activity. There was little devolution of initiative, and Scottish education has been disadvantaged by the lack of experience and stimulation which can arise from a network of practitioners experienced in teacher-based curriculum development.

PROFILING

The development of profiling and records of achievement highlights interesting points of comparison in approach and response to innovation north and south of the border. During the 1980s in England, an extensive programme of national and local initiatives produced a remarkable level of innovation. Even if the present government has, at the last minute, held back from making records of achievement a requirement for all school leavers, few English pupils will actually be unaffected by the developments. Despite the mounting of a major initiative in the field in 1977 (SCRE, 1977), there has been little or no further development in Scotland over the last decade, and interest has been sustained almost exclusively through the Training Agency and TVEI.

In England, Broadfoot (1986) claims that frustration at the delay in reform of the certification procedures resulted in grassroots action to promote profiling. There were, however, no such developments in Scotland; the agenda had been set by the SED, and the Munn/Dunning and Action Plan programmes all but eclipsed consideration of anything else. In Scotland there has been little interest and no public support shown by the central agencies (SED, SCCC and SEB) in and for the development of records of achievement. There was no governmental commitment to them, as there was in England through the DES policy statement in 1984. Other than through TVEI, there has been no national or local funding for development programmes, nor has there been a focus for reviewing experience and providing guidance, such as that available in England through RANSC (Records of Achievement National Steering Committee).

The existence of a large number of examining bodies in England and Wales has been identified as an obstacle to change. It is clear, however, that a stimulus to many of the developments in the area of records of achievement has been the range of alternative routes to certification available, through the various examination boards/groups and through formats such as the Certificate of Pre-Vocational Education (CPVE) and City and Guilds 365 programmes. In Scotland, all school certification procedures have been handled through the SEB; there has been no comparable certificate to the Certificate of Secondary Education (CSE) and certainly nothing like the school-devised and school-assessed Mode 3 format. Until the development of the SCOTVEC National Certificate, certification through SCE 'O' Grades and 'highers' was the only certification available. Most Scottish teachers had no experience of school-based assessment procedures for purposes of certification. Despite the efforts of the Dunning Committee, the assessment procedures which have characterised the Scottish Certificate of Education have, by comparison, been limited and conservative. It is possible to sustain a case that they have deskilled both teachers and students with regard to other, more flexible and imaginative uses of assessment, and that they have thus inhibited more fundamental changes in pedagogy.

TVEI Pilot

The TVEI Pilot provides a further interesting case study of innovation in Scotland. In Scotland TVEI developments bypassed, to a greater or lesser degree, the conventional and established curriculum development apparatus. For example, the SED, CCC and colleges of education played no real part in most of the Pilot developments. Indeed, in some projects there was little or no reference to the education authority advisory services either. The devolved nature of the Pilot projects gave to many teachers genuine opportunities to engage in school-based curriculum development. External and formative evaluations were essential features of the Pilot programmes, and the requirement for an annual review and development plans taught a wide range of Scottish educators some of the values of systematic reflection on practice.

TVEI has been the subject of considerable criticism. In the longer term, however, it may be recognised that it has made a very significant contribution, in that it has demonstrated, at least to those who have been involved in Pilot schemes, that alternatives to the more usual centrally controlled models of innovation are possible. For the first time since the establishment of secondary schooling for all in Scotland, a major innovation has taken place which was not devised and controlled directly by the SED and HMI.

Strategies for change

Commentators have identified three basic strategies for change in education (Dalin, 1975):

1 Power–coercive
2 Empirical–rational
3 Normative–re-educative.

According to the first, change can be achieved where the 'change agent' uses power or authority. This model applied to education takes the view of the teacher as a functionary. The teacher is expected to do what he or she is told and to follow central directives. The second model supposes that change is achieved by the presentation of logical argument or evidence to support the desired innovation. Such a model sees the teacher as a rational individual who will respond to reasoned argument. The third strategy sees change as a social and interactive process. For a change agent to intervene successfully, he or she requires a shared understanding of what those in the field perceive as the major problems and obstacles to change. Such a model sees the teacher as a co-worker and collaborator and the change agent's function as supportive and consultative.

Despite official descriptions of the approach as one of 'partnership', in Scotland traditional models of curriculum development have depended very considerably on the authority of the central agencies, in particular that of the SED and a single examining body. It is also true that the Scottish system is founded on the principle of rationality. Most of the major developments have been preceded by an extensive and elaborate exploration of issues, which have frequently been set out in detailed and well-argued reports. The 1947 Advisory Committee Report, 1965 Primary Memorandum, the Munn and Dunning Reports and the 16+ Action Plan are all examples of documents which provide a penetrating analysis of an aspect of Scottish education, together with an articulate and compelling case for change. Nonetheless, however impeccable the analysis or compelling the case for change, the subsequent developments have frequently fallen short of expectation. There have been very few examples in Scotland of the successful application of the third, collaborative or interactive, strategy for change. The successful mastery of such approaches is a key task for Scottish education in the 1990s.

REVIEW

This paper was written with the intention of highlighting some of the ways in which responses to the priorities and processes of curriculum design and development have differed north and south of the border during the 1970s and 1980s. The focus has been narrowly professional, although a characteristic of the period has been the growth in explicit political involvement in curricular decision-making. There is a certain paradox in the situation whereby in Scotland (where by tradition procedures for curriculum design and development have been centralised and directive) the 1990s begin with teachers enjoying greater autonomy over curriculum matters than do their colleagues south of the border. In England the longer tradition and greater depth of experience in grassroots and school-based developments have not protected teachers or schools from a determined political intervention, which has ultimately limited professional freedom of action. An analysis of this issue is beyond the scope and ambition of this paper, but is justification for the rejection of the view that there is a meaningful unitary British approach to curriculum development. It commends the investment of further time in comparative review of the different approaches to curriculum which exist *within* the UK.

REFERENCES

Broadfoot, P. (ed.) (1986) *Profiles and Records of Achievement*. London: Holt, Rinehart and Winston.

Brown, S. and Munn, P. (eds) (1985) *The Changing Face of Education 14 to 16: Curriculum and Assessment*. Windsor: NFER/Nelson.

Dalin, P. (1975) *Case Studies in Educational Innovation: IV.* Paris: OECD/CERI.

Gatherer, W. A. (1989) *Curriculum Development in Scotland.* Edinburgh: Scottish Academic Press.

Kirk, G. (1982) *Curriculum and Assessment in Scottish Secondary Schools: A Study of the Munn and Dunning Reports.* Ward Lock Educational.

McPherson, A. (1985) 'Address to Scottish Educational Research Association Conference, September 1985', reprinted *Times Educational Supplement*, Scotland, 11 October and 18 October.

Munn, J. (1985) 'Address to British Association for the Advancement of Science', Strathclyde University, 26 August.

Nisbet, J. (1976) 'Contrasting Structures for Curriculum Development: Scotland and England', *Journal of Curriculum Studies*, 8(2).

SCRE (1977) *Pupils in Profile.* Edinburgh: SCRE.

CONFLICTING APPROACHES TO THE REFORM OF JAPANESE SCHOOLING: ECONOMIC LIBERALISATION VERSUS EDUCATIONAL LIBERATION

4.4

TERUHISA HORIO

[...]

CONFLICTING APPROACHES TO EDUCATIONAL REFORM

There are two diametrically opposed approaches to the problem of how we should be reforming our schools. This cleavage reflects the fault lines that first appeared a century ago during the early Meiji era between those who advocated an 'enlightenment from above', administered by the state, and those who pushed for an 'enlightenment from below', which could only be worked out by the people themselves. This dichotomy has appeared in a number of guises over the past hundred years, but the nature of the conflict remains the same and is readily apparent in the bitter controversies going on today regarding the most desirable kind of educational reform.

In recent years the arguments of those advocating reform from above have followed the positions worked out by the Ministry of Education in the 1960s and 1970s under the direction of the ruling Liberal Democratic Party, in response to the manpower development demands of business and industry. These calls for reform are referred to by their supporters as 'the third reform of education'.[1] Needless to say, those proclaiming the need for a 'third reform' of education see it as a way to bring back the spirit of strict order and tight discipline which was instilled by the educational system of the pre-war imperial state. In other words,

Source: T. Horio (1988) 'Conflicting Approaches to the Reform of Japanese Schooling: Economic Liberalisation versus Educational Liberation', in T. Horio, *Educational Thought and Ideology in Modern Japan*. Tokyo: University of Tokyo Press.

the discourse on the need for a 'third reform' of education is an intrinsic part of the attempt to eradicate the liberalising influences of the post-war reforms.

But there are also important differences between the attempts to instigate reforms initiated by the government most recently and those launched in the 1960s and early 1970s. These differences do not result from a transformation of fundamental value orientations; rather, they reflect the response to the changed economic conditions Japanese business and political leaders found themselves in after the first 'oil shock' in 1973. Recognising that Japan's unprecedented rapid economic growth could no longer be sustained, they decided to reorganise the Japanese economy in line with the more modest aim of moderate growth. In this changed climate it gradually became clear to the shapers of national policy that a form of education suited to the country's altered economic agenda was required. Thus as Japan entered the 1980s, new calls for reform emerged as an important part of the Nakasone Government's attempt to enact comprehensive reforms of national administration.

One of the fundamental objectives of this programme for administrative reform has been an attempt to lighten the government's financial burden. To this end the national railways have already been privatised, and the government is beginning to sell off the telephone and telegraph monopoly. Education is the next area the government has targeted for privatisation. Concretely this means shifting the burden of educational expenses from the public budget to that of private individuals; however, it does not mean limiting the state bureaucracy's interference with the inner workings of the educational process.

It is worth noting that the original impetus for the recently proposed reforms did not arise within the government itself but emerged from a series of initiatives undertaken within Japan's economic and financial circles. Thus, for example, the Discussion Group on Problems Related to Education and Culture set up by the Nakasone Cabinet had originally been organised as a private group closely allied with the Kyoto Round Table for Thinking about the World, a body established by the industrialist Matsushita Kōnosuke to formulate long-range economic, social and educational policies for the twenty-first century. These efforts were supplemented by a number of reports issued by other organs connected with industry. It must also be pointed out that the Nakasone Government recruited the members of its Extraordinary Council on Education largely from the groups mentioned above. In short, it is not hard to tell whose interests were more than amply represented in this officially sanctioned body, and whose were totally ignored.

The other major impetus for educational reform has come from the non-governmental, non-industrial sector of society. These views are represented most clearly in reports issued by the Japan Teachers' Union Committee for Educational Investigation.

There have been other attempts to formulate the bases for educational reform, such as the programme advocated by the Japanese Society for Education, which attempts to mediate between the conflicting positions of those in the government-business alliance and those within the People's Education Movement. But given the extreme polarisation of these two approaches, the wish to reach a compromise is little more than a vain hope.

NEO-CONSERVATIVE REFORM

THE EXTRAORDINARY COUNCIL AND JAPAN'S EDUCATIONAL PROBLEMS

The main pillar upholding the thinking of the Extraordinary Council on Education[2] is the idea that Japan requires an educational reform that will prepare it to face the challenges of the twenty-first century. In particular this has been viewed in terms of the nation's need to reorganise education so that the members of society will be able to adapt to a form of life increasingly dependent upon new kinds of information. It has also been framed in terms of Japan's need to 'internationalise' and to prepare for an increasingly ageing society. These three objectives have been at the forefront of the Extraordinary Council on Education's deliberations about the kind of educational reform Japan currently requires.

The members of this Council have sought to alter dramatically the meaning of 'Japan's modernisation', to shift the focus of attention from a programme designed to help Japan 'catch up with the West' to one which will make it possible for the nation finally to overcome and surpass the West. Shifting the focus of attention in this manner certainly serves to place even greater emphasis upon the cultivation of those elites who will be responsible for leading the Japanese into the forefront of the post-industrialised world, because it is only these elites, the argument goes, who will be able to manage society's needs for new and ever greater amounts of information. By proceeding in this fashion, it has been claimed, Japan can both consolidate the economic gains it has won over recent years and increase its already powerful advantages in the global economy. In this sense, educational reform constitutes a vitally important part of the plans Japan's industrial leaders have for reaching an even higher and more dominant position in the world marketplace. Thus it must be remembered that the various debates on school reform which seek to 'liberalise' or 'diversify' education are in reality little more than attempts to streamline the cultivation of elites as the cornerstone of our nation's educational system.

There is one other major component in the Extraordinary Council on Education's proposals that requires careful analysis, namely, the emphasis placed upon Japan's 'eternal, unchanging traditions'. This theme, running throughout the work of both the Discussion Group on Problems Related to Education and Culture and the Kyoto Round Table for Thinking about the World, reveals that another agenda lies concealed beneath all the talk about internationalising Japan and preparing it for the twenty-first century. This is nothing other than the desire to restore to their previously privileged positions within pre-war Japanese life the mythic dimensions of Japanese nationalism and a tightly controlled form of moral education. The dangerous implications of this appeal to the values of chauvinistic Japanism are succinctly visible in the proposals of the Extraordinary Council on Education, which called for a reinvigorated pursuit of Japanology and which insisted upon the need to force the rest of the world to show more respect for Japan's unique national character and its unequalled traditions. Here we can see tangible signs of the birth of that culturally constituted form of nationalism which the Nakasone government has been promoting throughout the 1980s. [. . .]

EDUCATIONAL LIBERALISATION AND EDUCATIONAL LIBERATION

There was much discussion in the meetings and reports issued by and about the Extraordinary Council on Education regarding the need for 'educational liberalisation' and 'greater individualism' in education. In one sense this represented a criticism of the Ministry of Education, and reflects some of the reasons why this council was established as an organ attached to the Prime Minister's cabinet and not to the Ministry of Education, as is typically the case with such blue-ribbon deliberative bodies. But one should not be deceived by all the commotion raised in relation to this point, particularly the claim that the Council's proposals constituted an attempt to denigrate the Ministry of Education and take away many of its powers. After all, it should be remembered that, by the time the Council was disbanded in September of 1987, it had already become quite clear that the work of seeing its proposals through to realisation was the major new task facing the Ministry of Education.

The calls for 'liberalisation' voiced within the deliberations of the Extraordinary Council emerged from the earlier debates of the Kyoto Round Table, regarding the character of a desirable educational reform. Against this backdrop it can be seen that these ideas clearly reflect the desires of our financial and industrial leaders. Moreover, when these would-be reformers speak of liberalisation (*jiyūka*), they are most definitely not referring to the kinds of freedom and liberty which the post-war reforms of education attempted to make into the basic human rights of all citizens in the new Japan. What liberalisation has been viewed as meaning here is rather *deregulation*. In this highly limited sense, it can be said that the work of this Council was somewhat critical of the Ministry of Education's usual way of doing business, but the reader should not be deceived about the depth or extent of this antagonism. Indeed, it is closer to the truth to say that the members of the Prime Minister's Extraordinary Council on Education saw the challenges they construed in terms of the need for liberalisation not as a response to the need for a spiritually freer form of schooling but rather as a way to respond to the need to extend the 'unparalleled virtues of our educational system' well into the next century. [. . .]

THE PRINCIPLE OF COMPETITION AND THE PRINCIPLE OF INDIVIDUALITY

The reorganisation of our schools, which began in earnest in the 1960s following the introduction of unconstrained competition as the major principle of education, has had two important consequences. First, it has made educational activities totally subservient to economic ones; and secondly, it has prompted the growth of an educational industry in which teaching and learning are transformed from a social enterprise into a money-making one. In recent years, the argument has been put forward by those who believe that the principle of competition is the key to a good education that, in order to make it possible for the private educational entrepreneurs who run these academies to provide even more kinds of 'high-quality educational service', it is now necessary for the government to license and officially supervise the cram school (*juku*) industry.

The operators of these cram schools and private tutoring academies know full well that parents in Japan today will assume major additional financial burdens if they think that as a result their children will have even a slightly better chance of success at entrance examination time. However, education and scholarship lose their universal and public character when they fall under the domination of the logics of management and efficiency. Moreover, once the principle is established that the beneficiaries of education should predominantly shoulder its costs, it is hard to resist the tendency to view education and scholarship solely in terms of its personal or private pay-offs. In such an environment education can no longer respond to any aspirations of the people other than those for financial success. In short, if the thinking of the Extraordinary Council on Education fully finds its way into law, the people will no longer be masters of their learning and studies.

These arguments rest upon the contention that schools only become more individualised as a consequence of privatisation and increased competition between them for students. However, individualising our schools on the basis of the principle of free choice is fundamentally different from doing so on the basis of the principle of competition. In fact, it is closer to the truth to say that the values underlying these principles are fundamentally opposed to and in irremediable conflict with one another. In other words, because the principle of competition stimulates the standardisation of education, it can never encourage the principle of individualisation. [. . .]

EDUCATIONAL FREEDOM AND THE RIGHT TO LEARN

History shows that the struggle to liberate education in Japan from the tentacles of state control has repeatedly been energised by new ideas about the necessity of intellectual freedom and the importance of an independent form of pedagogic authority. In fact, this struggle is now being fortified by fresh ideas about why the freedoms of thought and belief are so vital to the success of the educational process.

Acknowledgment of the 'educational rights of the child' can lead to no conclusion other than that the child must be regarded as the sovereign or master of his or her intellectual fate. In addition to establishing that parents and society have an obligation to guarantee an education appropriate to the child's particular developmental stage, this new perspective makes it possible to view 'educational freedom' as indistinguishable from the 'right to an education' (*droit à l'enseignement*). In addition, as the inseparability of the ties linking popular sovereignty and the right to an education come to be more universally recognised, support continually grows for the movement to fulfil the child's educational rights.

Our new formulations of the child's right to learn have made it possible to fuse the concept of the 'right to an education' with already well-established ideas concerning the character of 'educational freedom'. Our calls for the popularisation of higher learning have been directed towards a realisation of these values. In particular, our discourse on the educational rights that belong to children by virtue of the developmental possibilities within them itself represents an attempt to awaken popular consciousness to the necessity of guaranteeing these most basic of all human rights in as concrete a manner as possible.

The idea of educational liberty demands that educational practice be autonomous and independent from the state. This means that guarantees must be provided to assure the freedom of the teacher's educational research and praxis, and that parents' freedom not only to choose the school but also to criticise and influence the kind of education their children receive must also be protected.

Jean Piaget has written about the 'right to an education' in his commentary on Article 26 of the Universal Declaration of Human Rights that was adopted by the General Assembly of the United Nations on 10 December 1948. Piaget saw this right as 'neither more nor less than the right of an individual to develop normally, in accord with all the potential he possesses, and the obligation that society has to transform this potential into useful and effective fulfilment':

> Affirming the right of all human beings to an education is to take on a far greater responsibility than simply to assure to each one reading, writing, and arithmetic capabilities; it is to guarantee fairly to each child the entire development of his mental faculties and the acquisition of knowledge and of ethical values corresponding to the exercise of these faculties until adaptation to actual social life. Moreover, it is to assume the obligation – keeping in mind the aptitudes and constitution that each person possesses – of not destroying or spoiling those possibilities he may have that would benefit society first of all, or of allowing the loss of important abilities, or the smothering of others.

From this vantage point, it is quite clear that thinking about the 'right to an education' should be premised on the freedom of educational choice, but should not stop there.

From the perspective of educational freedom, the right to an education should be conceived of as containing the rights to expect and receive an education as well as the right to reject one that is judged to be unsuitable. This perspective has played an instrumental role in helping us wage our struggle against the state's system of textbook censorship; it underlies our arguments that the authorship and adoption of textbooks should be undertaken in a free manner.

This flies directly in the face of the arguments put forth by the Ministry of Education that textbook authors do not suffer any infringement of their right to free expression, because even if their works are judged unfit for publication as texts for use in publicly supported schools they still can be published like any other book. However, textbook freedom is not a corollary of the freedom of expression;

rather it is part of the right to learn. In this sense the struggle for textbook freedom is an indispensable element in our effort to reconstitute educational authority within the context of a system that stresses popular sovereignty as the only legitimate foundation for educational practice.

[...]

NOTES

1 The first reform being that in which the Meiji statesmen established the Imperial educational system; the second, that in which the Occupation authorities attempted to democratise education after World War II.
2 A council established by Prime Minister Nakasone in 1984.

part five
POSTSCRIPT

5.1 Managing Curriculum Change

Michael Fullan

The purpose of studying the dynamics of curriculum change is to make the change process more explicit. This means identifying the key factors related to success, developing insights into the change process, and developing action programmes.

BACKGROUND

Studies of educational change have moved through several phases. In the 1960s research concentrated on tracing the adoption of innovations, for instance how many new schemes were actually in use in schools. It is obvious now, but it was not at that time, that such research information was of limited value. For one thing, adoption by organisations tells us almost nothing about how individual members feel or act. For another, reported use by individuals does not indicate whether an innovation is actually in use, let alone the quality of use.

We do not need to dwell on the reasons why researchers and policy makers were content to stop with adoption. Perhaps it relates to the symbolic value of having 'appeared' to change by launching a major reform effort; or to the naive optimism of the fifties and early sixties; or to the possibility that people were fully occupied with developing innovations and policies with little energy and resources for follow-through; or more basically to the fact that initiating projects is much more glamorous and visible than the time-consuming, laborious front-line work of implementing an innovation project; or more charitably to the possibility that worrying about implementation and actual use was a natural outgrowth of earlier adoption efforts that came with time.

Whatever the case, it was not until 1971 that the first works appeared analysing problems of implementing educational innovations (Sarason, 1971; Gross et al., 1971).

The 1970s were concerned with classroom practice and essentially resulted in documenting failure (see Fullan and Pomfret, 1977, for a review). We learned

Source: M. Fullan (1988) 'Managing Curriculum Change', from *Schools Curriculum Development Committee Curriculum at the Crossroads*. London: SCDC.

more about what not to do than anything else (don't ignore local needs; don't introduce complex, vague innovations; don't ignore training needs; don't ignore local leaders and opinion makers, etc.).

The 1980s have been concerned with identifying and analysing success and effectiveness in educational settings. Research has provided some evidence on the factors related to success. Depending on the study, the latter is defined in terms of increases in student achievement, degree of institutionalisation, or in more intermediate terms such as teaching skills, teacher change, teacher commitment.

We are now embarking on a new phase which can be called the management of change (or more accurately the management of change for achieving successful outcomes). At first glance one might think that the earlier descriptions of what constitutes success would have solved the management of change problem. But 'explanations' of situations are not the same as 'solutions' in new situations, although they can help. Our future efforts will need to concentrate on managing change and developing strategies for making it happen.

SIX BASIC OBSERVATIONS ABOUT CURRICULUM CHANGE

The six observations described in this section are ways of thinking or insights into the phenomenon of educational change that should give us pause for thought and provide important orientations prior to launching into any particular change project.

BRUTE SANITY

The problem of brute sanity was identified by George Bernard Shaw when he observed that 'reformers have the idea that change can be achieved by brute sanity'. The tendency towards brute sanity on the part of change initiators or planners is natural. What could be more rational than advocating a change which one believes in and may be in a position to introduce? The use of sheer argument and sheer authority can get a change 'on the books', but it is, of course, not a very effective strategy for implementing change. Research has demonstrated that persistence, patience and attention to detail in putting something into practice are critical. Brute sanity is the tendency to overlook the complexity and detailed processes and procedures required, in favour of more obvious matters of stressing goals, the importance of the problem and the grand plan. Brute sanity overpromises, over-rationalises and consequently results in unfulfilled dreams and frustrations which discourage people from sustaining their efforts and from taking on future change projects.

OVERLOAD

The overload of change projects on implementers is well known and there are frequently conflicting priorities on the agenda. One could say that the initiation of change projects represents a mixture of political and educational merit. As such, (1) too many projects are launched, (2) implementation is often attempted too early; that is, the political process often outstrips the educational development process, (3) overly ambitious projects are adopted, and (4) simultaneous multiple projects are introduced in an unco-ordinated way. The basic observation is: 'just because a change project is on the books does not mean that it should or could be implemented'. No theory or strategy can do the impossible, and the impossible in this case is to implement everything that is supposed to be implemented.

IMPLEMENTING THE IMPLEMENTATION PLAN

Many people have responded to the research of the 1970s, which documented implementation problems, by developing elaborate implementation plans designed to take into account factors known to affect success. This seems sensible enough on the surface but ironically has led to the problem of 'how do I implement the implementation plan?' It is useful to recognise that implementation plans, when they are first introduced, are *innovations* as much as, if not more than, curriculum innovations. Everything we know about the dos and don'ts of implementing curriculum innovations must be applied to the problem of developing implementation plans.

CONTENT VERSUS PROCESS

It is also helpful to distinguish between the content of change and the process of change and to realise that each represents distinct bodies of knowledge and expertise and each needs an appropriate implementation strategy. They are independent in the sense that it is possible to have expertise in one and not the other. It is possible, in other words, to be highly knowledgeable about a particular curriculum or curriculum development programme but yet be a disaster in working with others to implement it. Indeed, those most committed to a particular innovation may be least effective in working with others to bring about the change. Both elements of expertise must be present and integrated in any given change project.

PRESSURE AND SUPPORT

Recent research suggests that effective change, even if voluntarily pursued, rarely happens unless there is a combination of pressure and support. These are two important balancing mechanisms and success is usually accompanied by both. The positive role of pressure in change has been neglected until recently. Support without pressure can waste resources; pressure without support creates alienation.

CHANGE = LEARNING

Successful change, or successful implementation, is none other than learning, but it is the adults in the system who are learning along with or more so than the students. Thus, anything we know about how adults learn and under what conditions they are most likely to learn is useful for designing and carrying out strategies for implementation.

WHAT IS IMPLEMENTATION?

Implementation means curriculum change. For teachers in classrooms, new materials are important, but are ineffective by themselves. Change also involves new behaviours and practices, and ultimately new beliefs and understandings. It involves changes in what people know and assume.

It is possible to obtain some degree of change through policy decision and the initial process of getting new structures and materials in place, but this represents the more obvious, structural aspects of change in comparison with the new skills and understandings required of front-line implementers. In the absence of the latter, only superficial change is achieved. The effectiveness of a change project stands or falls with the extent to which front-line implementers use new practices with degrees of mastery, commitment and understanding.

FACTORS RELATED TO SUCCESSFUL CHANGE

These can be grouped within the three broad project phases of initiation, implementation and institutionalisation.

INITIATION FACTORS

There are four requirements:

- educational need should be linked to an agenda of political (high-profile) need
- a clear model should exist for the proposed change
- there needs to be a strong advocate for the change
- there should be an early active initiation establishing initial commitment, as an elaborate planning stage is wasteful of energy.

IMPLEMENTATION FACTORS

Some critical needs include:

- careful orchestration. Implementation requires the clear direction of many players; a group is needed to oversee the implementation plan and carry it through
- the correct alchemy of pressure and support
- early rewards for implementers
- ongoing in Service Education for Teachers (INSET), to maintain commitment, as behaviours often change before beliefs.

INSTITUTIONALISATION FACTORS

An innovation will be more successful if it:

- becomes embedded into the fabric of everyday practice
- is clearly linked to classroom practice
- is in widespread use across several classrooms and schools
- is not contending with conflicting priorities
- is subject to continuing INSET for new staff, to consolidate commitment.

IMPLICATIONS FOR ACTION

I would offer finally the following eight basic guidelines or insights:

- Effective entrepreneurs exploit multiple innovations.
- Overcome the 'if only ...' problem; for example, 'If only more heads were curriculum leaders ...'; 'If only the government would stop introducing so many policies ...'.

- Manage multiple innovations. 'Do two well and the others as well as possible.'
- Get better at implementation planning – more by doing than planning. Start small but think big.
- Beware of 'implementation dip'; that is, the risk of temporary deskilling as innovators learn new skills.
- Remember that research shows that behaviour changes first and changes in belief follow.
- Recognise that project leaders need to have a vision of content and process and the relationship between the two which will promote change. To have a vision of content change without a vision of process change is an example of brute sanity.
- Acknowledge the importance of ownership and commitment and that ownership is a process where commitment is increasingly acquired.

CONCLUSION

The process of curriculum change is complex and the search to understand it continues. If the teachers are to be convinced, those in authority positions in LEAs and schools must believe and understand the change sufficiently to convey its meaning. The psychiatrist Ronald Laing (1970) has captured the essence of this in one of his poems:

> There is something I don't know
> that I am supposed to know.
> I don't know *what* it is I don't know,
> and yet am supposed to know,
> and I feel I look stupid
> if I seem both not to know it
> and not know *what* it is I don't know.
> Therefore I pretend I know it.
> This is nerve-racking
> since I don't know what I must pretend to know.
> Therefore I pretend to know everything.

REFERENCES

Fullan, M. and Pomfret (1977) 'A Research on Curriculum and Instructive Implementation', *Review of Educational Research*, 47(1), pp. 335–97.

Gross, N., *et al.* (1971) *Implementing Organisational Innovations: A Sociological Analysis of Planned Educational Change.* New York: Basic Books.

Laing, R. D. (1970) *Knots.* London: Tavistock Publications.

Sarason, S. (1971) *The Culture of the School and the Problem of Change.* Boston: Allyn and Bacon.

Index